*An Unlikely Journey from Negro Policeman to
Florida's First Black Parole & Probation Commissioner*

Justice
in the
Jim Crow South

CHARLES J. SCRIVEN

© 2022 by Charles J. Scriven

All rights reserved. No part of this book may be reproduced or transmitted in any form whatsoever without prior written permission from the published except in the case of brief quotations embodied in critical articles and reviews.

ISBN 978-1-958174-10-4

Published by Susan the Scribe, Inc.

Disclaimer: I have made every effort to ensure the information in this book is correct. This work depicts actual events in my life as truthfully as my recollection permits. I cannot unequivocably verify the authenticity of every event presented nor the representation or characterization of individuals described herein. I realize and willingly grant the possibility that others may dispute some of these events and characterizations. I hereby disclaim any liability for damage or harm which could result from possible mischaracterization or misrepresentation. I have done my best to tell a truthful story.

Dedication

This book is decicated to the courageous Black police officers who, despite racial prejudice and discrimination, paved the way for acceptance and equality in the ranks of law enforcement, and to all the fine officers who served with honor and dignity in Jacksonville, Florida's Precinct Three.

It is dedicated as well to Martin P. Garris, a true friend and brother, a man of God, and one of the finest men who ever wore the uniform of a law enforcement officer.

Acknowledgements

I wish to offer my sincerest and heartfelt thanks to my wife Jeannetta Scriven, whose love and encouragement have sustained me throughout this and all my life's endeavors, and to my son Lansing Scriven whose caring support was invaluable to this project.

I also want to thank my publisher, Susan D. Brandenburg for her guidance and extensive knowledge; Andrew J. Skerritt, my chronicler; my friend Debbie Floyd whose impetus and enthusiasm kept this project alive; and Joney Perry for her graphic design expertise and knowledge of formatting and printing.

Table of Contents

BOOK I – ORIGINS

Chapter 1: The Letter 1
Chapter 2: Origins 11
Chapter 3: A Mother's Love 15
Chapter 4: Daddy 19
Chapter 5: Jean 23

BOOK II – MY EARLY EDUCATION

Chapter 6: High Price of Free Candy 27
Chapter7: The Feel-up Frame-up 31
Chapter 8: Stanton High 35
Chapter 9: Stanton Sports Lesson 39
Chapter10: Jeannetta 49
Chapter 11: The Call 53

BOOK III – IN THE SERVICE

Chapter 12: Korean War 57
Chapter 13: Enlisting 59
Chapter 14: Fort Jackson 65
Chapter 15: Integration 69
Chapter 16: Basic Training 71
Chapter 17: Living with Integration 73
Chapter 18: Unrest 75
Chapter 19: 200 Miles of Standing 77
Chapter 20: Military Police 81
Chapter 21: Black MPs 83
Chapter 22: Camp Stewart 87
Chapter 23: Out West 89
Chapter 24: Going Home 93

BOOK IV – RETURNING TO JIM CROW

Chapter 25: Returning Home 97
Chapter 26: Saying I Do 99
Chapter 27: Wedding Night 103
Chapter 28: Civilian Work 107
Chapter 29: Maxwell House Coffee 109
Chapter 30: The Advertisement 111
Chapter 31: The Test 113

BOOK V – POLICING AND POWER

Chapter 32: Arresting the President...117
Chapter 33: Policing and Power 121
Chapter 34: The Powerless and the Punished..123
Chapter 35: Few Black Police Officers...127
Chapter 36: The History of Black Police Officers in Jacksonville 131
Chapter 37: Black Peril and White Policing..137

BOOK VI – THE ROAD TO THE NEGRO PRECINCT

Chapter 38: Haydon Burns 143
Chapter 39: Mayor Burns' Historic Role in Precinct Three...................147
PHOTOS 155
Chapter 40: Becoming a Negro Police Officer 173
Chapter 41: The Rookie 177
Chapter 42: Policing While Black..183
Chapter 43: Chaos Theory 187
Chapter 44: Charlie Sea 191
Chapter 45: School Patrol 195

BOOK VII – LEARNING DOESN'T STOP

Chapter 46: Further Education 203
Chapter 47: A Student of Phi Beta Sigma Founder, Leonard Morse 205
Chapter 48: Sheriff Dale Carson 209
Chapter 49: A Pastor with a Pistol 213
Chapter 50: Martin P. Garris 219
Chapter 51: Blackballed 225
Chapter 52: A Bullet Above My Head 229

BOOK VIII – THE 60S

Chapter 53: Ax Handle Saturday 233
Chapter 54: The Gas Station 235
Chapter 55: Frank Hampton..239
Chapter 56: Closing the Negro Precinct 243
Chapter 57: Consolidation 247
Chapter 58: After Consolidation 251
Chapter 59: Lieutenant Scriven 257
Chapter 60: Chief Scriven 263
Chapter 61: Civil Rights Commission 267
Chapter 62: Approaching the End...273

BOOK IX – PAROLE AND PAROLE COMMISSION

Chapter 63: Going to Tallahassee 279
Chapter 64: The Last Luncheon 285
Chapter 65: Leaving St. Marys 287
Chapter 66: Alone in Tallahassee 293
Chapter 67: The Outsider 299
Chapter 68: The Knowledge of Socrates, the Wisdom of Solomon 303
Chapter 69: Justice and Mercy 307
Chapter 70: Prison Visits...309
Chapter 71: Chairman Scriven 313
Chapter 72: Murph the Smurf 317
Chapter 73: Crime and Punishment..319
Chapter 74: The Hazelton Controversy 323
Chapter 75: In Hindsight..327
Chapter 76: The Lawsuit, Still Fighting.....................................329
Chapter 77: An Overdue Apology 333

Introduction

Nearly seventy years have passed since I first took the oath and swore to protect and serve the residents of Jacksonville, Florida. As I watch the current unrest and protests against police brutality and racism in America, I am compelled to reflect on my own career as a Negro policeman.

I know what it is like to be the only person who stands between a criminal suspect and chaos. I have worn the uniform. I spent almost my entire adult life as a sworn officer of the law.

I am also a student of history. The protests against inequality in America remind me of other moments in history when the tide against injustice and the momentum for change seemed unstoppable, of the 1950s and 1960s when Black men and women across the South protested to end racial segregation and to secure the voting rights promised to our ancestors almost a century earlier.

There has been progress in those nearly seven decades since I first took the oath to serve. More than fifty-five years have elapsed following the passage of the 1964 Civil Rights Act. But race equality remains an ongoing problem of American law enforcement, and racism and racial bias continue. Many of America's largest law enforcement agencies remain bedeviled by this dilemma, and I am frustrated that in the twilight of my life, answers to some of our nation's most pressing problems still elude us:

How does a populace historically oppressed and discriminated against obtain and secure equal justice under law?

How does this country police its most marginalized residents, its citizens of color, with equity?

How do people of all races enjoy their constitutional rights of life, liberty and the pursuit of happiness without fear of police brutality?

As a former lawman and as a Black father with sons and grandsons, there is an urgency, in light of my advancing age, to tell this story. *Justice in the Jim Crow South: An Unlikely Journey from Negro Policeman to Florida's First Black Parole & Probation Commissioner* is my attempt to answer some of those questions.

The struggle to get Negroes in uniform was part of African Americans' struggle for equal protection under the law. Negro police squads and precincts in the South were proposed as the solution to the persistent complaints of white police brutality of Black citizens in their segregated neighborhoods. The Negro police officer was a phenomenon of American racial oppression. He was viewed as more salve than solution, more reaction than a remedy. The push for Southern cities to hire Negro policemen was integral to our fight for equal rights. Black police officers and Black political power walked in tandem. The campaign to see Black men patrolling city streets, even if only in segregated Black neighborhoods, was part of our centuries-old struggle to exercise political power.

This is more than the story of one Black police officer, in one Negro squad, Precinct Three, in one Southern city, Jacksonville, Florida. It is about justice in the Jim Crow South. My journey parallels the twentieth century struggle for civil rights and equal opportunity in America. This covers a period in history when the Sunshine State emerged from its status as a tropical backwater akin to the banana republics of Central America, and took its rightful place among the rising states of America during the 1950s and early 60s. My journey begins in a segregated squad room beneath a public swimming pool for Negroes and ends at the pinnacle of Florida's prison-industrial complex, as chairman of the once-powerful Florida Parole and Probation Commission.

In telling my story, I bear witness to history; I complete the historical record; I pay tribute to the hundreds of other Black men and women, especially in the South, who wore the uniform proudly, who swore to protect and serve and did so honorably, even though they did so with one arm handcuffed, in hand-me-down uniforms and using second-hand equipment.

Mine was an improbable journey from a wood house on a dirt road to the top echelons of the Jacksonville Sheriff's Office and beyond. I did rise through the ranks, and like so many others, did not compromise my honor. The fact that I am here to tell this story is a measure of our success, but what we accomplished should be regarded as progress rather than victory.

BOOK I:
ORIGINS

Chapter 1:
THE LETTER

Spring 1955, Jacksonville, Florida

I couldn't wait to get home from work each afternoon. As soon as my shift ended at 4 p.m. at the Maxwell House Coffee factory, I climbed into the backseat of a friend's car with my fellow co-workers. As we drove out of the factory parking lot at 735 East Bay Street, the powerful aroma of coffee awakened our senses. That spring, gas cost a nickel per gallon. My fellow co-workers and I paid our friend a few bucks each week to cover gas and wear and tear on his vehicle. Seated in the back seat, I counted the eleven minutes as we drove across town to my apartment at 1777 West 11th Street. Each block along the way, my excitement grew. I wanted to get home and rush inside. Even before I hugged and greeted Jeannetta, my wife of just one year, and my baby daughter, Rosemary, I wanted to check the mail.

Did the mailman bring any letters for me? I asked Jeannetta. Was there an envelope from Jacksonville City Hall? Each day the letter didn't arrive was one more day of agony. I had a wife and a daughter to support. My wages at Maxwell House Coffee paid the bills, but I wanted something more. I yearned for a career, a better, more meaningful life.

A year earlier, after my discharge from the Army, I had applied to join the Florida National Guard. Those extra monthly wages would have gone a long way toward supporting my household. But my application was denied. National Guard units in Florida and across the South remained segregated. Those "Dixie" National Guard units had no room even for honorably discharged Black veterans like me. The only option for me was an all-Negro infantry unit. I didn't want to join the infantry. Even though Black men were largely considered cannon fodder during the Korean War, I had avoided the infantry during my three-year tour of duty. I was a military policeman, a proud MP and criminal investigator. But when I returned home, all I could find were menial, laboring jobs.

Initially, I had worked as an orderly cleaning blood and gore at University Hospital. When I got there, the nurse promised me $1 an hour. But when I received my first paycheck, I was paid 75 cents an hour.

"You promised me $1 an hour," I told her.

"No, this is your pay," the nurse replied.

"I quit," I replied in disgust.

"You have to give me two weeks' notice," she said.

"You just got my notice. This is it. I quit," I said and stormed off in disgust. When I returned home early, Jeanetta asked me what I was doing home.

I told her I quit. Afterward, I earned $1 an hour carrying cement mortar for my boss, a brick layer. After working long hours in the hot sun, I returned home and collapsed in bed, exhausted until the next morning.

Months later, I was one of dozens of employees at the Maxwell House Coffee plant, which had opened in 1910. Introduced in 1892 by wholesale grocer Joel Owsley Cheek, the brand was named for the Maxwell House Hotel in Nashville, Tennessee, his largest customer.

Being a tow motor operator was a decent job. I drove the forklift-like device in air-conditioned comfort. The job paid about $200 a month. My bosses liked my work. Under the right circumstances, I could remain with the company for years. After all, Maxwell House Coffee was the best-selling brand in America.

• • • • • • • • • • • • • • • •

It had been more than a year since my discharge from the U.S. Army. It was more than a year since I returned from San Francisco to my native Jacksonville. I loved living in California. I loved the freedom of being able to walk into a restaurant or store without having to check for the "White" or "Colored" signs. Out West, I experienced life as a free Black man, free of the chains of Jim Crow, for the first time. With its lush valleys, soaring mountains and appetizing, unsegregated beaches, California seemed a world of limitless possibilities. For the first time in my life, I didn't always have to remember I was a Black man. I could live as a man, proud, respected, in uniform, in service to my country and my fellow man. I embraced life in California. I reveled in it from the mountains to the sea and all the glitz and glamor in between. I wanted that life in California for Jeannetta and our children.

But because I loved California, and I loved Jeannetta, this didn't mean she also loved California. She had never been away from home. She was still a teenager and had never lived away from her parents and sisters. She wanted me to come home so we could get married. My mother and father, Mary and L. J. Scriven, also lived in Jacksonville. I cared for their well-being. My monthly Army paycheck helped them make ends meet while I was in the Service. They had reached middle age. If I remained in California, who would care for them as they grew older? Although I had three older siblings, there was no guarantee they would care for my parents the way I would.

And so, I had come back home to Jacksonville, to Jeannetta, to marry, to raise a family. In returning to Jacksonville, I had chosen to return to Jim Crow segregation. I had come home to a life of struggle, bereft of opportunity. The signs over the restrooms and water fountains were rustier and more aged than I remembered. But their message remained as unmistakable as ever: Jacksonville was a Black and White world, still separate, more unequal than ever, even though in 1954, the United States Supreme Court ruled that segregated schools were unconstitutional.

As a Negro, I was repeatedly reminded that my place was at the bottom. Whites ran the show. They felt superior. We lived off the scraps whites allowed us to have. Despite my high school diploma and my honorable military service, my hometown seemed determined to sentence me to a lifetime of menial labor, confinement to the lowest caste in society, to a life of subsistence and struggle, just like my parents.

But I was not my father. I was educated far beyond him. Not only had I graduated from high school, but I had also started college.

Months after I returned home, I took advantage of the GI Bill. I enrolled in Walker's Business College, a small school started by a Black couple in the Black town of Durkeeville. Walker would be the first step in an educational journey that would take me to Edward Waters College, Stetson University and Florida State University, a dissertation short of earning my doctorate. My knowledge expanded. My horizons grew. My ambition blossomed. I also had dreams. I had dreams for myself, for my wife, and for my children. I believed deeply that the answer to the fulfillment of those dreams lay in the letter from the City of Jacksonville, which I eagerly awaited. Had I passed the Negro policeman's exam? When the letter arrived, what would it say?

• • • • • • • • • • • • • • •

The advertisement appeared in the Negro section of the Florida Times Union, Jacksonville's daily newspaper. Until that moment, in spring 1955,

I was fairly content at Maxwell House Coffee. But transporting coffee containers back and forth across a factory floor was not my destination. It was an interval on my journey to economic and social improvement.

The listing advertised a test for Negro police officers. It gave the date and location for the test. When I saw it, my heart leaped with excitement. This was the better job I craved. This was the career that would provide the life and opportunities I desired, and I was qualified for it. I had experience in police work. I had done the job. As an MP at Fort Jackson, I had patrolled streets in Columbia, South Carolina. I could be a policeman in my hometown. I could treat Negroes on the streets and in their homes with the dignity they deserved. I would be a role model for young Black boys to look up to. After all the lessons I learned about fairness, I would make a difference. As an investigator in the Provost Marshal's Office, I understood criminal investigative procedures.

· · · · · · · · · · · · · · · ·

In 1955, hiring a Negro policeman was still a relatively new experiment for my hometown. Five years earlier, in the fall of 1950, during my senior year, the first Black officers began walking the beat on Ashley and Broad streets not far from where I went to Stanton High School. Six Negro officers broke Jacksonville's impenetrable blue line that had stood for 61 years. Although I didn't know them, their names were etched into the collective memory of Jacksonville's sizable Black population: Henry Harley, Edward Hickson, Alvin James, Beamon Kendall, Marion Massey and Charlie Sea.

These men stood tall and erect. They conveyed authority and demanded respect. I believed I could stand among their ranks. I could earn a place among the Black men in blue. I would make my parents and my wife proud.

· · · · · · · · · · · · · · · ·

For generations, law enforcement was the exclusive preserve of white men. No Black men in uniform had walked the streets of Jacksonville in Florida's Duval County since 1889. White supremacy, the notion that Blacks were inferior and inherently unfit to exercise political and legal authority, demanded that Blacks be kept from public office and law enforcement by any means necessary. Jacksonville's white power structure had effectively erased the memory of Negroes in politics and policing. Yet, we had a proud history. We once won elections. We once governed. We used to serve in public office. But I didn't know it. My friends and family didn't know that in the years after the Civil War, Black freedmen and Reconstruction Republicans won elections and controlled Jacksonville politically.

In 1870, five years after the Confederate surrender at Appomattox, Jacksonville elected its first Negro police commissioner. That year, five Black police officers, two Black jailers and two Black constables also wore the uniform. One of those men, George H. Mays, became Jacksonville's first Negro sergeant and would become the second Black town marshal in 1878. He served in that role for three years. E. Fortune made history in 1872, when he was elected to a two-year term as the first Black town marshal. (Source: 1976 Bicentennial Report). A decade later, the Jacksonville police department would include 24 Negro officers among its ranks.

I was wholly ignorant of my hometown's history of Black law enforcement accomplishment. Generations of Black boys were raised to believe that being a policeman was a white man's domain. That was no accident. More than half a century of racial oppression had effectively wiped the slate clean of our past law enforcement accomplishments and political triumphs. While Jim Crow perpetrators tried to rewrite my history, they could not destroy my aspirations and my ambition.

....

In Jacksonville, Black citizens paid taxes just like whites, but we were largely deprived of the benefits of those taxes. We were educated in segregated, substandard, poorly equipped, and poorly maintained schools. Police protection and public safety were an especially sore point for us. Each encounter with white policemen was fraught with danger. They despised us. They felt superior to us. They mistreated us. They rarely appeared in our neighborhoods except to respond to calls and complaints. By the time they arrived, the violence or the theft had long occurred, and the suspect had vanished. By the time the white police officers left, Black residents often felt twice victimized, by the criminals and by white police officers. Police often tout their mission to serve and to protect. White officers neither served nor protected us.

Under the written and unwritten code of the Jim Crow South, my siblings and I could be arrested for just about any minor infraction that occurred on streets, public buses, and street cars. I could be arrested for demanding the right change from the bus conductor, for refusing to give up my seat in the back section of the bus or for speaking to a white person in the wrong tone. I could be arrested for being, God forbid, in the white section of town after dark. White officers can be discourteous to me and my parents, but we could be arrested for responding in kind or addressing them in a way considered sassing a police officer. They called our fathers "boy" and our mothers by their first name with disdain.

· · · · · · · · · · · · · · ·

Such was our plight that whites didn't even have to be in uniform to exercise police authority over us. One day when I was in high school, I was driving the football coach's car. At a traffic light, I pulled out in front of a white man, changed lanes and moved in front of him. Next thing I knew, he pulled up alongside me and signaled for me to pull over to the side of the road. Of course, I complied. After he pulled me over, he climbed out of his vehicle and walked up to my side of the vehicle as the Cadillac idled at the side of the road.

"Whose car are you driving, boy?" He asked. His question felt like a slap in the face. His demand pricked my teenage anger, as the word "boy," like a three-syllable insult, rolled derisively off his Southern lips.

In the early 50s, only Black football coaches and Black preachers drove Cadillacs.

Where are you going? Stanton High School Football Coach James P. Small had sent me on an errand. I was in his car with two other students. The white man gave me a stern warning just like a police officer.

"Be careful with your driving," he yelled at me. He didn't identify himself. He didn't need to. The man wore no uniform. He never flashed a badge or a pistol. It never occurred to me to question his authority. He was a white man. His skin color gave him authority. He could have had me arrested. His word was unquestioned when stacked against mine. I drove away nervously.

As part of the code that governed our lives, breaking the rules against one white person was a violation against all whites. It must be treated and punished as such. In the ensuing years, I better came to understand that the Southern white policeman was much more than law, someone who brandished a badge and his revolver. His word was final and unimpeachable, his authority unquestioned. In the courtroom, his testimony was the only one that counted. He was the viceroy of the white community to the Negro community, as one writer put it. He represented civic order and symbolized white supremacy, whites as lord and master over us, Negroes. The white policeman in the South was the sheriff, judge, jury and often executioner. He was the delegated inquisitor and punisher. His power was social as well as legal. Courts granted him latitude to act extrajudicially without fear of sanction. He could take the law into his own hands without fear of punishment. After all, he was acting in the best interest of white society. To question his actions and his motives white society held, was to undermine the status quo, the very framework upon which Jim Crow rested. His words and testimony were sacrosanct. They must always be accepted against a Negro's, even in situations when the facts in evidence stated something to the contrary. To do otherwise would threaten his prestige and weaken his authority, as Swedish sociologist Gunnar Myrdal so astutely pointed out in his groundbreaking work, *An American Dilemma*.

• • • • • • • • • • • • • • • •

Although I didn't have the words to describe it at the time, I now understand that by taking the Negro police officer's exam, I was taking my stand against white supremacy. By taking the test, I lent myself to the struggle for civil and equal rights. In taking the test, I was assuming my rightful place in the long, proud line of Black law enforcement officers in America. This was a privilege long denied those like me. Now that the door had been pried slightly ajar, I was determined to barge through it, claim my badge and my pistol, and stand in the gap to provide protection and equal justice for my family, my friends, and my neighbors. As a Negro policeman, I would finally breach the blue wall and put on the uniform. But like the rest of life in the American South, the unbreachable wall of Jim Crow would separate me from my white fellow officers. Negro officers were not allowed at the Jacksonville Police Headquarters, then located at 711 Liberty Street. They were billeted in a building at 1205 North Davis Street in a property we shared with a public swimming pool built by Mayor William Haydon Burns for the city's Negro residents.

The presence of Negro policemen on the streets of Jacksonville was the direct result of an election payback from Mayor Burns. But even that act of political expediency was a recognition and response to the Black struggle for civil and equal rights in America, especially in the South, in Florida, Alabama, Georgia, Mississippi, Louisiana, South Carolina and other states of the former Confederacy.

• • • • • • • • • • • • • • • •

The coming of the Negro officer to the downtown streets of Jacksonville in November 1950 would change that. The arrival of the Negro police officer changed the Black social order. The job carried considerable social status. If an officer attended a church service, in or out of uniform, he was introduced and recognized. In Jacksonville, the Negro policeman was treated like a minor celebrity. He was an asset to the community. And he was much more than a social symbol.

The Negro policeman helped change the attitude of white folks to Black folks. The Negro police officer made a big change in the attitude of the entire city of Jacksonville. At that point no Blacks were in city government except the sanitation department. No Blacks had held any authority in the city since before the turn of the twentieth century. Other than our postal workers, teachers and our preachers, most Black men like my father eked out a living doing menial labor. When it came to economic opportunities, it always seemed as if we had to enter through the back door. The front door was always marked with the word "white." We couldn't enter.

Because of the novelty of the experiment, the Negro policeman was selected from the best of the best. Their ranks were filled by college graduates and military veterans, men of proven character. They were not just handpicked. They had to pass a test. Things were different for our white counterparts. Many had little more than elementary school education. Some had an eighth-grade education. Prior to the introduction of civil service standards, white men, if they were not blind or crippled, had no criminal record and could meet the height and weight requirements, could be hired to wear the uniform.

The Negro policeman, unlike his white counterpart, was respected and well regarded by the community he served. He knew the people who lived and worked in the neighborhoods he patrolled. His presence was welcomed, not despised. He was seen as an ally rather than an occupying enemy force. With the badge and uniform came social status. The Negro policeman created a new rung in the Black social order. At the top were doctors, dentists and lawyers, what few we had. Then you had your preachers, teachers, and postal workers. Now, with the Negro police officer, there was nobody who could match their status. Growing up poor, I yearned for that. I wanted to be part of the city government. I wanted to have the authority of the white power structure.

Our presence on the streets in uniform was revolutionary. It was a new day. It changed white policemen. For the first time, Southern white men were forced to view Black men as equals. After all, we were sworn law enforcement officers, with an equal badge and revolver, even though we could not arrest whites.

The white police officer's behavior had to change because of the Negro policemen. His behavior had to change because in court the Negro police officers were also there. We could hear his testimony; we could discern the truth from his lies. He could no longer freely call our neighbors and friends "Nigger."

As a Negro policeman, I would go to places that the average Negro couldn't go.

The uniform would give me a certain access. The uniform would give me respect. I learned to use respect as a tool rather than a weapon. It made the Black community feel they had someone in authority whom they could trust, someone who believed they should be protected. I was one of this special brotherhood. I was Black in blue.

The uniform gave me status, authority and power, legal, legitimate white power.

So many people never had an interaction with a Black man in authority. Substation 3, the Negro Precinct was just a starting point. Patrolling the streets of the Negro business, entertainment, and residential community, chasing dice throwers and muggers, and greeting merchants was one step along my journey that began during the depths of the Great Depression and paralleled the course of America's 20th century history — World War II, integration of the Armed Services, the Korean War, the unrest and protests of the 1960s and the rise of Black political power in Jacksonville and across the old South. Along the way, like Jackie Robinson and other pioneers, I broke racial barriers to become the first Black man named a division chief in Duval County law enforcement history before being named the first African American appointed to the Florida Parole and Probation Commission.

Along the way, I saw America's system of unequal justice in black and white. I battled stereotypes and America's propensity to judge me and those who look like me by the color of my skin rather than the content of character. But I, the son of barely literate folks from South Georgia, refused to be stopped.

Chapter 2
ORIGINS

I was born in Jacksonville, Florida, but my ancestral roots are bound up in the rich, fertile South Georgia soil. My mother, Mary Scott, was born in Albany, Georgia, on March 11, 1904. She came from a place W. E. B. Dubois described a few years earlier as the heart of the Black Belt. She was one of the 10,000 Negroes who lived among 2,000 whites in Dougherty County in the early years of the twentieth century. Back then, the Albany in which my mother grew up was a placid Southern town with stores and saloons. It was a land of fertile soil, home to king cotton and forest lush with pine, oak, ash, hickory and poplar. Mary and her folks must have loved the arrival of Saturdays when all the Negroes went to town, walked up and down the streets, greeted their friends and gossiped with their neighbors. In between they shopped in stores for provisions for the week. The summers in Albany got hot and humid, dull, when even nature took an afternoon nap. There wasn't much to stay in Albany for as a young woman.

One day, Mary boarded a bus out of town. Unlike some of her neighbors, Mary didn't head north for the big city, Atlanta. Instead, she traveled east for the Atlantic Coast. She disembarked in Brunswick, a bustling port city in the southeast corner of the state.

In Brunswick, my mother found herself among a population mostly descended from the slaves who worked in the rice fields and the ports. Some of them must have boasted ancestors who were among the shipment of 409 Africans transported from the Congo and landed at Jekyll Island seven miles down the Georgia coastline in 1858. In 1921, when my mother was merely 17 years old, she got pregnant. She soon gave birth to a son, Robert Lee Quinn. Being a struggling single mother, she sent Robert to be raised by her parents back in Albany. Soon afterward, my mother met Lifton James "L J" Scriven, a short, wiry young man who hailed from Dorchester, Georgia, a dusty town almost 50 miles north on State Road 25. James, as his friends called him, was born in 1902. His parents died when he was very young, and he and his siblings were left to fend for themselves.

His father was Charles Scriven, one of the scores of Scrivens bound to the land in the Low Country Georgia community founded by Quakers and Puritans who moved from South Carolina with their slaves a century earlier. Dorchester was part of the Midway District where Quakers and Baptists allowed the enslaved to hold worship services in their building. In 1810, Baptists provided accommodations for the slaves in their new church at Sunbury. A Reverend Charles O. Screven, a minister and his assistant, Samuel S. Law, held services every Sunday afternoon for the enslaved members. I don't know if the good reverend is an ancestor, but the name Charles Scriven is quite common in my family tree.

• • • • • • • • • • • • • • • •

The courtship between Mary, a young mother, liberated from child rearing duties, and the energetic James was short. They were married in Brunswick in 1922. That was before Highway 17 was constructed, providing a scenic north-south thoroughfare along the Intracoastal Waterway and the Atlantic coast corridor.

My mother and father had each other's undivided attention for five years before their first child arrived. She gave birth to George on September 18, 1927. My sister, Mary, followed 14 months later, on November 23, 1928. When Frances Marie arrived on October 18, 1930, my parents found themselves raising three children younger than four years old.

By then South Georgia, along with the rest of the country, was gripped by the Great Depression. In the South, Black men like my daddy found themselves in dire straits. During boom times in the Jim Crow South, employment options for educated Black men were limited to teaching or preaching or operating their own business. For uneducated Black men like my father, without a trade or a skill, the choice was to be a laborer in the fields or a janitor or to pump gas and clean customer windshields at the corner gas station.

Daddy was a laborer. He also worked at a gas station. I have an old black and white photograph of him looking young and energetic at the gas station where he worked. With my mother at home taking care of three young children, Daddy's meager wages were all the family had to survive on. I imagine Mother and Daddy scraping together vegetables and ham hocks and frying flour in oil to put food on the table. For my father, who was barely literate, it was especially difficult. Soon, the family decided to move 70 miles south and try their luck in Jacksonville, a city of more than 130,000, once known as Cow Ford.

At the time, Jacksonville was a haven for winter tourists from the Midwest and the Northeast. The struggling family looked south across the state line for a new start, for a better life, to have more children.

Chapter 3
A MOTHER'S LOVE

A child of what everyone now calls the silent generation, I was born on Wednesday July 13, 1932. Amelia Earhart made big news that day when she set a new record for a woman by flying from Los Angeles to Newark in just over 19 hours. Our country remained in the grip of the Great Depression and hapless Herbert Hoover still occupied the White House.

I was the first of my parents' children to be born in Jacksonville. I was the fourth of J. L. and Mary Scott Scriven's six children. I was born at Brewster Hospital, Jacksonville's Negro hospital, which was opened in 1901 by the Methodist Church Women Missionary Society. White hospitals in the South didn't treat or train Black people. Named for Mrs. George A. Brewster, the facility located at 915 West Monroe Street in the Black LaVilla neighborhood, was the first training hospital for Blacks in the country.

My older brother George was five years older than me. My big sisters, Mary and Frances Marie, were three and four years older, respectively. Our age and gender differences created a gulf between us. They seemed to live in a whole other world. Girls had their own things. They had their own friends. By the time I was born, Daddy had been hired as a janitor at the Florida Times Union newspaper. We lived in a two-story house at 1863 Kings Road in northwest Jacksonville. The house had six bedrooms. We used four rooms for our family. The girls slept together. The boys slept together. We rented rooms to other families. They paid around $2.50 per week. That helped us with the light bill and water bill. Everybody shared one bathroom.

· · · · · · · · · · · · · · · ·

My mother never worked outside the home. Her job was to raise her children. With two older sisters and a brother, I was the center of my mother's life for at least eight years until my baby sister was born. Those formative years meant that I had all the love and affection from both of my parents

— a privileged childhood in that neighborhood and in those days. While I wasn't spoiled, I did truly learn the meaning of a mother's love in my early developing years, and that made leaving home for elementary school at six years old more difficult than it might have been.

Regardless of what happened, I knew my mother loved me. Those times she took care of me when I wasn't feeling good cannot be erased. She rubbed me down in the metal wash tub. She gave me kerosene to drink for the cold. She bathed me with Epson Salts and tree bark. Being from Georgia, she had a lot of old home remedies. I never went to see a doctor. We practiced our own medicine at home.

• • • • • • • • • • • • • • • •

While Daddy never could reconcile what church people said and how they behaved, Mother was a regular worshiper. When I was an infant, I sat on my mother's knees watching her singing and clapping and thanking God at house churches. That was my first Christian experience. It was in somebody's living room.

There was a woman who preached. She wasn't ordained in the church, she was a lay preacher. She was called Mother Helen. My mom took me with her to see Mother Helen. I was two or three years old. There was also a barely literate woman preaching, singing and praying. The early seeds of my Christian faith were sown as my mother followed prayer bands in people's homes. We arrived around six or seven o'clock, but we didn't get home until midnight. They sang and prayed and testified until after 12 or one in the morning. As I sat there fighting sleep, the women spoke in tongues, strange words gushed from their lips. Others fell out on the ground as if they were possessed by a spirit. They were. They were filled with the Holy Spirit. These were people in the community who worked a day job as a maid or a cook and felt touched by the spirit of God to pray fervently and to preach passionately. They believed the Second Coming was imminent. They desperately wanted to save their neighbors and family from the destruction they believed was soon to come.

The nights when I didn't accompany my mother to a house church or a prayer meeting, I'd climb into bed with her to sleep. When Daddy returned home late at night from his job at the Florida Times Union, he'd find me sleeping in his bed with Mother.

"What are you doing in bed with my wife?" he'd ask in jest. Although the question sounded judgmental, it lacked the venom that preceded punishment. He was only joking. He knew the bond between my mother and me. He understood how much I enjoyed her comfort. He appreciated how much she enjoyed my company.

Chapter 4
DADDY

My dad, J. L. Scriven, was quite a man. He was on the short side, but his character made up for his lack of size and formal education. He was born in the small town of Dorchester, but it's unlikely he was able to attend the Dorchester Academy, a school for Negroes which was established in 1869. Daddy might have had a second or third grade education because as a young father, Daddy could barely read and write.

Daddy was a very gentle man. He hardly ever spoke above a whisper. You had to know him. He wasn't the person you'd start a conversation with. He was very quiet and unassuming. He seldom spoke in public. When my dad talked, he spoke with purpose. He wasn't boisterous in any way. He was very direct and honest. Although he was not religious and never professed to be a Christian, Daddy possessed a high sense of integrity and truthfulness. The thing I always admired about him was his personal dignity and his truthfulness. He judged a person on how that person kept his word.

Jobs were scarce in Depression-era Jacksonville. For uneducated Negroes like my father, finding a decent job was like winning the numbers. Daddy was a hardworking man. He often worked two jobs to support his six children and a stay-at-home wife. A proud man, he didn't believe in accepting charity.

"You need two jobs to keep one," Daddy said.

During the week, Daddy worked at night cleaning up at the Florida Times Union newspaper. He spent about 12 or 15 years there as a janitor. They used hot type. Once the paper was printed, the hot type was melted and used again. He cleaned up the spare type department. He had to use a blow gun to get it cleaned up. Each night, they picked up all the metal and reused it. Sometimes he took me to work with him. I would fall asleep on the papers as he completed his tasks. His shift ended around 11 or 12 o'clock. When it was time to go home, he woke me up. That experience of my father taking me to work to see how he made a living made an indelible impression on me. From early on, it gave me a sense of how hard he worked — without making much money.

Perhaps because he was left to fend for himself at a young age, my dad never depended on anybody. He was always trying to do something to help himself and to help his family. On weekends, I used to go on the truck with him as he drove through our Black neighborhood to deliver ice, wood and kerosene, and to sell watermelons. He went to the market and bought 30 or 40 watermelons, put them in his truck and drove through the neighborhood. If he bought one for $1, he would sell them for $1.50 each. He also sold ice. Daddy bought 25 or 50 pounds of ice and sold it to housewives for their icebox. Our neighbors had kerosene heaters. He sold them the kerosene oil to keep their homes warm and lit. He also supplied firewood to those with wood-burning stoves.

· · · · · · · · · · · · · · · ·

My father didn't drink. He didn't imbibe any of the moonshine liquor flowing in our neighborhood. He didn't smoke. Still, he wasn't religious. On Sunday mornings, he didn't put on a suit and drive to church with my mom. Although he wasn't a church-going man, he set an example for me to follow. He didn't lie. He didn't swear. As far as I know, he didn't cheat on my mom. He taught me my word is my bond.

My dad was so different from a neighbor who lived across the street. Every Friday night he came home drunk and raised hell. I could hear his anger and feel the terror for his children.

Daddy was a generous man. Although he always worked two and three jobs, he was generous with his time. He didn't mind helping a friend. He was generous with his food. If we were sitting at the table eating and there was a biscuit left over, that biscuit was always mine. If he had anything left over on his plate, he would put it on mine. We never wanted for any food or clothing. He prided himself in taking care of his family.

When he was a boy in Georgia, my daddy didn't go far in school. He could barely read. But he always had a passion to improve himself. When he was grown and in his 40s, I remember him riding his bicycle to an adult learning center in Jacksonville where he learned to read and earn his GED. Afterward he loved to read. Daddy loved to read the Bible. He lived out the teachings of the Bible, not in words but his actions. Sitting at the dinner table, he talked passionately about the contradiction in the way church people talked and the way they lived. Daddy never could reconcile with people who were religious but whose lives contradicted the faith they preached and did not practice.

In those days, if you were a Christian, you didn't drink liquor or run around with women. He knew a man who claimed to be a Christian, but the man drank liquor and ran around with women. My Daddy judged people not by what they said but how they lived.

• • • • • • • • • • • • • • • •

We lived on a dirt road, so each time we stepped inside our house, the dust from the street entered with us. That required a lot of sweeping daily. When we got up each morning, we swept the house. We made up our own bed. My father was the kind of man, if things didn't look right, he said something about it.

After we came home from school, we took off our shoes and went outside to play in the street. We played in our bare feet. When it rained, the streets turned muddy. Everybody in the neighborhood went around in their bare feet. We played football and softball in the street.

By nightfall, when we went inside for dinner, our feet were clothed in north Florida dust. We sat around the table with Mother having dinner. Daddy's seat was usually empty since he worked the night shift at the Times Union building. After his shift ended, Daddy didn't go to the juke joint or the bar. He came straight home. And when he did, he was fastidious about our hygiene.

Daddy was particular about us going to bed with clean feet. When he arrived home late at night, he walked into our room to check on each of us. In each room, he turned on the light and pulled up the covers. He didn't look anywhere else but our feet. He checked to see if we had gone to bed with unwashed, dusty feet. It was one of the things he would not abide — dirty feet.

"Wash them!" he said, his voice pierced my deepest sleep.

He didn't have to say anymore. It's one thing going to bed at six or eight o'clock. It was something else having to get up at 11 or 12 o'clock to wash my feet. In the winter, the penalty for going to bed with dirty feet was worse. We didn't have hot running water. If I was going to get hot water, I was going to have to start a fire to warm the water. I was sleepy. I was tired. Washing dirty feet in cold water at midnight felt like torture, even in the summertime. And don't even talk about winter. Jacksonville may be in Florida, but our winters were cold. In the winter, we didn't have a warm house. Someone had to get up early in the morning and put in the wood to get the house warm. In the evening we tried to go to bed before the house got too cold. I shared a room with my older brother, George. When I was much younger, we slept in the same bed. On cold nights, he would give me a nickel to get in bed first and warm up the bed for him. Later, my parents bought us bunk beds.

By the time Daddy came home, you were usually fast asleep. By the time he said "wash 'em," it meant getting up in a cold house. Daddy didn't play. He didn't ask you twice. When he said "wash 'em," that was what he meant. If they were not washed, there was an old leather strap he named "Nick." "Nick" was the answer to every childhood misdeed. If you didn't do what he said, he'd say, "Go get Nick."

Daddy wasn't a brutal man. There was never a question about the punishment we earned for specific misdeeds. The number of licks with Nick depended on our transgression. Whenever we did something wrong, we knew exactly how many licks were forthcoming.

• • • • • • • • • • • • • • • •

When I was in middle school, I played hooky for one day, then the next, and the next four days. When I returned to school, my teacher asked me what happened. I said we moved across town, and we moved back. He had heard that lie before. When my daddy learned about my delinquency, he took care of that right away. I got a severe dose of "Nick," the leather strap. He had a nail behind the door, and that's where "Nick" stayed.

Daddy dealt with the severity of our offenses. He never punished us in anger. I never saw him angry. He was calm and deliberate. If it was egregious, he would put me across his lap and use one leg to hold me down. When he beat us, we took off all our clothes except our underpants. By the time he was through, I was convinced to amend my ways and keep to the straight and narrow road.

For my sisters, he left all the discipline to my mother. I never can recall him disciplining my sisters. Maybe he was afraid of hurting them.

Chapter 5
JEAN

For most of my elementary school years, I didn't have to share Mother with my older siblings. They didn't demand her attention. It was just me and her. We went places together. I sat in her lap and listened to her. When I was eight, my mother became pregnant. She told me she was having a baby. I watched her small frame get bigger and bigger. Then one day in 1940, Daddy drove her to Brewster Hospital. When she returned a few days later, she brought home a newborn baby girl. She named her Jean.

Jean didn't look like Mother or Daddy. She was born with slightly odd facial features. Jean was born with Down's syndrome. She was different, but she was always happy. She didn't fuss, and she never got angry or upset. At the time she was born, most babies like Jean were put away in government asylums, far away from their families and their friends. But Mother would never let anyone put Jean in a home.

After Jean was born, everybody loved her. Being born with that condition means one doesn't have bad days. One doesn't have personality clashes with one's brothers and sisters. We played with Jean. We all loved her.

Mother spent every day trying to keep Jean alive. Mother was so protective of her. Mother felt she was responsible for Jean's condition. I don't know why she felt that way, but she blamed herself. Mother was in her mid-thirties when Jean was born. It wasn't as if Jean was a child of her old age.

They would sit down to dinner together and watch TV or listen to the radio together. Mother wouldn't let my baby sister out of her sight. Mother wouldn't let Jean get on a bus or go anywhere by herself. The only time she was out of my mother's presence was if she went to the bathroom. Mother had a special love for her.

In those days, children like Jean didn't go to school. Children with Down's syndrome didn't learn to read and write. Mother would never let

Jean go to any type of training. Much later in life, when societal attitudes had changed about men and women with Down's syndrome, Jean was able to go to training centers, but by then, she was much older and it was too late. She couldn't benefit from the training. Jean didn't learn much.

In the 1940s and 1950s, babies with Down's syndrome usually didn't live past 12 years old. Mother's love was like medicine for Jean. Mother's love kept Jean alive. It kept Jean strong and happy. She lived much longer than anyone could have expected. She lived into middle age. Jean lived with Mother all her life. Mother worried what would happen to Jean after she died. Where would she live? Who would care for her? Would Jean live with me or with my older sisters? Mother died in 1998. Losing Mother must have broken Jean's heart. She lived for less than a year after Mother died. Jean breathed her last in July 1999. She was 59 years old.

BOOK II:
MY EARLY EDUCATION

Chapter Six:
HIGH PRICE OF FREE CANDY

My schooling got off to a rocky start. It turned out that being so close to my Mommy was bad medicine. She was overly protective of her baby boy. I was overly sheltered. I was prepared for the class education but unprepared for the lessons of my young life. I flunked the first half of first grade at LaVilla Elementary School because I was frightened.

There were not many Negro schools in those days. At six years old, I walked three miles to LaVilla and three miles home. I was terrified all the way. There were no other boys in my neighborhood to walk with. My two sisters were older than me, so I walked alone through strange neighborhoods where the houses were so unfamiliar, it was easy to get lost. I imagined that bigger boys would be coming out of those houses to attack me at any time as I walked past. By the time I finally got to school, all I could think about was the walk home and if I'd make it without getting jumped by older boys. I couldn't concentrate on what the teacher said. The words on the blackboard seemed like a blur.

Finally, when my mother realized what was happening to me in the second half of the first semester of first grade, she enrolled me in College Park Elementary. It was much closer to home — only about two or three blocks from our rented two-story house at 1460 Kings Road. It wasn't until many years later that I understood one underlying reason for my fears as I walked to school.

There was a service station on the corner about three doors from our house. The old white proprietor operated a garage and gas station. Motorists could fill up and get serviced with an oil change. Inside the store, customers bought cigarettes, ice-cold sodas and groceries. The proprietor lured us kids inside with an array of tooth-decay-inducing candy. My parents didn't mind me walking a few doors from the house at 1460 Kings Road to buy candy.

I went there to buy candy or cookies. One day, as I walked by, the owner of the store asked me if I wanted a piece of candy. My pockets were empty. I didn't have any money. The old white man knew how much I loved candy. Intuitively, he understood I would be disappointed to walk home empty-handed without the sweet taste of candy on my tongue. Since I didn't have a single penny, the old white man offered me what he and I inherently knew to be an indecent proposal.

"You can have a piece of candy," he said. "But you have to pay for it."

He knew I didn't have any money. What was his price?

"I will give you a piece of candy if you let me put my penis in your mouth," he said.

As he uttered the words, my head must have spun as my young mind tried to comprehend the ignominy of his offer. My youthfulness, my innocence, my naivete, my ignorance of the evil in the world handicapped my judgment. Nothing in my brief life would have prepared me for what he proposed. Nothing ever should in any young boy's life. My parents had never seen the need to warn me about the predilection of evil men who preyed on innocent young boys like me. I don't recall if I consented with a nod of my head or with words. My lack of recollection mirrors the shroud with which I cloaked that abominable memory for an entire lifetime. I must have felt the shame of my acquiescence as I walked home, my head bowed, my eyes downcast. The bitterness of my shame must have erased the sugar sweetness of that ill-gotten candy. There could have been no enjoyment that day. What I didn't know then but understand fully now, was that I had exchanged a lifetime of shame for a moment of joy. Such a trade, life has taught me, is a fool's bargain. That decision marked me, although I didn't quite know or understand it until many years later.

I walked home that day, my mind racing with confusion, my heart heavy with shame, my lips sealed with a dark secret. I told no one — not my older sisters, not my brother George, not my mother, not my father. As a matter of fact, I was afraid to tell my parents. My father was a gentle, dignified man who hardly ever raised his voice, but I feared he would have killed my abuser if he had found out. So, I buried my secret in years of forgetfulness.

I kept that traumatic, demeaning secret to myself for decades. I went through elementary school, middle and high school and into adulthood suppressing the incident until the memory resurfaced when, as a police officer in Jacksonville, I began to see children being abused and I realized I had a deeper understanding of their trauma. I didn't know it then, but I know now, that my passion for working with young people and for keeping them safe must have been a consequence of my childhood, when my innocence left me vulnerable to a man who must have harmed other children before and after me. That memory lay buried so deeply that it didn't resurface for more than 60 years until it came back one day, and I told my wife, Jeannetta.

• • • • • • • • • • • • • • • •

After being transferred to College Park Elementary, I did much better in school and learned a great deal, although I don't remember ever seeing a new textbook. The school was a three-story wood frame building leased from Edward Waters College. It was later moved to 1666 Pearce Street.

All our books and desks throughout my public schooling were hand-me-downs, equipment left over from the white schools. I remember broken seats with names carved in them — sent to our schools instead of to the city dump. I never saw a new textbook. All the books I used came with the pages torn out and covers ripped and names scratched in.

Often Negro students attended double sessions because of overcrowding. A group of students attended school in the mornings and another group went to class in the afternoons. While white students enjoyed a whole day of classwork, we often got shortchanged. And that's not even accounting for time lost when the boilers broke down during the North Florida winter. We had a boiler we called Big Jim. When the heat went out, we went home. Many days we were forced to stay home because our school building had no heat. That made a big difference when it came to academics. While white children attended school 180 days a year, Black children on average spent 120 days a year or less getting instruction.

All those days of missed classes and abbreviated sessions took their toll on our ability to get a decent education. From my youth, I knew the system was stacked against us. But I was determined to persevere. I refused to fail. I refused to make excuses for myself. I knew I would succeed.

Chapter Seven:
THE FEEL-UP FRAME UP

One day when I was at Davis Street Junior High School, I was walking up the stairs on my way to my next class. One of my female eighth-grade classmates walked up the stairs in front of me. When she reached the top of the stairs, I tried to pass her and almost bumped into her. Such occurrences happened dozens of times each week as we walked our school's crowded hallways and climbed the congested stairways to get to our next class on time. That day didn't strike me as being any different.

To avoid knocking her over, I stepped around her and continued on my way. Before I could get far, she reached out and slapped me in my face. She slapped me so hard, it stung. I was startled.

"Why did you slap me?" I asked.

"Because you felt me."

"What?" I asked, my eyes about to tear up.

"You felt me," she repeated.

I had not touched her. I didn't know anything about touching girls. That girl had a reputation for slapping boys, but I had never run into anything like her — and didn't know anything about feeling girls. My face still stung as I turned around and went directly to the principal's office to complain that she had slapped me in the face. After I filed my complaint, the principal summoned her. When she arrived, she said she slapped me because I felt her up.

"Scriven is always picking on girls," she lied. "He felt me in the stairway."

The principal wore a frown on his face. My heart raced. The atmosphere in his office felt like a courtroom, a place of punishment and judgement. Here was I, making a complaint because I was slapped, only to be accused of touching this girl.

Her accusation stunned me. We were in the same class, but we weren't friends. Other than my three sisters and the girl whose parents rented a room in our house, I didn't associate with girls. I must have been about 12 or 13 years old when this happened, but I had led a sheltered life when it came to doing things with girls.

I was a late bloomer. Perhaps because of my mother's strict religious life and my father's no-nonsense, no smoking, no drinking, no cussing lifestyle, I was shielded from so much that occurred outside our door in Jacksonville. I was way behind my classmates on matters of sex and love.

I had no crushes in elementary school or middle school. My heart was a clean slate when it came to matters of love at my age. When it came to feeling girls, I was way behind. Boys around me boasted, "I felt her." I didn't know what it meant to feel a girl.

To bolster her charge, my classmate called another girl who sided with her. She also accused me of picking at her.

In junior high school, boys and girls begin to explore what it means to be sexual. Teenage girls are attracted to boys, and boys are tempted to touch girls. In his position, the principal had seen such situations before. The accusations were often true. Maybe, he thought, I did feel her. He heard such complaints all the time. There were boys who felt girls. I wasn't at the age when touching a girl meant anything to me.

I was dumbfounded. I had never ever contemplated feeling up girls. I had never had the urge to touch a girl. I had done nothing. Yet, the principal believed the girl instead of me. The only thing he knew was what I told him and what the girl who slapped me said. I learned people told lies about you. Not only did she do it, but she got somebody to cover what she said.

I didn't cry. Even if I wanted to, I couldn't. Disappointment and anger stopped any tears I would shed.

My heart hurt at being wrongly accused for something I didn't do. But even though I was too young to know the excitement of touching a girl, I was old enough to understand the larger implications for Black boys like me being accused of such behavior. Anything involving sex and a Black boy was dangerous ground. A Black boy could be lynched for touching or even looking at the wrong girl — a white girl.

The principal meted out punishment that was more degrading than harsh. He sentenced me to janitorial duty for five days. Each day after school, I reported to the custodian. He handed me a mop, a bucket and a broom. Each afternoon, as I emptied the dust bins and swept and mopped the floors, I seethed inside. I was innocent. I hadn't touched her. I was not even aware enough to think I accepted the punishment for the pleasure I had received of touching that girl. I was thirteen years old. I had never kissed a girl. I had never even thought of kissing a girl. I was my mother's son. I accompanied her to church meetings. I knew nothing about what went on between men and women, boys and girls.

Yet here I was being punished for an act, I later learned, that could be considered a crime, a sexual assault. That crime could land a Black man in prison doing hard time. And if he's accused of touching a white woman, the punishment could be far swifter and so much harsher.

That lesson about innocence, guilt and punishment stayed with me in the years to come as I donned a police uniform and encountered Black men and women in similar situations, where accusations carried life altering consequences, when to be Black and accused was to be Black and guilty. As Dubois wrote half a century earlier, "It was not then a question of crime but rather of color that settled a man's conviction on almost any charge."

The unwritten laws of the South had not changed. And so, I learned early on that it didn't matter who was the accuser or who was the judge. A Black boy or Black man who stood accused was guilty.

Truth didn't matter. Evidence didn't matter. That day in my Black, segregated junior high school I learned my first lesson about crime and punishment. I knew I was innocent. But my version of the facts didn't matter. In the principal's eyes I was guilty. He could suspend me; he could expel me; he could refer me to the Jacksonville Police Department for criminal charges.

But, as an adult Black man who had survived life under Jim Crow, the principal must have understood that punishment, even if unjust, was a suitable deterrent. He must have understood what I was too young and too naïve to appreciate — that he needed to punish me whether I was guilty or innocent. By punishing me, I would see the big picture and come to understand that such actions had consequences. Too many Black men had already paid too high a price for not having learned that lesson earlier in life.

The penalty I got really helped me in life. You can be penalized and be innocent. I would take nothing for that experience. It guided me while I was on the police force. I would see people doing something that under normal conditions I would arrest them for, and I wouldn't. It gave me a spirit of giving somebody a break.

The lesson that I could be punished when I was innocent stayed with me as I became an MP in the U.S. Army. It stayed with me as I was sworn in to become a Jacksonville policeman. It stayed with me every day as I walked on patrol. It stayed with me when I returned to the schools in charge of the safety patrol. It stayed with me when I was the first African American to serve on the Florida Parole and Probation Commission.

    I never wanted anyone to be punished for my mistakes. It's one thing to make a mistake. In my situation, if I made a mistake as a policeman, somebody could go to jail. Depending on the extent of my mistake, they could spend time in jail, a penal farm, or worse, a state penitentiary. Most of the time, the punishment was usually 60 days. Unlike my middle school punishment, that was too high a price for a miscarriage of justice.

Chapter 8:
STANTON HIGH

I graduated from Davis Street Junior High School in 1948, but I was unable to participate in the graduation ceremony because my parents could not afford to buy me the blue trousers, white shirt and blue tie that were required of each boy to wear for the commencement exercise.

Money was always scarce. By then, my older brother George was grown and had left home to serve in the Army. Daddy did all he could to provide for his six children and his wife on a salary of $18 a week. I was just grateful I was able to finish the 9th grade and would be going to historic Stanton High, the only Negro senior high school in Duval County at the time.

For 80 years, Stanton had stood as a symbol of Black aspiration and progress, not just in Jacksonville but in all of Florida. Stanton's history is Florida's history. Florida history is my history. My history is Jacksonville's history.

Depending on whom you ask, the Stanton School was either the first or second school for Negro children in Florida. The honor for the first school for black children in Florida, some say, belongs to the forerunner to Edward Waters College, which dates back to 1866.

Jacksonville, like many cities in the defeated Confederacy, struggled in the years after General Robert Lee surrendered at Appomattox. Among the most pressing problems facing civic and political leaders was the education of children of the formerly enslaved Blacks.

Soon after the Civil War ended, a group of Blacks in Jacksonville organized the Education Society. This was a forerunner of many attempts by Blacks to organize themselves for uplift and self-improvement. In 1868, the group acquired property to build a school they planned to name the Florida Institute, but they ran into money trouble. The following year, the Freedmen's Bureau, the federal agency created in 1865 to assist millions of formerly enslaved Blacks, stepped in with financial assistance to complete the school. The wooden structure was named in honor of President Abraham Lincoln's second Secretary of War, Edwin McMasters Stanton, who championed free public education for Negro boys and girls.

In its earliest years, Stanton was operated by the Freedmen's Bureau, which employed white teachers from the North to educate the Black students. Later, the building at Ashley, Broad, Beaver and Clay streets was leased by Duval County, which took over running the school. The education of Black children in Duval County was interrupted when a fire destroyed the building in 1882 and again in the Great Jacksonville Fire of May 1901. At that time, Jacksonville native James Weldon Johnson was serving as principal.

Born of freeborn middle-class parents from the North, Johnson had graduated from Stanton before attending Atlanta University. As a young man, Johnson saw Frederick Douglass during his appearance at the Jacksonville Subtropic Expo in 1886. After he graduated in 1894, he returned to Jacksonville and taught at Stanton, which under his leadership began to develop a high school department.

The addition of a 12th grade in 1894 made Stanton a Comprehensive School that opened its doors to Negro students throughout Duval County and surrounding areas of Northeast Florida. The school, which had begun as an elementary school with six grades, was known throughout Florida for its high educational standards.

In February of 1900, while principal of Stanton, Johnson wrote "Lift Every Voice and Sing" for a school commemoration of Lincoln's 91st birthday. Set to music composed by his brother Rosamond, the song became known in Johnson's lifetime as the Negro National Anthem.

Johnson left Stanton the following year to pursue a songwriting career in New York City. There he became a supporter of the presidential campaign of Teddy Roosevelt, who later appointed the Jacksonville native as a U.S. consul in Puerto Cabello, Venezuela, and head of the U.S. consulate at Corinto, Nicaragua.

Stanton remained a comprehensive school until 1938, when under the leadership of Principal F. J. Anderson, the campus became a senior high school exclusively. While there were two junior high schools and several elementary schools that catered to Black students, Stanton remained the only Black public high school for hundreds of square miles in every direction.

By the time I walked through the front door of the campus on Ashley and Broad Streets in 1948, Jesse L. Terry occupied the principal's office.

Principal Terry was a Morehouse man, and was well respected throughout the community.

Head Coach James "Bubbling" Small had been patrolling the sidelines for football, baseball, basketball, and track for more than a decade. Small also coached the girls basketball, drill team, and majorettes.

While white teens attended high schools in the north, south, east and west of Duval County, Black students had only one option — Stanton. Situated in the heart of the Black business and entertainment district, Stanton High School provided an education for Negro students from neighboring rural counties that lacked a Black high school.

If you lived in Green Cove Springs, 33 miles away south in Clay County and New Berlin, outside Duval, there were no high schools for colored students. You had no choice but to come to Stanton.

If you were an educated Black person in Jacksonville, born before a certain time, say 1935, the only place you could have attended was Stanton. Whenever you met a Black person from Jacksonville, the question was not where you graduated from, but what year did you graduate from Stanton. Everybody Black graduated from the same school. Their mother and grandmother went to the same school. My family was different. My parents didn't attend Stanton. They had moved from South Georgia as adults and were unschooled. But my three older siblings attended Stanton. George graduated from Stanton in 1945. My oldest sister, Mary, graduated from Stanton in 1947. Frances Marie graduated from Stanton in 1949.

There was no diversity in color in Stanton, just geography. We lived in a Black world inspired by Black teachers who had earned college degrees at places like Edward Waters College, Florida A&M College and Bethune-Cookman College, Morehouse and Spellman.

The all-Black world of Stanton Senior High was my world. It was the only world I knew. It prepared me to venture forth into a world that had two distinct shades — black and white. My feet were firmly placed in the Black world.

· · · · · · · · · · · · · · · ·

My high school years were rough socially and financially. My parents couldn't afford to buy me the latest styles everyone else wore. I spent weekends with my daddy as he drove around in his pickup selling watermelons, kerosene, wood and ice. But many days, I struggled to afford lunch at school.

Things began to look better for me during my junior year in high school when Vickie James, manager of the school cafeteria, offered me a deal. If I took out the trash after lunch each day and mopped and scrubbed the dining room floor, she would pay me $2.50, and I could eat as much lunch as I wanted. It was a blessing to be able to eat to my heart's content.

After two weeks, though, she said the best thing they could offer was $1.25 a week, but I could eat as much as I wanted. After another two weeks, she saw how desperate I was, and she told me that they would not be able to pay me anything, but I could still eat as much as I wanted to for lunch if I kept on taking out the trash and cleaning up the dining room. Subsequently, she said she would have to limit the amount of food that I could eat for lunch. I felt betrayed. I had kept my side of the bargain. She kept changing the terms. She realized I was in no position to refuse. But, not for the first time, my sense of fairness came to the forefront. The trust between us was destroyed. I could no longer work for her, even if it meant the end of my free lunches. It was another valuable lesson I learned early on in life. Free lunches are not really free. That day I quit my job as a dining room orderly.

I had been eating as much as I could for lunch because it was my main meal. I weighed 150 pounds and was tall and playing football. After I quit the job, I somehow scraped together enough money to pay for lunch. I never missed a meal.

Years later, after I had joined the police department and led the school safety program, I would cross paths with Miss James. By then she was over all food services at schools throughout the county. When we exchanged greetings, I'd say to her with a smile, "I am still eating."

I had come a long way from being unable to afford lunch for twenty-five cents.

Chapter Nine:
STANTON SPORTS LESSON

As I entered high school in 1948, my home situation remained the same. Although my two oldest siblings had left and gone into the world, the Scriven household on King Street was still poor. George finished school and went to the Army. Mary, my oldest sister got pregnant with a baby boy and left school without graduating. Rose Mary was a senior and would graduate in 1949.

Football, in a way, rescued me. It gave me direction. Success brought a sense of pride.

I found my love for football and started playing my freshman year on the varsity team. It was all I needed to distract me from our troubles, if even for a short time, at school.

The highlight of my time at Stanton Senior High School was playing football for the Blue Devils under Coach James P. "Bubbling" Small. Coach Small stood about six-foot-two, two hundred and twenty-five pounds. He was built like a line-backer. He was a graduate of FAMC in Tallahassee. All the Black boys wanted to play for Coach Small. The legend is that Coach Small earned the nickname "Bubbling" for the 1926 Kentucky Derby winner "Bubbling Over" because of his speed as a young boy.

Small began his coaching and teaching career at Franklin Street Grammar School in 1934. When I met Coach during freshman year in 1946, he had been at Stanton Senior High School for 12 years. He was a very dominating man. From the start, Coach Small's drive was to educate Black youths, to instill in them character, discipline, and the will to win. He told me they brought him from Franklin Street because Franklin's Coach Everett was unable to keep order. A football coach was expected to be a disciplinarian. What the principal couldn't do, Coach Small could do because of his authority as a coach on the field.

Coach Small was a man of prodigious energy and talent. He was Mr.

Everything. He did it all. He was the only coach at the school. A musician, Coach Small directed the band. He coached the drill team. He choreographed the majorettes. He coached football. He coached baseball. He coached basketball. He coached track. He was athletic director. Later on, about the time I arrived at Stanton, the school had a second coach, but for years, Coach Small had to do it all. And he also had to drive the bus when the team played out of town, which was pretty much every other week during the football season. White schools had decent buses and paid bus drivers, but Black schools had to scrape together buses and drivers.

Ours was not a regular school bus; it was a vehicle someone gave us. We put it together and made it a bus. We pushed it as much as we drove it. Sometimes, we stopped at service stations. They didn't want to service you anyway. You had a bus full of young Black boys. We couldn't use their facilities.

• • • • • • • • • • • • • • • •

Coach Robert E. Lee and Andrew Jackson High and Landon High Schools were located in the affluent areas of Jacksonville. Coach Small would visit the schools to collect their used equipment. We went to these high schools when their season was over, and they would have a pile of equipment, old jerseys, old pants, old pads, old shoes, and old helmets for us to use. Our colors were blue and white, but on the practice field it was not unusual to see players wearing colors from other schools. When we dressed out, we were limited in the number of players who could dress because we lacked equipment. Coach Small took equipment from these different schools and outfitted two teams when we played. He wasn't just the coach. He was the equipment manager and a goodwill ambassador who knew how to get things his teams needed. I never saw him demean himself when he was around the white coaches. He recognized white coaches' positions. They called him "James." He always referred to them as Coach "Joe." He never put himself on the same level with them. He couldn't because he came with his hand outstretched asking for surplus equipment. He recognized the disparity that existed between them and us that allowed them to have access to more equipment and staff.

Until 1948, he was the only coach until he was allowed to get an assistant. Coach George Narin coached the B-team and taught biology. He didn't have a degree in athletics, but helped coach the B-team anyway.

• • • • • • • • • • • • • • • •

I learned to drive at age 16. I also drove the team travel bus during basketball season. I did it as a favor for Coach George Narin, the biology teacher and coach for the junior varsity, the B-team. One night I almost got the whole team killed as we drove home from a game in Hawthorne. After we arrived for a road game, I usually slept while the team played. But that night, rather than resting up for the drive home, I sat in the stands and watched the game. By the time I got behind the wheel for the trip home, I was as tired as the players who were on the court.

As we drove northeast toward Jacksonville that night, my eyelids grew heavy. Sleep and fatigue took hold of the steering wheel.

"Coach, I feel tired."

"Can't you drive?" he asked.

It was after 11 o'clock, heading toward midnight. There's no darkness like a Central Florida moonless night on a country highway surrounded by nothing but swamp land and citrus orchards. As we drove on the highway, the night screamed loud with the call of nocturnal creatures. But the chorus of nature was not nearly enough to keep me awake. My eyelids drooped. Sleep felt irresistible. In desperation, I put the bus in the middle of the road and closed my eyes to steal a few minutes of sleep. The next thing I knew, I was awakened by the sharp pain inflicted by a slap across the back of my head.

"Scriven, Scriven, wake up boy!" the assistant coach yelled.

I opened my eyes to behold the headlights of an approaching car. A head-on collision seemed certain. Inexperience, sleep, and fatigue dulled my reflexes. I was too slow to respond.

The other driver swerved and ran off the road into a ditch.

I didn't stop to see what happened. I was desperate to get us home in one piece. I was scared awake for the rest of the 73-mile trip home.

Somehow, by the grace of God, I didn't hit that car. Usually you would have those large 16-wheelers hauling loads of timber barreling at you. That night, God was on my side.

Not all team bus driving stories have happy endings. Unreliable buses, tired drivers and dark roads often made for a deadly combination. The week after my near mishap, a team from Waycross, Georgia, came to Jacksonville for a basketball game. On the nearly two-hour drive home, the team's bus driver and coach were killed in a wreck.

· · · · · · · · · · · · · · ·

Other than my father, Coach Small was the person who influenced me most. By far, his mannerisms and words became my words. He loved to use the word "definitely." It became a big part of the vocation. My teammates called me Coach. They also called me "Small's Boy" when we were on the road and he was not around. They knew that Charles Scriven would let him know what went on. I was Small's Boy. My concern was doing the right thing. If it wasn't right, I would tell him. I was his eyes and ears when he was not around. My teammates accepted me for that. I was a good player. If there was anything untoward, it wasn't done around Scriven because it would be just as if Coach Small was there.

Girls admired Small for his strength and authority. He decided who made the cheerleading squad and the majorettes.

From the moment I first met him, I found a true mentor in Coach. In those days, Coach served as our disciplinarian, especially if we played football, and he knew about any off the field misdeeds. He understood discipline. The boys really looked up to him. We wanted to be like him.

· · · · · · · · · · · · · · ·

We didn't compete against white schools. Since the Stanton Blue Devils was the only Black high school in Duval County, all our rival schools were out of town as far as Burke High School in South Carolina and Beach High School in Savannah, Georgia. We played them annually. We drove to Miami to play Booker T. Washington. Either they traveled to Jacksonville to play against us, or we drove hours to play against them. Playing an away football game usually meant boarding that old, hand-me-down bus to drive to play Miami's Washington Tornadoes. Some seasons, the bus transported us southwest to play against the Jones High Tigers in Orlando. We even drove west to Tallahassee to play against Lincoln High Tigers, a school whose history dates to 1869, as far back as Stanton's. Miami's Booker T. Washington and Tallahassee's Lincoln High were always our toughest opponents.

My senior year before we were allowed to play in the Gator Bowl, we played at the Myrtle Avenue Baseball Park. In 1949, 1950 when Mathew Gilbert became a high school, we played against them in the East-West Classic in the Gator Bowl. All of the other white high schools played in the Gator Bowl. Stanton High didn't have the kind of fan support to fill the Gator Bowl. We could fill up the Myrtle Avenue Baseball Park, which was designated for Black athletic events and activities. It was ours. We didn't go across town and play in the Gator Bowl.

Riding the bus to games was a new experience for me. Throughout elementary and junior high, I always walked to school. From home, I walked northwest. From Myrtle Avenue to Eighth Street, I followed the railroad track all the way to 15th Street and on to Davis Street. The Davis Street Junior High School's name was later changed to Isaiah Blackburne.

To get to Stanton, I walked along Davis Street to Ashley and Ashley to Broad Street. Stanton sat at the corner of Broad and Ashley. Whenever white kids in the bus passed us on the street, they threw cups and food, and fruits, like oranges, out of the bus window.

All year long, the boys on our street played tackle football on any field of grass we could find. We played without helmets, pads or protection. It was our way of learning to be tough, to take a hit, to get knocked down and get up again. I impressed Coach Small and made the team my first year in high school. I played the second year and the third year. I was five-foot-ten. At my heaviest, I weighed one hundred and sixty-five pounds soaking wet. If a strong wind came, it would have blown me over. I was skinny, but I was tough.

The bus that transported us to away games was old, decrepit, and unreliable. Whenever it broke down on the road, we would push it for what seemed like 30 miles, and then push it some more. It seemed like we spent more time pushing the bus than riding in it. But many nights we drove home happy. Winning made even long bus rides feel shorter.

In 1949, my junior year, we went undefeated. My highlight from that season came against Jones High of Orlando. On offense, I played end, what modern footballers call tight end. On the key play of the game, I got behind the defensive back. It was the fourth quarter. As I ran toward the end zone, quarterback Baxter Warner unleashed his pass. The ball soared in a tight spiral over the defense and descended as I reached the end zone. I reached out, grabbed the pass, and clutched it to my chest — touch down! We won the game 7-6, preserving our unbeaten season.

As that season ended, I was looking forward to my senior year. Coach promised to make me team captain.

• • • • • • • • • • • • • • • •

At the end of my junior year, Coach made me a promise.

"Keep your grades up and I'm going to name you captain senior year," he said. As he spoke his voice reverberated through my whole being. He towered over me. I looked up to him physically and emotionally. His words were like gospel to me.

After school each afternoon, I worked at Willie Smith's Drugstore. He owned two locations — one across from the school and the other on Fifth and Florida Avenue. He was a very smart businessman. I delivered medicine to customers' homes. Initially, I rode a bicycle back and forth delivering their blood pressure and heart medication. I needed the money. My parents couldn't afford to give me the things a high school senior needed, but as my senior year approached, I desperately wanted to play football. I wanted to go out on a high. College was not in my dreams. My senior year was my final chance to play the game I loved. But football practice was after school. In order to make the team I had to practice. I couldn't attend football practice if I had to work after school, and I wanted to play football. So at the start of the school year, with football in my plans, I quit. I told the owner of the drugstore I wanted to play football.

Mr. Smith wasn't happy. He had bought a motorcycle with saddlebags for me to make deliveries. For him that purchase was an important investment. He invested in me. I was a reliable employee. Clearly, Mr. Smith was hoping to expand his business with my diligence and the new motorcycle, but I had other plans.

A dark frown framed his face when I told him of my intention to quit. He even tried to change my mind. But he paid me the wages he owed me, and I left. As I walked away from the store that afternoon, I had no idea that my decision to quit my job would have implications that would linger for years to come.

· · · · · · · · · · · · · · · ·

As I returned to Stanton that fall, each afternoon I couldn't wait for practice to start. This was going to be my year. My senior year. I was going to be captain. I had earned it. I was the only player who had lettered, playing the first and second year, and he had promised to name me captain in 1950. It was a source of pride. I was poor. I couldn't afford fancy clothes. I didn't own a car. Being a team captain was going to be my badge of honor.

But just before practice started, Coach Small called me into his office. His mood was somber. He seemed weighed down by the moment. The season hadn't started. I had kept my nose clean. I had kept out of trouble. My grades were decent.

When I walked in, he was seated behind his desk. I remained standing. He started slowly.

"Charles, there's going to be a change of plans."

I held my breath. He wasn't looking at me. He cleared his throat.

"Unfortunately, I will not be able to name you a team captain this year."

The news stunned me. My head spun. The pain of his words felt like a stab in my flat chest, as if I had been blindsided by an opponent on the football field.

I let his words hang in the air. I couldn't think of a response.

Finally, I spoke up. My words were barely audible. My mouth was dry like sandpaper.

"Why, Coach? My grades are good, I am a good player."

"I received a complaint about you," he said. "From our sponsor."

"Who, Coach?"

The drug store owner Willie Smith was a sponsor for the school. Stanton survived on a shoestring. The generosity of Negro business owners was important to keeping the school programs operating. Smith provided means for the visiting teams after home games. His financial support was vital for the athletics department at Stanton. His contributions to the school were far more valuable than the captaincy for me.

At that moment, I recalled the afternoon I gave Willie Smith my notice. When I walked out of the door of his drugstore, I never imagined he would be plotting his revenge.

Now Smith was paying me back in a way it would hurt me the most.

"He threatened to withdraw support from the school, if I named you captain, Scriven," I heard Coach Small say. His words hit the floor just before my heart did.

"What do you mean, Coach?'

"If I named you team captain, Charles, he would withhold his financial support," Coach said. "I can't afford that. I have to think of the whole team."

The words stung my face. I could feel my eyes burn with the tears of betrayal. How could Coach Small break his promise? How could he punish me in school for a matter that happened outside school? I tried to understand how he sacrificed me on the altar of expedience and financial support.

I quit my job so I could play football. I had done nothing wrong.

How could they take away my most prized football honor for a reason that had nothing to do with football? The unfairness stunned me. The power and influence of that local merchant mattered more than the bond of Coach Small's word. If his decision was related to my conduct, I would understand. But it wasn't, and it was painful.

"This had nothing to do with my performance in school or on the field," I told him in frustration.

Somebody took something from me that was mine. Their action was outside of the spirit of brotherhood or conduct. Nothing I did pertaining to the team warranted that punishment. I hurt Smith's feelings to a point that he wanted to get vengeance against me. The only thing he could do to get back at me was to take something I desperately craved. I really wanted to be a team captain. I was a poor, skinny teenager without family connections. Being team captain was going to be something I could hold on to. He took it away from me.

The pain of disappointment hurt to the deepest part of my being. Coach Small was my mentor. He was my role model. I looked up to him. How could he allow himself to be blackmailed? I felt as if I was being held hostage. My captaincy was the price Coach Small was willing to pay to keep the sponsorship. I had to live with his decision. But that day in late summer 1950, I grew up. I came of age that day. In that short conversation, I understood that adults made decisions for reasons I didn't always understand. I discovered that sometimes the consequences of those adult decisions fall on the innocent. That innocent was me.

I struggled to find words to describe how much Coach's decision hurt me. Until then, I had lived a very sheltered life. But this was the real world. Life could be cruel and unfair. That was my first taste of it. I couldn't accept it. It was painful. Being captain of the football team was something to be proud of. That was one of the first disappointments in my life. Coach Small was my idol. I looked up to him. But his actions gave me a whole new perspective on life and on adults. I learned early that all heroes have faults. There are things that make an impression on you. Time doesn't erase the incident. It will always be a part of my life. That fall I played with a broken spirit. It didn't affect my play on the field, but my eyes didn't shine nearly so brightly that final season. A man who always told me to do the right thing had broken his word. Should I have stayed working at the drugstore? The owner made an investment in his business with the expectation that I would be available to make deliveries. But those were his plans. He told me there was no future for me in football after high school. I knew that. This was it for me. I understood and accepted that. We were coming off a championship season. My choice was to make the team and be captain. To a sixteen-year-old, that was the most important thing in the world.

After I graduated, I stayed in touch with Coach Small. He remained my mentor. I celebrated with him when in 1957, Stanton High School Blue Devils football team won the All-City and All-Conference championships. They were the first black school in Jacksonville to win the double. Coach Small retired in 1969 after 35 years of coaching football, basketball, baseball, and track. Parks around Jacksonville bear his name. A former student, Nathaniel Farley Jr., created the J. P. Small Foundation in Coach's memory. Years later I, along with a number of other former Stanton players, was inducted into the James P. Small Foundation Hall of Fame. I remain an active member of that Foundation.

Chapter 10:
JEANNETTA

In January 1951, I was a senior with my eyes firmly set on graduating. I was proud of playing for the football team. I had given up my job at the drugstore, but I was getting by. I was a lanky and unimpressive-looking senior. One morning I was one the students selected to speak at the school assembly. Standing on the stage as I waited my turn to walk up to the microphone, I noticed her.

She stood along with the freshmen. She was brown-skinned, slim, and petite, about 105 to 110 pounds like my mother. Maybe that's what caught my eye. I was attracted by her demeanor; she moved with an understated grace that made it hard for me to pull my eyes away. I had never seen her before. Her face stuck with me.

I don't remember what I said in my speech, but I remembered her. She remembered me too. I made quite an impression. She remembered what I said that morning. I spoke about what I learned from my father.

"There are two things a man likes to have — a beautiful woman and good food," she recalled.

She liked the way I spoke. She liked the way I looked. She knew I was a football player. I wasn't the team captain, but I was a senior of Coach Small's team. I wanted to see her. I wanted to get to know the first girl in high school who ever caught my eye. I didn't know it then, but she was also looking forward to seeing me again, to meeting me in person.

I got my chance to meet her soon afterward. One day, we encountered each other in the halls of Stanton. She was a hall monitor. She was on patrol. She directed student traffic as we walked up and down the crowded stairs and along congested hallways between classes. To lessen the chaos, there was an order to the way we got from one class to the next. We could go up one way, but you couldn't come down the same way.

I was walking in the wrong direction. As a senior, I should have known better. I must have felt the need to exercise some senior privilege, to flout the rules. So she stopped me and told me I needed to turn around.

I was not skilled in dealing with girls, but seeing the one girl who caught my eye on the day I gave my speech, I quickly found my footing. We chatted for a few minutes. Her name was Jeannetta Latimer. Her friends called her "Net."

She lived on the other side of town. She had attended a different junior high school, so we had never seen each other before Stanton.

She was cordial. She was a freshman. I was a senior. Freshmen and seniors didn't associate. She might have been flattered that I paid attention to her. She was 13 or 14. I was 18.

I later learned that Jeannetta was the oldest of Rose and O. D. Latimer's three surviving children. The second child, a boy, died at age two. Her mother told her that her baby brother died of worms. That wasn't unusual. At the time, they lived in the country in Mitchell, a tiny town in rural southwest Georgia. It was the height of the Great Depression. Tragedy visited the wood shacks of Negro families in the South for all kinds of reasons.

I don't remember what Jeannetta and I said to each other during our first encounter, but that day I asked for her phone number.

We didn't have a home phone. I don't remember calling her. I didn't own a car so it would have been hard for me to visit her. We didn't visit girls then unless you got permission from their parents. Some girls took company. She was not taking company. Her family was strict. There were no dates or even chaperoned visits. I either saw her at school or I didn't see her at all, but I was attracted to her.

Lacking social graces, I said very little to Jeanetta whenever I saw her in the hallways and stairs of Stanton High. When I saw her, I usually just said hello. There wasn't much more than the first grains of affection, unexplored. But even though I didn't talk to her much, the image of her face lingered in the back of my mind, her demeanor, how much her disposition resembled my mother's, captured my imagination. I liked her. I hoped she liked me.

But what could I really offer her?

I didn't have much going for me. My family was very poor. The only thing that made a difference was I was a member of Coach Small's winning football team. I had made a pretty good name for myself as a player, but I was not a star. I wasn't the best-looking fella, but being a graduating senior made me feel somewhat important. At the same time, my family was somewhat known at Stanton. My older brother George had gone into the

Service after he graduated. Both of my sisters, Mary and Frances Marie, had attended a few years earlier. But I burned with ambition. I vowed to rise above the poverty of my humble circumstances. I would make something of myself. I couldn't wait to leave high school.

The streets of segregated Jacksonville offered few options to a young colored man — either a life of crime, menial labor, or both. There was one clear path for me to follow.

I was a young man of a few words. I was not a sweet talker who could charm teenage girls. I was tongue-tied around my female classmates. So Jeannetta heard none of my words about my hopes and my dreams until I had left Jacksonville when I joined the U.S. Army and began writing letters home.

Jeannetta was excited to hear from me. She cherished my letters. She kept them and reread them when she missed me.

I told her about life in the Army. I told her about my plans for a future I desperately wanted to share with her. I even told her I felt called to the ministry, to be a preacher. Yes, I trusted her enough to tell her things that were close to my heart, although that news might have turned off some young girls since being married to a pastor is a big responsibility. Not every young woman wants to live with that burden. Jeannetta didn't discourage me. Her silence on the matter brought me comfort. After that, she still answered my letters. She was still interested.

The United States Postal Services facilitated our budding courtship. Hours away in places like Fort Jackson, South Carolina, and Fort Stewart, Georgia, I found the courage to say to Jeannetta on paper things I could never muster the courage to say to her face to face. She had won my heart. No one had ever done so before or ever since. No one else ever could.

Chapter 11:
THE CALL

In high school when I went to church there was no commitment other than a sixteen-year-old wanting to be with his high school friends. We came together for socializing, and we were all together in a class. It was not something I was conscious of other than I wanted to be a minister.

Around the time when I was sixteen, I got baptized at Shiloh Baptist Church, where the Reverend A. B. Coleman was the pastor. But that baptism was like going to the mall. It was merely a social ritual, something I did as I got to a certain age. There was no moment of light. No voices of assurance whispering in my ears. No descent of the Holy Spirit, the Spirit of God on my shoulder. I went down dry and came up wet. But inside, in my mind and heart I remained untouched.

It was social. I did what my other friends did. This was baptism from peer pressure.

. . . .

When I was 17 years old, I woke up one day with the urge to preach. I had the sudden, overwhelming desire to become a minister, to spread the word of God to my fellow man, to do everything I could to straighten out the world.

I felt called by God to do it. I didn't receive a vision or have a dream. I didn't have a Damascus Road experience. There was no blinding light, no disembodied voice calling my name from above. There was no heavenly encounter like the ones described in the Bible, yet the unmistakable knowledge of my calling seemed to fill my head and heart. To be called is to be imbued with an undeniable certainty of my destiny. Regardless, His call on my life was clear to me. In time, His call became my burden, His summons, my passion.

It was as unexpected as it was real. I was unaware of any preachers in my family. It was not something I aspired to of my own volition. But for the first time in my young life, I understood the journey of my life would be filled with purpose. I would be a man of God. Unlike my classmates, I was chosen to do a special work, to uplift the hearts and minds, to save souls, to lead the Lord's sheep out of the desert.

At the time, I was a junior at Stanton High School. My family was not overly religious. My mother was a regular churchgoer, but my father wasn't. For me, church was social, somewhere I went with my friends. No matter what I did on Saturday evenings, church on Sunday mornings always seemed to be the right place to be. Those mornings of sitting in the pews with my friends seemed so disconnected from the nights when as a young boy I sat on my mother's lap in the living room of a house in Jacksonville as women prayed and sang and preached late into the night. Although I was much too young to understand all that was going on around me, being in the presence of God had become part of my DNA. Like the biblical Samuel being in the temple since boyhood, all those nights in my mother's prayer meetings had marked me as one of God's children, no matter what personal ambitions I harbored.

· · · · · · · · · · · · · · · ·

I didn't talk to my dad or mom about my calling. It was hard to tell them I was called to be a preacher as a 17-year-old because I continued to see my family struggling to meet the daily necessities of life. Being a preacher offered no promise of wealth and comfort, just more poverty. That's why I decided to volunteer for the Army.

The only person I told was Jeannetta, the freshman I met my senior year. I'm not sure why I told her, but I felt compelled to tell her about my vision for my life. I had no visions of a life together with her, but I wanted her to know where I was headed. I was called to the ministry. No matter what else I did, mine would be a religious life.

Looking back more than seven decades, I had crush on her but had no dreams of marriage. It was too early for them. But she admired me, and I felt comfortable sharing what I felt my life would be like. I wanted to be a minister.

In retrospect, my naivete is glaring. Some girls dreamed of marrying a preacher. Some Black women saw being first lady of a church as a high honor, while others shied away from that position. They were unprepared for the kind of commitment and sparse rewards required of a preacher's wife. Jeannetta didn't say it then, but she was skeptical. She hadn't experienced much in life. Being a preacher's wife seemed like a prescription for sensory deprivation, a life shut off from all the wonderful things the world and adulthood had to offer.

    My strong calling ebbed and flowed for a few years, but it never deserted me. God's voice would grow distant, even faint, and His presence often felt like an estrangement in the years after I left the hallways of Stanton High School and donned the green army uniform to serve my country. After I became a military policeman, I faced all the temptations of the flesh, women and wine, sex and drugs. My arm band, helmet and baton were symbols of power. Men and women were always willing to cater to my every whim, to offer me favors, to entice me.

BOOK III:
IN THE SERVICE

Chapter 12:
KOREAN WAR

As I enjoyed my summer vacation at the end of my junior year in high school, my thoughts turned toward the fall, senior year and football. Halfway around the globe, the five-year lull of military conflict that followed World War II was about to end.

With the blossoming peace, our military was cutting troop numbers and announcing peacetime base closures. Fort Jackson, South Carolina, was on the list of Army installations targeted to be downsized. By June 1950, Fort Jackson was largely deserted. Basic training had ended, and the Fifth Division had moved on two months earlier. Fort Jackson was scheduled to be deactivated that month. The once-bustling military installation was on the way to becoming a ghost town. City fathers in nearby Columbia, the capital of South Carolina, bemoaned the projected loss of $1.2 million in revenue with the departure of eleven thousand, two hundred and seventy-five soldiers.

But events on the Korean Peninsula changed all that. Between 1910 and the end of the Second World War, Koreans were brutally colonized by Imperial Japan. But our defeat of Japan created two independent Koreas — Communists in the North and western-supported capitalists in the South. Communist China and the Soviet Union supported North Korea. America and our European allies backed South Korea. The nature of our commitment was sorely tested when on Sunday, June 25, 1950, the Communist forces from the North overran much of South Korea. Two days later, President Harry S. Truman pledged military support to our battered ally. By Wednesday, North Korean troops controlled the streets of Seoul, South Korea's capital. President Truman immediately dispatched Army and Marine Corps units from Japan. Even as my buddies and I were having a great time on American Beach, eating hot dogs and watching fireworks on Independence Day, the first of our soldiers were landing in South Korea.

With America defending our ally, the Defense Department canceled its planned draw-down of soldiers. America needed fighting men to stop the advancing Communists. The draft was reinstated. President Truman called up the National Guard and the Reserves. On July 10, twenty thousand American boys were drafted. With war back on, Fort Jackson was back in business. The Fort Jackson replacement training center reopened. On July 17, the post was revived. It would be a destination for troop training. By Labor Day, about twelve hundred officers and enlisted men were stationed at Fort Jackson headquarters for the newly created Eighth Infantry Training Division.

· · · · · · · · · · · · · · · · ·

During my senior year, as I contemplated my life beyond Stanton High, events on the Korean Peninsula seemed distant, way outside my consciousness. I needed a job, and the Army would provide. But the reality of war and its demands on young men like me were becoming clearer to the general populace, if not to me. That fall, the names of local boys killed while fighting in Korea began to appear in the local paper, the Florida Times Union. Army Private First-Class Wherry Abercrombie was killed on July 16, 1950. During my senior year at Stanton High, I was too busy to read the notice in the Times Union announcing the death of Marine Corps Private First Class Eugene Whitney Bowden who was killed in combat on November 13, 1950. Three weeks later, Elvin Boswell, an Army Private First Class, was killed in combat. He was 25.

A year later, after I enlisted and was stationed at Fort Jackson and praying for God to protect me from being shipped to Korea, Army Private Larry C. Alleman of Jacksonville, who was born the same year as me, was killed in Korea on September 23, 1951, and shipped home in a body bag. By the time the guns fell silent on July 27, 1953, more than thirty-three thousand American boys had died in Korea. Of those boys, four hundred and fifty-eight were from Florida.

Chapter 13:
ENLISTING

While young men from my Jacksonville neighborhood were being drafted into the military, others like me saw the Army as an organization that offered a steady paycheck, room and board, and three square meals, and a ticket out of my hometown.

I also joined the Army so I could earn enough to help support my parents and two younger siblings. I didn't join to fight. It never entered my mind that I could end up in combat. I never wanted to be a hero. Many of the boys had little or no education. The Army was looking for bodies. Only by the grace of God I didn't end up in Korea. I wanted to travel, but I didn't want to travel under the threat of going into battle. I was proud to be an American, but I wasn't trying to die fighting to defend America.

During World War II, Black men toiled as longshoremen, cooks, mechanics, laborers, truck drivers, machine operators, MPs or guards for German prisoners of war. Black soldiers toiled alongside women and civilian white men who were physically unfit for combat. Our brothers and uncles knew about the aerial accomplishments of the Tuskegee Airmen, but there were few opportunities for combat glory for Black men in the Army. White folks believed Black men did not perform well in combat. Despite our history of bravery in France during the First World War, they believed we were cowards, that we were not intelligent enough to understand military tactics, that we broke under pressure. For many of us Black men in the South, the military, especially the Army, was not a place for military glory, but to learn skills and earn a steady, decent paycheck away from the hardship of sharecropping and the oppression of Jim Crow. As the Korean conflict heated up, Black units that finished their basic training were being sent to Korea. I needed a job, a place to sleep and a place to eat. When I joined the Army, I wasn't looking for a fight.

When I was 17, I was tired of being broke. I was tired of my family being poor. In desperation, I lied to try to enlist in the Army. I tried to up my age at the recruitment office in Jacksonville. I could not find a birth certificate. Back then, if I had an old insurance policy, the recruiters would accept that if I didn't have my birth certificate. I tried to get an insurance policy to certify that I was at least 17 years of age, as some of my classmates had done. It worked for them, but it didn't work for me. I was tall and slim. I weighed no more than 150 pounds on a good day. I didn't even have an inkling of growing a beard or moustache. No one would mistake me for an 18-year-old. After the recruiters turned me away, I returned to Stanton, dejected.

Out of frustration, I decided to leave home and drop out during my senior year. It was the spring of 1951 and my final six months in high school. I boarded a bus to Miami, thinking I'd find riches in South Florida. I had an aunt in Miami, but I didn't have any friends down there. Once I got there, I came face to face with adulthood. My aunt loved me as her own, but she refused to let me sit around her place while she fed me. But things were still rough. I had to fend for myself. I was hungry all the time. All I found was a job on a mule-drawn ice wagon.

Meanwhile, although I was not at school, some people refused to forget about me. One of those was a teacher, Ms. Thelma H. Jones. She was one of my mentors at Stanton. Ms. Jones saw my potential. She refused to give up on me. She kept sending me messages through other students, telling me that I needed to get back in school. She stressed the importance of getting an education. In 1951, things were difficult enough for Black men in Jacksonville. A Black man without a high school diploma was condemned to a life of struggle and hardship. Her words of encouragement finally did the trick. If it wasn't for her, I would have stayed in Miami.

When I came back from Miami, my mother was overjoyed. She hugged me. Like the prodigal son, I was glad to be home. I was tired of being hungry. I could return to the house on Grothe Street, sit down and have a meal at the table with my parents and my younger sister and brother.

Luckily, I didn't miss too many weeks of schoolwork. I was able to return and pick right up where I left off. But my parents were still poor. I still could hardly afford the 25 cents or 50 cents for lunch in the Stanton cafeteria. Being in school felt like a luxury neither I nor my family could afford. I felt like a burden to my parents. I had to do something to help them and my younger sister and brother. I had to find a way to help myself.

In 1951, the average Negro youth in Jacksonville had nothing to look forward to after high school. Unless we migrated north to New York City, Newark, Philadelphia, or Boston like many of our friends and neighbors, we had very few options other than lives of hard labor and poverty. There were no jobs available for colored men in the city government except the Sanitation Department, and they had a long waiting list. You couldn't get a job with Duval County or the state of Florida. If your family had money, you might be able to afford Florida A&M College or Bethune Cookman, or Florida Memorial. Closer to home, Edward Waters College in Jacksonville was a place one could take classes to earn a degree. Although I sometimes dreamed of college, it was never part of the conversation between my parents and me. They couldn't afford it. And I wasn't fast and big enough to earn a football scholarship.

If you were poor like everyone else, you could sign your name and if you didn't have a criminal record, bad eyes, sickle cell anemia, or a limp, you could try to join the Army. Our choices were slim. Either we enlisted to serve in the Army or stayed home to be a laborer or to do janitorial work. Most of those jobs were taken. My father had one of them at the Florida Times Union paying him $18 a week. Many Black fathers kept their job hoping to pass it down to their sons. As a child, I went to work with my father as he cleaned the press room after the first edition of the paper was printed. I had no intention of growing up to be a janitor.

• • • • • • • • • • • • • • • •

The Korean War had broken out on June 26, 1950. I had just completed my junior year at Stanton. Senior year, with its accolades and prestige awaited me. At the time, talk about war, fighting Communism and men dying seemed so far away from my life in Jacksonville. But in 1951, as graduation approached, it forced me to pay attention to life beyond Broad and Ashley streets.

Following the peacetime lull after America defeated Nazi Germany and imperial Japan in the Second World War, young men stopped worrying about being drafted into the Armed Services. But after fighting broke out on the Korean Peninsula, President Truman re-instituted the draft. I was 18. I was of fighting age. Even if I didn't volunteer, there was a strong chance I would find myself in an Army uniform sooner rather than later.

Meanwhile, local authorities were happy to supply the young men needed for America's military machine. The Duval County School District adopted a rule: if you passed two semesters in your senior year and you went into the service, they would give you the average you had, and you could graduate with your diploma.

I had passed two semesters. I was ready to leave home. I was tired of my parents struggling to make ends meet. I was ready to leave Jacksonville. I was ready to face the world.

Although I had turned 18, I didn't want to return to the Jacksonville Army Recruitment Office in case the recruiters recognized me and rejected my application. My maternal grandmother lived in Brunswick, Georgia, so I took the bus north across the state line and walked into the Army Recruitment Office. They gave me a test, which I easily passed. They were glad to have me.

The U.S. Army was my ticket out of Jacksonville. The Army was my way to get out of my parents' rented house and become an adult. The Army was the only branch of the service that would let me in. Recruiters didn't talk to us Black boys about going into the Air Force or the Marines. They rarely talked to us about going into the Navy. The only thing in the Navy was to be a cook. I grew up in a house with my mother and three sisters. I never learned to cook.

The Army was trying to get Blacks to join so they could send us overseas to Korea to fight. We were no longer restricted to being truck drivers, mechanics, cooks, and laborers in the Army. America's war machine needed young Black men for combat.

Recruitment was high among Blacks, especially in the South. Thanks to teenagers like me, Army recruiters had no trouble meeting their monthly and quarterly quotas. We didn't have anywhere else to go. The Army was much more attractive than working in cotton or tobacco fields. The pay and benefits were better. The Army promised better treatment than the daily insults to our manhood under Jim Crow. After all, President Truman had ordered the integration of the armed forces in 1948.

On Saturday, March 24, 1951, I walked into the Army Recruitment Office in Brunswick, Georgia, and volunteered to serve my country. That morning in South Georgia, as I swore to serve and defend the Constitution against all enemies foreign and domestic, halfway around the globe, United Nations forces, led by American troops, were pushing the Chinese People's Volunteer Army and North Korean People's Army north to the 38th Parallel as part of Operation Ripper.

When I returned to Jacksonville to share the news with my family, my mother was happy. I could learn discipline and grow up to be the kind of man she would be proud of — not like my older brother, George, who by then was struggling with alcoholism and would lose his job with the Post Office. But I could be like my daddy, J. L. Scriven — disciplined, moral, and hardworking.

Once I enlisted, I made an allotment of $50 per month from my $97 a month private's pay to send money home to my parents. They still struggled to support themselves and my two younger siblings, Jean and James. My dad was still only making about $18 a week at the Florida Times Union. The Army would take the money before I saw it. I wouldn't miss it. My family needed it.

Chapter 14:
FORT JACKSON

After I enlisted in the Army, I remained with my grandmother Frances White in Brunswick for a few days. Then on April 24, 1951, I boarded a Greyhound bus from Brunswick to Macon, Georgia. From Macon, I caught another bus for the northwest journey to Fort Jackson, South Carolina. As I climbed aboard the bus, I was wholly unprepared for the world I was about to be thrust into. I was 18 years old, but I knew little about life beyond the confines of my neighborhood and Stanton High School.

As I drove to Fort Jackson for basic training, I was unaware of the history of Black soldiers at Fort Jackson during the previous decade. I was ignorant of the hostility of Jim Crow toward Black men in uniform, the history of the brutality of white MPs against Black civilians in Columbia and the role that would play in my life. I was leaving home to discover the world for myself. I was going to be a soldier.

I had no idea that Fort Jackson, my destination for basic training, was, in the words of United Press International reporter Lee Nichols, a fully racially integrated military base next to Columbia, the capital city of one of the most viciously segregated states in the South. The commanding general took the initiative and mixed Blacks and whites together in the summer of 1950. Even as I prepared to enter my senior year in high school, the Army was laying the foundation for the next few years of my life.

· · · · · · · · · · · · · · ·

Fort Jackson was a 53,000-acre Army cantonment near Columbia. Named for President Andrew Jackson, Camp Jackson was created in 1917 from sandy hills and extensive swamp land. The Army designed the camp to train men in the 30th and 81st Infantry Divisions after the United States entered World War I on the side of the Allies. At the time, Negroes comprised a majority — 55 percent of the South Carolina population. Of the 135,000

South Carolinians who registered for the draft, Blacks outnumbered whites by 7,500. Black men were desperate to escape the poverty of sharecropping and the unmitigated uncertainty of life under Jim Crow. Military service offered dignity. Many of the Black draftees arrived in rags, without shoes. Some came with guitars and banjos.

Blacks had a long history with Fort Jackson. We helped build the barracks and roads when the cantonment was first established. Fort Jackson was the home of the legendary all-Black 371st Infantry Regiment. Comprised of men drafted from Florida, Georgia, North Carolina, and South Carolina, the 371st was initially designated a labor battalion but after vigorous protests was assigned as a combat unit. On February 22, 1918, the unit paraded through the streets of Columbia to resounding applause from the city's white residents. Four months later, the 371st deployed to Europe, where the unit fought the Germans alongside the Fourth French Army. Though they took heavy casualties, members of the 371st distinguished themselves in combat. The decorated survivors returned home with honor. One of their own, Corporal Freddie Sowers was killed in combat and was awarded the Medal of Honor by President George Bush in 1991, seventy-three years later.

Americans have short memories. By World War II, the heroism of the 371st, two decades earlier, had long been forgotten. Black soldiers were once again relegated mostly to labor battalions. We worked as longshoremen, truck drivers, cooks, engineers and military policemen. Young Black men were once again drafted in large numbers. Fort Jackson became a major training center for the war effort. The huge influx of young Black and white men in uniform infused the sleepy, segregated South Carolina capital.

Of the average Black soldier, many were laborers. Many could look up and read the weather from the clouds overhead, but could barely make heads or tails of the words on a piece of paper. They were largely illiterate. They struggled with the entrance exam. A small minority were like me, high school graduates. In one month in 1943, during the height of World War Two, the Fort Jackson induction station rejected two thousand, three hundred — approximately fifty percent out of four thousand, seven hundred and fifty-six Black men for poor scores.

• • • • • • • • • • • • • • •

In the years before President Truman's desegregation executive order, Black soldiers in the South faced harsh discrimination on and off base. Outside the gates of Fort Jackson, pubs and service stations on Jackson Boulevard and the drive-in theater at the Garners Ferry Road intersection were off limits to Negro soldiers. For entertainment, Black soldiers went to the Waverly District, home to Columbia's Black elite. The neighborhood was dominated by two Historically Black Colleges and Universities — Allen University which was named for Bishop Richard Allen, founder of the African Methodist Episcopal Church, and Benedict College, founded by northern Baptists in 1870. Both campuses were surrounded by Black-owned businesses. Whites derisively called that section of town "Burma Road." Black soldiers attended dances at the Township Auditorium on Taylor Road, or at two non-white USO venues. The Carver Theater on Harden Street also welcomed Black soldiers.

A long bus ride would take Black soldiers to the heart of Black downtown Columbia on Washington Street. Black owned dentistry, pharmacy, funeral home and doctor's offices lined the street. As they walked west on Washington Street, between Assembly and Park, the neighborhood went downhill as the red-light district approached. Among the venues were the Big Apple dance hall and the Dew Drop Inn. The Blue Palace Cafe was among the most popular with soldiers assigned to Fort Jackson in the early 1940s. Soldiers were attracted by cheap liquor and sex for sale. Whites derisively called the area "Congo Square." At one point during the war years, the Fort Jackson brass forbade white GIs from frequenting Columbia's Black neighborhoods.

Chapter 15:
INTEGRATION

The Korean War saved Fort Jackson. The Korean War sped up integration at Fort Jackson while Columbia, its civilian neighbor next door, remained rigidly segregated for decades to come.

Once fighting began, America needed fighting men to stop the advancing Communists on the Korean peninsula. The Defense Department canceled its planned drawdown of soldiers. America needed fighting men, so the draft was reinstated. President Truman called up the National Guard and the Reserves. On July 10, 20,000 American boys were drafted. With war back on, Fort Jackson was back in business. The Fort Jackson replacement training center reopened.

On July 17, the post was revived. It would be a destination for troop training. By Labor Day, about 1,200 officers and enlisted men were stationed at Fort Jackson headquarters for the newly created Eighth Infantry Training Division. With America trying to push back North Korean and Communist Chinese forces, Fort Jackson ramped up as a training center for new soldiers and mobilized National Guardsmen.

Because the Army decided to assign Black soldiers elsewhere in 1947, it meant that Fort Jackson lacked a segregated infrastructure. Integration happened at Fort Jackson in September 1950.

• • • • • • • • • • • • • • • •

One of the most momentous days in American history occurred when on July 26, 1948 President Harry Truman signed Executive Order 9981, desegregating the armed forces. "There shall be equality of treatment and opportunity for all persons in the armed services without regard to race, color, religion or national origin," Truman stated.

In the years immediately afterward, the military dragged its feet on integration. But in January 1950, Army Secretary Gordon Gray issued Special Regulation 600-629-1 Utilization of Negro Manpower in the Army. "The policy of the Army is that there shall be equality of treatment and opportunity for all persons in the Army without regard to race, color, religion or national origin."

After the policy went into force, Black men across America saw the peace time Armed Services as a place of opportunity. We had General Benjamin Davis and the Tuskegee Airmen as role models. Many young men like me signed up. Black enlistment spiked from 8.2 percent in March 1952 to 25.2 percent in August 1952. Not surprisingly, the military officials in Washington worried that if they lifted the 10 percent enlistment cap for Negroes, African Americans would overwhelm the Army. The policy worked because the Truman administration instituted desegregation not by integration but equal opportunity. Unfortunately, it took the rest of America until much later to discover the efficacy of the military's approach. Years later, as a Negro policeman in Jacksonville, I learned to use the same argument.

Desegregation in the Armed Services meant not just integration but opportunity, training and promotion opportunities that had long been closed to Black men in the Armed Services. Black men who excelled in uniform expanded our prospects later in civilian life. My law enforcement career is living proof of that.

While many military garrisons resisted President Truman's order to integrate, things changed rapidly at Fort Jackson. The arrival of thousands of young Black and white men draftees after the outbreak of the Korean War in summer 1950 contributed to Fort Jackson becoming one of the first Army installations to undergo desegregation. At the time, the 8th and 31st Infantry Divisions trained here. The elite 101st Airborne Division also served at Fort Jackson.

Chapter 16:
BASIC TRAINING

Basic training was six to eight weeks of physical exercise, conditioning, marching, rifle marksmanship and other fundamentals. After basic training, two months of advanced individual training followed as infantrymen prepared for combat and deployment overseas. Because of the mobilization for the Korean War, 65,000 soldiers came through Fort Jackson in 1951. The base was the reception center for draftees and enlisted soldiers from across the South, regardless of whether you lived in Florida, Georgia, North and South Carolina, Alabama and Mississippi. All-white National Guard "Dixie" Units also trained at Fort Jackson. That is where they ended up. Us Southerners, Black and white, did our basic training there.

• • • • • • • • • • • • • • • •

Many of the recruits and draftees had no education. When a boy got to a certain age, he had to help support himself and the family, especially if there were other younger children. In our family, my parents had two younger children, Jean and James, who were 10 and 8 respectively, to care for.

My basic training at Fort Jackson was in an area called Tank Hill, which was named for the 90-foot high, 60-feet in diameter, 1.8-million-gallon beige water tank. As America geared up for its war effort, the tank was installed in March 1941 at a cost of $400,000 to supply the whole of Fort Jackson. When we went on long runs during basic training, the tank was my destination on that steep hill. If I could just reach the top of Tank Hill, I knew I could survive basic training. We lived in the wooden World War II barracks that stood in a line beneath the tank. Our unit was designated heavy mortar. The usual physical training was done each morning and we were taught to kill. My units were basically made up of whites from the South who would occasionally look over and use the "N" word without remembering where they were. Later, they would apologize to us, their darker brothers in arms, and we would go on as if it didn't happen. And, really, it didn't matter. They just forgot for a moment that they were not responsible to themselves but to the Army.

The Army taught me the most valuable lesson in life — the art of self-discipline. To get out of bed, make my bed, get to breakfast on time, stand in the chow line so I could get fed in time to go back to where I was supposed to be afterward, I learned that I had to listen to authority and follow orders without regard to what I thought. I was told when to go to bed and when to get up, when to eat and what I would be doing each day. I learned that there would be penalties that I would have to pay if I did not follow the regimentation.

If my uniform didn't look right, I would get punished with cleaning toilets and other unpleasant assignments. I also learned the value of teamwork. One man couldn't operate a mortar gun. Someone had to calculate the coordinates, someone had to load it, someone had to fire. Each soldier had to remember his assignment.

It didn't take long for me to learn how much could be accomplished if each one did their assigned job as a team member. I further learned that the Army did not need my advice. They knew what they were doing, and if I did not cooperate fully, we would not accomplish our goals. They had a place for dissidents called the stockade that used different methods to get your attention. I never went to the stockade. I was never disciplined for disruptive behavior or failing to follow the rules. If I was told to jump, I asked how high.

I also learned that the cultural behavior that I practiced outside in civilian life didn't matter in the Army. We all ate in the same mess hall. We all slept in the same assigned barracks, and we all had to pull together to get the job done the Army way. My first assigned unit was located across the street from the stockade. We saw soldiers going through their exercise regimen while those of us in our barracks were going to town.

After basic training, the entire unit was on alert for travel. We had 30 days. I had no idea where we would be sent. At that time, when you finished basic training, you would be sent to Korea. I would wake up early just about every morning and go to the chapel and pray that I wouldn't be sent to Korea. At that time, 80 or 90 percent of the combat units from Fort Jackson went to Korea. That's where they needed you. For the young men who didn't return home alive, their sacrifice was not in vain. Their family received $10,000 from the military for the soldier's death insurance. That was more money than most Black men in the South earned in their lifetime.

Chapter 17:
LIVING WITH INTEGRATION

By the time I arrived in the late spring of 1951, integration was a way of life on the Army base. Being integrated was a new experience for everyone — both Black and white. It was comical, to a certain extent. One of the white soldiers told me he'd never been stuck sleeping in a room with a black man before. I told him I'd never slept in a room with a white man. The next morning, when we woke up, I asked him, "How do you feel?" He said he felt all right. I told him, "I feel all right, too."

It was difficult to discriminate in the Army. We all were assigned various unpleasant duties such as having to peel potatoes in the kitchen or guard duty. I did not go to Germany, but I was assigned to a military police detachment. All of us were assigned to a particular barracks. It was the first time I'd experienced an all-Black unit. I had a Black master sergeant who lived off post in charge of us. It was quite noticeable that none of the Black military policemen were assigned to duties on post. All Black military police officers were assigned to work in pairs, or they would be assigned to work with a police officer in a predominantly Black section of Columbia.

Chapter 18:
UNREST

Despite the Army's efforts at integration and harmony at Fort Jackson, life beyond the gates was still very difficult for Black soldiers. Jim Crow laws required Black soldiers to drive in the back of the bus once they left the base. That was often a source of friction and sometimes violence. We could not sit next to whites. Residents of Columbia viewed Black soldiers as troublemakers. We could be rowdy. In December 1945, a group of African American soldiers threatened to shoot up a civilian bus. African American soldiers at Fort Jackson started several near riots in late 1945 and early 1946. Unrest in March 1946 prompted a commander to order Blacks on guard duty to be armed with broomsticks instead of rifles.

Conflict between Black soldiers and white civilians erupted across South Carolina. We are prone to fights. I didn't drink or smoke, which made me an exception rather than the rule. Soldiers drink too much. When they do, they become disorderly. The flesh traffic thrives whenever thousands of healthy young men are billeted nearby. The houses of prostitution spurred the spread of venereal diseases. Soldiers brought business but at a high price. Local Black men resented soldiers because they often stole the hearts and virtues of local young women. But more seriously, Black soldiers often ran afoul of white police officers and white citizens.

A Black man in military uniform seemed like an affront to Southern whites. The uniform conveyed an authority and a legitimacy long denied us. It endowed the wearer with power. It contradicted the mythology of Jim Crow that Black men were weak, powerless, inferior. A Black man standing ramrod straight, his uniform pressed crisp and clean, defied the white imagination. Not surprisingly, the Southern landscape was stained with the innocent blood of Black soldiers killed by whites who escaped justice.

In November 1942, a Columbia city policeman shot and killed Private Larry Stroud at a house on Harden Street after a domestic disturbance. Although Stroud was shot in the back of the head, the officer claimed self-defense and the coroner declined to bring charges.

In Darlington, South Carolina, in December 1945, a police officer arrested two Black soldiers for being drunk and disorderly on a civilian bus. In April 1945, a Black soldier was arrested for sitting next to a white girl. In August 1945, a white man in Elmo shot a recently discharged veteran. In November 1945, a Johnsonville policeman killed another veteran with a pistol. While some of these incidents were fatal, none was perhaps more notorious and consequential than the blinding of Isaac Woodard.

Chapter 19:
200 MILES OF STANDING

While I remained within the gates of Fort Jackson, the burden of my race did not limit my choices so much as my aspirations. But outside that chain-link fence, white Southerners never lost the opportunity to remind me of my inferior place.

After I came home for leave, I boarded a Greyhound bus for the return trip back to Fort Jackson. As whites entered the bus ahead of me, each opted not to sit next to anyone but took a seat in an unoccupied row. Before long, many of the rows to the front each had an empty seat. The Black passengers sat in the back of the bus.

Seeing no more vacant seats at the back of the bus, I asked one white guy "Can I sit next to you?" "No," he said.

I asked another and got the same response.

Another white passenger just looked at me and shook his head. I didn't even bother to ask white women passengers.

As I slowly made my way to the back of the bus, I was acutely aware that the bus driver was looking at me through his rear-view mirror. His gaze burned through my uniform shirt. He was the person who could handle the situation. He had the authority to force one of the white passengers to move so I could get a seat. In my view, the bus driver could make things right, but the right thing for him and the right thing for me were very different. He not only controlled the bus, but he was empowered to enforce segregated seating. He was Jim Crow's captain on board. His authority was unquestioned. He heard me asking for permission to sit. There were empty seats throughout the bus. All were situated next to a white man or woman. None offered me a seat. None honored my uniform. None valued my service.

The bus driver kept looking in his rearview mirror to see what was going on, but he didn't ask. I was in uniform. I remained calm. One Black fellow was angry about having to stand up. He yelled at the driver and seemed ready to fight him because he was unable to sit. I didn't have that attitude. I had grown up in the Jim Crow South. I learned to hold my tongue. Saying the wrong thing at the wrong time in the wrong place could get me killed. My uniform, denoting service to my country, would not save me. As a matter of fact, it would only make matters worse.

From all the stories circulating in the Black newspapers, it appeared that a Negro in uniform seemed to inflame the worst passions in whites. I'm talking about the story of Sgt. Isaac Woodard. His story was all over the Black newspapers. He toured the country telling his story. Woodard was 26 years old when he was discharged February 12, 1946, at Camp Gordon, Georgia, and boarded a bus to Columbia. After Woodard got into an argument with the driver, he was accosted in Batesburg by the police chief Lynwood Shull and police officer Elliott Long.

Woodard was accused of drinking and using language offensive to a white female passenger. One of the officers struck Woodard as he tried to tell his side of the story. During a scuffle, they beat Woodard in the head causing both eyeballs to rupture. Woodard pled guilty to drunk and disorderly conduct for which he was fined $50. He had $44 in cash and the magistrate accepted that amount. He spent the next two months at a veterans' hospital in Columbia. When he was discharged, Woodard was blind. Woodard's sisters took him to New York, where the NAACP took up his case.

The federal government brought civil rights charges against Chief Shull, but he was acquitted after his lawyer successfully argued that, if he were convicted, police would no longer be able to protect wives and children. The Southern white man's appeal to protecting white women from marauding Black men once again proved effective. The jury deliberated for less than an hour before acquitting Chief Shull. Jim Crow won that day in that Charleston courtroom, but that injustice to Sgt. Woodard added a nail to the coffin of racial segregation in the Army. Outraged by the not-guilty verdict, President Truman signed an executive order to end segregation in the Armed Forces.

Federal Judge J. Waties Waring, who presided over the case, was so angry with the jurors' refusal to hold the white police chief accountable, that he became an ardent advocate for change. He ruled in cases outlawing closed Democratic primaries in South Carolina and across the states of the old Confederacy. His decision on school segregation cases in South Carolina paved the way for the United States Supreme Court to hear and rule in favor of outlawing separate but equal in America's public schools in its 1954

Brown v. Board of Education decision.

I was oblivious of that history as I stood up for the next 200 miles from Jacksonville back to Fort Jackson, and for every stop in every small town in between. At the time, as my legs grew tired on the six-hour trip, I was vaguely aware of what happened to other Black men in uniform. Each time the ache of fatigue tempted me to look longingly at the empty seats next to whites on the bus, I remembered the story of what happened on another bus in South Carolina half a dozen years before.

I didn't have the mind to fight to have a place to sit. That was not me. My approach to change was never violent. I was never one to protest and make a big fuss. That wasn't because I was less angry than those who marched and were beaten. Each insult fueled my determination to find ways to beat the white man at his game.

Years later, young Freedom Riders like John Lewis would ride the bus to end segregation on interstate travel. But that was way beyond a horizon I could not dare dream about. I wasn't looking for a fight. I was looking for a place to sit down traveling 200 or so miles back to camp.

Just like the northward journey of that Greyhound bus, the train of racial progress was also moving. Even though I was totally oblivious to the change that was coming, it was. Standing on that hot bus on a pair of tired legs for six hours, all I could think about was my discomfort and the darkness and evil in the hearts of those Southern white men and women who refused to allow me to sit next to them. Somehow, I knew that things had to change. And that change would come with or without their consent.

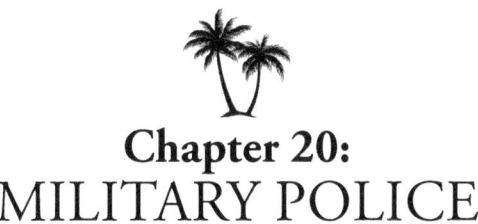

Chapter 20:
MILITARY POLICE

After basic training ended, I waited to be assigned to a unit. With the Korean War raging, I expected to be assigned to a combat battalion. As a matter of fact, my battalion was set to be assigned to West Germany. In the aftermath of World War II, the defeated Germans were divided into Communist East Germany and capitalist West Germany. My fellow soldiers and I were bound for one of the massive American Army bases that sprouted up in West Germany in the six years since Adolph Hitler's defeat.

Some of the guys who underwent basic training with me were assigned to the Military Police unit. In the military police, you could either be basic combat support or a corrections specialist. MPs served as law enforcement on military installations, protected lives and property, controlled traffic, prevented crime and responded to emergencies.

The Fort Jackson MPs were commanded by the Provost Marshal General, who at the time was Major General Edwin P. Parker Jr. He had made a name for himself in the European theater during World War II and served with the U.S. occupied forces in West Germany until 1948.

The newly designated MPs were headed for Fort Gordon for nine weeks of special military police training. Named for Confederate Major General John Brown Gordon, the installation was located not far from Augusta in southwest Georgia. While the MP trainees headed for Fort Gordon, I was nervous about going to Korea.

• • • • • • • • • • • • • • • •

Initially, I wasn't assigned to the military police unit. Perhaps I was too skinny. Even with the MP armband on my sleeve and a baton in my hand, I didn't cut an authoritative figure. I wasn't going to intimidate those Southern country boys who Uncle Sam was trying to turn into fighting men. Even though the Army didn't see me as an MP, I did. Those men from my unit who had been selected to be MPs had already been bussed off to Fort Gordon for training, when I took matters into my own hands.

One day soon afterward, I walked into the Vice Provost Marshal's Office and asked the officer in charge if I could be assigned to that unit. Being an MP was my ticket to avoid combat. Any fights I got into would be with men on the same side who swore allegiance to the red, white and blue. I wanted no part of shooting and killing. Since there were several members of my unit who were assigned after basic training to the local military police detachment I wanted to be added to their number. To my surprise, the officer said yes. He said yes to my non-combat request. He said yes to a job choice that would later prove to be a career-altering choice.

At the time, my youth blinded me to the prospects offered by being an MP. I didn't connect being a policeman in the Army with being a policeman in civilian life. I lacked the foresight to appreciate that MP training and experience could bolster my job prospects once I was discharged from the Army. In the back of my mind was still my calling of being a preacher. I could never have imagined that my role as an MP in boisterous, unruly, segregated Columbia would lead to a career as a Negro policeman in segregated Jacksonville. It was just by chance that I became aware of and needed a job and I applied. But none of this was in my mind when I was in the Service. I was trying to get out of going to the frontlines of combat and make it back home to become a preacher.

After I finished basic training, my unit didn't go to Korea but was assigned to be stationed in West Germany. Since I became an MP, I remained at Fort Jackson. I was a bit disappointed because I wanted to travel overseas. But my disappointment was assuaged by relief. My biggest fear was going to Korea. If I had any inkling I could go to West Germany, I wouldn't have gone to the military police. The only way to travel as a poor man was in the Service.

Chapter 21:
BLACK MPs

The significance of race in America parallels the abuse of power. Problems Black people had with civilian police officers also existed between Black soldiers and white MPs. White MPs abused Black soldiers when they were arrested. White MPs abused Black civilians on the streets of Columbia. One of the Army's solutions to curb the abuse was to deploy Black MPs to patrol predominantly Black areas in Columbia. After the end of World War II, cities across the South hired Negro policemen in response to concerted pressure from Black civic groups. Black police officers were seen as the solution to generations of white police brutality against Blacks. Even as conflict raged overseas, on the home front an uncivil war simmered. Black MPs were introduced to Fort Jackson as a solution to the rampant incidents of white MPs beating and mistreating Black soldiers and civilians.

In 1942, white MPs attacked Black civilians in Columbia. An Army investigator sent from Washington found that white MPs went out of their way to look for trouble, provoked confrontations with Black civilians and took advantage of their authority as military policemen. They deliberately insulted and mistreated Black folks. The investigator recommended that the commander order MPs to stop calling Negroes "Nigger." Regrettably, however, he recommended that the War Department take no action.

As a result of the flare ups and complaints, the Fort Jackson commander barred all white military soldiers from the area around Washington Street, the heart of Columbia's Black business district. He instructed white MPs to drive instead of walk on patrol, an approach that typified the way white city police officers behaved in Black neighborhoods. During the thriving World War II years, the Black section of Columbia included such venues as the Capitol Theater, which was owned by prominent Jewish businessman Sidney Friedman, the Big Apple, Blue Palace Cafe, and the Moses' Café, which Friedman also owned. There was also the Township

Auditorium on Taylor Street.

The situation changed after African American MPs began patrolling Washington Street. Although this was part of a War Department nationwide program to introduce the use of Black MPs, local activists in Columbia saw the use of Black MPs as a victory and a result of their agitation. White MPs were equal opportunity brutalizers. Color rather than class influenced their daily interactions with Blacks in and out of uniform. White MP brutality galvanized support by presenting a common danger that affected Columbia's lower and Black middle classes. Out of that struggle later emerged leaders who would spearhead the larger battle for voting and equal rights in South Carolina. I began to patrol the streets of Black Columbia a decade after the cauldron caused by World War II. My ability to do the job rested on so much that had gone on before.

• • • • • • • • • • • • • • •

Being a policeman in the Army was like being a policeman in civilian life. People catered to me. They did things to entice me to come and get favors. I didn't know how to handle it. I was like a kid in a candy store for the first time. There were older soldiers around me who knew the danger of the things I would encounter. Being in a military town, people catered to me because of the power I had or the power they perceived I possessed. Most times I didn't feel powerful. I knew the only thing that separated me from my fellow soldiers was the armband on my sleeve, and it could be taken at any moment. Still, people recognized the power of the uniform, the helmet and the armband. They tried to entice me with cigarettes, alcohol, and drugs. Women threw themselves at me. I had no defense at all. They offered me favors I struggled to resist. I didn't know how to handle it. There were older soldiers around me who knew how to navigate the dangers. I was the new kid on the block.

I was fortunate, however. I didn't drink. I didn't smoke. I didn't do drugs. I didn't gamble — I couldn't afford the habit. But I was susceptible to attractive, adult women. They threw themselves at me. As a young man I had little defense. I had no sense at all. I was an 18-year-old, and someone armed me with a pistol and a baton and told me to go to town and keep order. What were they thinking?

• • • • • • • • • • • • • • •

Since I received my MP armband after my fellow soldiers had left for MP school at Fort Gordon, I was forced to learn on the job. I had defensive training and firearm training. I didn't grow up around guns. My father, J. L.

Scriven, wasn't a hunter. He didn't take me and my brothers hunting deer and wild turkeys each fall. So, when it came to guns, I had to start nearly from scratch. What I picked up in basic training. I had to learn to use a .45 pistol and, of course, my baton. With soldiers, a situation can easily get out of hand. I received my on-the-job training working alongside senior military policemen. That made a difference. It was like getting vocational training on the street. Still, I was not ready for Fort Jackson.

It was quite noticeable that none of the Black military policemen were assigned to duties on post.

I was assigned as an MP to an all-Black unit. We were not associated with the white military policemen. We had separate barracks. We had a Black sergeant who assigned the Black policemen to walk the beat. We walked on patrol with a Black policeman from the Columbia Police Department. Often when we encountered soldiers not in uniform, we stopped them and questioned them.

"Are you a soldier?" I'd ask. "Produce your ID."

Soldiers were easy to pick out because of their clean shave and Army regulation haircut.

• • • • • • • • • • • • • • • •

Once when I was stationed in Fort Jackson, the FBI picked up a white deserter in the South Carolina low country. The sergeant assigned me and a white MP to drive to return him. After we collected the white prisoner, we stopped at a gas station to fill up and get some snacks to eat. They allowed the white prisoner in uniform to go inside to buy snacks, but I had to wait in the car. There was a window out back for Blacks. I thought being in uniform and carrying a .45 on my side would make a difference. But it didn't. They refused to serve me, so I got back in the car and waited for the white MP and white deserter to return.

• • • • • • • • • • • • • • • •

After more than a year of being stationed at Fort Jackson, we got a new provost marshal. He heard about the reckless way military police conducted themselves at Fort Jackson. He told us if there was any shooting, if someone was injured or killed, the offending MP was going to be transferred elsewhere immediately.

One night, soon afterward, I and another military policeman confronted two Black paratroopers from the 82nd Airborne. I was patrolling on foot. Soldiers were only able to travel so far with a pass. After I arrested these two paratroopers, we were walking when they saw several of their buddies.

As we walked, one of the arrested soldiers stopped.

"I'm not going any farther," he said to me.

The two soldiers gave their buddies a signal and we started fighting.

Those 82nd Airborne soldiers were tough. I feared for my life.

One soldier was giving me a tough time until I used my club. I hit him a few times. Suddenly, a small group crowded around us.

"Kill that MP," someone shouted. But given the situation, I could only imagine the names those angry, drunk Black soldiers called me. My MP emblazoned helmet and arm band represented authority they didn't respect. I felt threatened. My life was in danger. I needed more than my baton to protect myself.

I pulled out my firearm. I flipped the safety switch on the .45 pistol and pointed the weapon straight up above my head. I squeezed the trigger and shot in the air.

Bang. Bang. Bang.

The report of the pistol tore through the night air as I squeezed the trigger once, twice, three times. As the shots echoed through the night air, the crowd scattered in a hundred directions. Soldiers training for combat ran like cockroaches in a dirty kitchen after you switched on the lights. Things quieted down after that.

The next morning the provost marshal summoned me to his office. He demanded an explanation of what happened the previous night. Calmly I explained. I was trying to bring order to a volatile situation. Apparently, my explanation of events didn't satisfy him. A few days later, I got orders to be reassigned to Camp Stewart, Georgia.

Chapter 22:
CAMP STEWART

Two days after the bust up at Fort Jackson, I got an order from the Provost Marshal Investigator transferring me out of that unit. I was reassigned to Camp Stewart, Georgia, an installation about 40 miles southwest of Savannah. Named for Revolutionary War Hero Brigadier Daniel Stewart, Camp Stewart was still relatively young when I arrived in 1952. A dozen years earlier, with most of Western Europe reeling from the might of Nazi Germany, and America still officially at peace, Congress authorized funding for the creation of an anti-aircraft artillery training center near the Georgia Coast. National Guard troops on active duty conducted live artillery training at Camp Stewart in preparation for the conflict that seemed inevitable. That foresight proved prescient after the Japanese attack on Pearl Harbor in December 1941. Later, Camp Stewart housed German and Italian prisoners of war captured in North Africa. Camp Stewart was deactivated after the end of World War II, but like Fort Jackson, the installation sprang to life when the Communists invaded South Korea. As the Korean conflict raged, Camp Stewart was re-designated the 3rd Army Anti-Aircraft Artillery Training Center.

Soon after I arrived, the War Department shifted the focus at Camp Stewart from just anti-aircraft training and added training for armor and tank firing. As Camp Stewart's primary mission changed, so did its size. From an initial purchase of 5,000 acres, Camp Stewart had grown to 280,000 acres spread across five Georgia counties. The large space was needed for live artillery training. Although Fort Stewart was geographically the largest Army installation east of the Mississippi, in terms of the men and women stationed there, it was a much smaller post than Fort Jackson. There were also far fewer distractions and attractions. I did not have the temptations nor the dangers. Nearby Hinesville, which years later would earn the dubious distinction of being voted the most boring city in Georgia, didn't offer soldiers much by way of night life and entertainment. I was able to clear my head, think straight and grow up.

That was the best thing that happened to me. If I had stayed in Columbia, I would have killed someone, or someone would have killed me. I was given a .45 and told to keep order on the streets of Columbia. It went to my head. I couldn't handle it. In a city where police officers were the controlling authority, I lost my way. I lost contact with my family. I lost contact with Jeannetta. There was temptation everywhere I went. It was only by the grace of God that I didn't kill anyone. I didn't have any sense. I was a 19-year-old boy living in an adult world.

• • • • • • • • • • • • • • •

At Camp Stewart, I was assigned to the Provost Marshall Investigation Unit. Military police patrolled, dispatched 911 calls, liaised with civilian law enforcement agencies, handled administrative records, traffic accident investigations, escorted funds, and returned deserters. In Columbia, I mainly patrolled the streets looking for GIs getting rowdy or visiting off-limit establishments. In Camp Stewart, I was assigned to the investigation unit investigating crime among military personnel. I investigated thefts, robberies, homosexuality. At that time, soldiers didn't have the freedom to love who they wanted to love. On the base, they had these stalls in the bathroom. They dug a hole in the wall of the stall and homosexuals would come and sit in that stall and peep through the hole in the wall at men using the stalls.

• • • • • • • • • • • • • • •

We Black MPs labored under a double burden. As a Black MP, I got the same humiliation and disrespect suffered by other Black soldiers, but I was also a tool of the authorities. With my baton, my helmet, and my armband, I was an instrument of enforcing the existing, unequal social order. I patrolled segregated military housing and civilian black neighborhoods.

My time at Camp Stewart was a brief interlude for my favorite Army adventure. I enjoyed the responsibility of being an MP. I loved the challenge of investigating cases. But one thing I hated about the Army was how little control I had over my day-to-day life. At any moment, the Army could assign me to go anywhere, and I had no say in the matter. I remained at Camp Stewart until I was transferred to Los Angeles, California.

Chapter 23:
OUT WEST

The first Army division to undergo complete desegregation was the Fourth Infantry Training Division at Fort Ord, a 45-square-mile installation created in 1917 for artillery training on the Pacific Coast. Fort Ord was considered the most beautiful army base. It became a launching point for soldiers bound for the fighting in Korea.

But that was not my destination. From Camp Stewart, the Army sent me to Fort McArthur in San Pedro, Los Angeles. Named for Lieutenant General Arthur McArthur, whose son, General Douglas McArthur, led U.S. Pacific forces during World War II, the installation was created to protect the prosperous Los Angeles port during World War I. At that time, it was a large gun training center. During the Second World War, it was a key part of the Pacific coastal defense. The garrison protected the massive shipbuilding and aircraft factories so vital to the American war effort. By the time I arrived in 1953, Fort McArthur had become a key cog in the American anti-aircraft defense system during the Cold War. Members of the 47th Anti-Aircraft Artillery Brigade were stationed at Fort McArthur.

My role was to investigate crimes and to retrieve deserters from local lockups throughout southern California. The FBI would detain deserters and place them in the local jails. My partner and I drove from our home base to return the detainees, in handcuffs and leg irons, to face a court-martial. I enjoyed the freedom of the job and exploring a state so similar and yet so very different from my native Florida.

In California, I breathed the fresh air of racial freedom for the first time in my life, and I loved it. I loved it when I was about to enter a business to buy something to eat, I didn't have to look for the "colored" or "Negro" signs. I didn't have to worry about using the right bathroom or drinking fountain. It felt like a huge weight had lifted from my shoulders. California possessed a reputation for freedom and opportunity for Black folks. For decades Black young men and women from Louisiana and Mississippi and even Texas ventured west to the vast state bordering the Pacific Ocean in search of jobs. California had its own share of discrimination but lacked the color bar of the South. Once I got to the Golden State, I didn't have to look around for a place to relieve myself or buy a hamburger. I felt like I was in hogs' heaven.

• • • • • • • • • • • • • • • •

When they integrated the Army, troops from the north and west came south, and I was transferred to Fort McArthur in Los Angeles, California.

After a few months, I was transferred to the 8th Army headquarters in San Francisco at the Presidio. During that assignment there was a Woman Army Corps unit stationed there. A former Stanton High School classmate, Lois "Skinny" Randolph, had joined the WAC. I met her when I moved to San Francisco. One day when we met at the gym, she introduced me to a white fellow WAC member. Being around white women was a big adjustment for me. Being a Southern Black boy, I had never socialized around white women; I had never held conversations with them, gone dancing with them or even dreamed of dating them. So, imagine my discomfort one day when this young white woman extended her arm for me to shake her hand. I was so dumbfounded that I didn't let it go. She made a joke of it, saying, "Look, he wants to hold my hand."

Later, an incident occurred when I visited a small city in Oregon as an investigator for the Army. My assignment was to bring back deserters who had been picked up by the FBI. This small Oregon city was in lumberjack country. The Swedes were as big as trees and there were absolutely no Black people to be seen. I dreamed one night that I woke up in my hotel room at about three or four o'clock in the morning and looked out to see the whole street lined with people. They were all shouting "Pull him out of there! You know he doesn't have any business being here!" I yelled at my partner to get me my pistol, but by then people were coming into the room and pulling on my leg and the pistol was just out of reach. I was still reaching for my pistol when I awoke in a cold sweat — it had been a terrible nightmare — one I never forgot.

• • • • • • • • • • • • • • • •

California was a whole new world. I experienced a freedom I didn't think possible. The saying was "Go west young man." I was out West, and I felt as if I had found my home. But the woman I loved, Jeannetta, was back east. I wanted her to come out there rather than me returning to life under Jim Crow in Jacksonville. Hardly a minute passed without thinking about

Jeannetta. I longed to have her share my life. I missed her dearly. I wrote to her often. The more I wrote, the better I got at expressing my affection for her. Gone was the shyness of my boyhood in high school. I had become a man of the world. Life in the Army had changed me. I had grown in confidence and stature. But I was looking forward to a life out of uniform — a life in California with Jeannetta. My letters left no doubt about my intentions. On December 27, the Sunday night after Christmas, 1953, I was stationed at the headquarters of the 30th Engineer Base Topographic Battalion, Fort Winfield Scott, California. I had seen her a week earlier when I returned home to Jacksonville on leave. I was lovesick. I missed Jeannetta. I missed my parents. The joys of California could never substitute for my love for her. So, I sat down and wrote Jeannetta.

"My Lover Chica," I wrote. The greeting was imbued with passion and desire, accented with a California flavor. It reflected my state of mind in the middle of that Hispanic culture and those beautiful Mexican-American women.

In my typewritten letter, I held back very little:

"It seems as if every time that I'm not doing anything that keeps my mind fully occupied, I can't seem to do anything but write to you, and each time that I do I never feel that I've really said I loved you enough. Oh well, as you can very well see, I'm just in love so I'm not really responsible for the way I am acting. Well today was the eighth day that we have been apart, and I sure miss you very much, but with the idea in mind that one day we will be able to get married and have that ball team of boys.

I'll be content to wait a bit longer, it's like you once said, that 'anything that is worth having is worth waiting for,' and my Cherub you are worth your weight in silver — all that hundred and one pounds of you (smile)."

I was enthralled by her slim, lithe figure. California, Army life bore its temptations, but my heart was fixed on Jacksonville.

"Well, I know you had an enjoyable Xmas. Sorry that I wasn't able to spend it with you, but we still have about a hundred more to spend together (smile). You never did tell me whether or not you wanted to come out here to California, but I presume that you had a good reason and maybe it would be best if we could wait until or at least another year before we get married, besides I haven't even asked your mother yet and gee, that's going to be a job in itself (smile)."

In some families you sense the stronger party. In her family, her mother, Rose was the stronger person. Once she made up her mind about an issue, that was it. Children know the difference between the members of the family. They know which one to play on to get what they want. Jeannetta's dad was a gentle, soft-spoken man. He didn't want to be controversial or to go against anything his wife said. In that household, her mother was the person who mattered, not her father. We called her Momma Rose.

For me, it was just a matter of getting Jeannetta to come to California. She had just turned 17 and had never ventured far from home. That prospect frightened her. Instead, she wanted me to come home so we could get married and then return west to California. So, I decided to go home.

That decision gave us time to think, time to plan. It was the second-best thing I ever did other than stay on the police force and preach. I also realized that I needed to be near my parents, Mary and L. J. Scriven. As they grew older, who would care for them? Even though I had other siblings, my relationship with my parents was different than their relationship with my parents. My relationship was such that if one of my siblings did something my mother didn't like, she'd say, "I'm going to tell Charles on you." My parents were getting old. Who would care for them if I was a thousand miles away in California?

Chapter 24:
GOING HOME

During my enlistment I had bought a Chevrolet with my savings. After I was discharged from my unit in San Francisco, I climbed in the sedan with an Army buddy from Georgia. We drove back together.

On the road trip from California, when we stopped in Mississippi for gas, it didn't take long for me to be reminded that I was no longer in California. A white fella asked me if I wanted some water, so I leaned over to drink from the water fountain. As I did, the attendant tapped me on the shoulder and pointed to a cup. Living in California, I had forgotten the rules — in the South, Blacks and white don't drink from the same fountain. Living in California, I had gotten used to using public accommodations without fear of racial reprisals. How quickly I forgot the old rules. So as I returned to the South, I felt the South with every mile. The change was most acute in Mississippi. There were bathrooms for white women and white men. The colored bathroom would be more of an outhouse detached from the main building. I was not prepared to return to a racially segregated South.

At that moment, as the white gas station attendant handed me the cup, so much flashed through my mind. He didn't need to say another word. The hand on my shoulder was caution enough. I stopped and reached for the cup. I walked out of that gas station that day fully aware of where I was and where I was headed. I had returned to the South. California might have been free of the "white" and "Colored" signs. But the South had not changed. Jim Crow was still the law in Jacksonville. If I was going to survive, raise a family and do better than my struggling mother and father, I would have to abide by the rules, keep my head down. But I was determined to get more out of life than my parents. I loved them dearly. But their lack of education limited their prospects for their entire lives. I had finished high school; they didn't. I could read and write. I could count on veteran benefits. I could take advantage of the GI Bill. Uncle Sam would pay for my college education if I wanted to pursue a degree. And I desperately wanted to earn a college degree. I wanted to make something of myself. My determination grew with every mile as I drove east toward home.

But returning to Jacksonville, I thought at that moment, was only a prelude to my big adventure with Jeannetta back west. I wanted to enjoy the rights of full citizenship. I wanted to be more than a janitor.

And Jeannetta...she was looking forward to marrying me. We would make a life together. We would raise our children. We would give them opportunities our parents couldn't afford to give us. Ambition and desire fueled me and my car for every mile. It brought me home to Jacksonville. It was springtime 1954. My life was about to begin in earnest.

BOOK IV:
RETURNING TO JIM CROW

Chapter 25:
RETURNING HOME

I took the long road home to Jacksonville that spring. Heading east from California, my companion, an Army buddy from Georgia, and I drove through Arizona, Texas, Louisiana, Mississippi, and Alabama. For each mile of pavement and asphalt, I saw the impoverished plight of the Black man in the Deep South. The landscape filled me with dread, but knowing I was driving home to see my sweetheart Jeannetta, brightened my mood. On the radio we listened to Dinah Washington, B. B. King, and Joe Turner. In my mind, I made my own movies from their lyrics of love and loss, hurting and crying. I was young and strong and determined to succeed even though my hometown remained largely unchanged. Black folks were still confined to our neighborhoods like LaVilla, Hansontown, Grand Boulevard, Durkeeville, Sugar Hill, Hogan Creek, Springfield, and Mixontown. Whites controlled the waterfront and the wharves. The Black businesses were congregated around Ashley and Broad streets.

The city was also unchanged politically. It was still run by the white men. But more and more whites were moving to the Beaches, leaving the city to an increasingly restive and no longer subservient Black community.

Blacks have always had a strong presence in Jacksonville. Union troops raided the city three times during the Civil War. Black troops were instrumental in helping Union forces hold on to Jacksonville. After the war, Black veterans joined with the newly freed to organize politically and economically. Many of the newly freed were attracted to Jacksonville by the availability of cheap land and jobs on the bustling waterfront.

For a long time, we had the numbers in our favor. By 1870, the small seaport was home to 3,989 Blacks and 2,923 whites. Half a century later, 48,294 Negroes constituted a majority of the city's 91,558 residents. By 1950, my hometown's population had ballooned to 204,517. But thanks to the Great Migration, as thousands fled Jim Crow and boarded trains north for New York City, Philadelphia, Boston, Newark, New Jersey and other cities in the Northeast, Jacksonville's Black population had dwindled to a mere 30 percent. My family was among those who stayed. Jacksonville was our home.

That summer of '54, the Jacksonville Braves entered their second season. They played at the newly built Wolfson Park on East Duval Street named for their owner and founder, prominent businessman and philanthropist Samuel, W. Wolfson.

A year earlier, while I was in California, I heard the news that the Braves were one of the first two teams in the Southern League to integrate. The Braves added not one, not two but three Black players, Horace Garner, Felix Mantilla and "Hammering" Hank Aaron. The racial insults and verbal abuse Aaron and his Black teammates endured were a reminder of how little had changed in Jacksonville. Aaron was undeterred. Each of his 22 home runs that year was an act of defiance.

• • • • • • • • • • • • • • •

My hometown was a popular stop for the top Black entertainers. The Jacksonville Library boasts a black and white photo of Duke Ellington and his band members playing stickball on the streets of one of the Black neighborhoods. As famous as he was, white hotels refused to accommodate the Duke. From time to time, performers roiled the social compact of Jim Crow. In 1952, Marian Anderson sang to a racially integrated audience at the Old Duval County Armory after refusing to sing if Black and white audience members could not be together. Anderson's Jacksonville and Miami shows were the first integrated concerts in Florida since Reconstruction. Despite that symbolic victory, the vestiges of racism still gripped Jacksonville. The city was still being led by a segregationist, Mayor Haydon Burns, who understood how to use appeasement and payoffs to gain Black support at the polls.

Chapter 26:
SAYING I DO

Jeannetta graduated from Stanton in January 1954. Back then, graduation was twice a year, January and June. She had graduated early. She had just turned 17 in late December 1953, but I couldn't wait to marry her. I wanted her to come West to be with me. The thought of returning to Jacksonville and the life it symbolized was discouraging. I wanted her to come to California to meet me so we could marry and start our life together. She was four years younger than me, but she had a mind of her own. She was emphatic.

She wanted me to come home so we could get married in front of her parents and her two sisters. She wanted my parents to enjoy the moment. She told me we could move to California after we got married.

Nearing the end of my service I was looking to being discharged and returning to civilian life. What do I do after that? I wanted to serve in the Florida National Guard unit. White veterans usually served in the unit that corresponded with their active duty service. Artillery veterans served in artillery units and infantry vets served in infantry units. The rules were different for us Black veterans, however. The Florida National Guard units were largely closed to Blacks. We only had one option — there was one infantry unit reserved for Negro veterans. But I had been an MP and a criminal investigator with three stripes on my arm. I had no interest in being in the infantry. National Guard infantry units are often deployed to combat zones. I had avoided war when I was active duty; I wasn't going to join the infantry. I was a military policeman and an investigator. There were no opportunities for Black men who were military policemen in the National Guard outside the infantry units.

I was promoted from private first class to corporal to sergeant in my three years in the Army.

• • • • • • • • • • • • • • • •

I was spoiled by living in the West. I didn't want to come back to the segregated South. There were limited jobs opportunities for a Black man without a college education. But job prospects in the West were not nearly as constricted because of my color. Defense industry jobs provided a decent living to Blacks living in California. You couldn't apply for certain jobs in the South unless you were the right color. I certainly didn't want to return to that.

For her part, Jeannetta had her misgivings about leaving home. She had never been farther from Jacksonville than Gibson, Georgia, where her grandparents lived.

"Just the idea of leaving home and being alone was frightening to me. I had never been more than two hundred miles from home. It's frightening to think of leaving home," Jeannetta told me. "In my head, I had no idea how far California was. I would have to live there by myself if for some reason you didn't show up. And I was concerned about my mom."

• • • • • • • • • • • • • • •

When I came home to Jacksonville, I returned for Jeannetta. Her family became my family. Her religious life became my religious life. Before I left for the Army, my church attendance was sporadic, more social than spiritual, despite the yearning of God's call on my life. In the Army, I didn't attend church. Most of my praying came during the weeks after I first enlisted. Uncle Sam was selecting soldiers to ship off to the war in Korea. I wanted no part of that fighting. I prayed in my barracks every day not to be sent to Korea. In exchange for those answered prayers, I ignored God.

So, fresh out of the Army, Jeannetta's church life became my own. Jeannetta and her parents and siblings attended Saint Paul Baptist Church. I had been baptized as a teenager. But that immersion was more social than spiritual. I did it as my other friends were doing it. At the time, it seemed like the right thing to do. Jeannetta and her family were grounded in the church environment. That wasn't the case in my family. While my mother was a devout Christian and a devoted churchgoer, my father L. J. Scriven didn't attend church. He wasn't anti-Christian, he was anti-church, although he attended adult night school and had become a devout reader of the Bible. Still, the difference between what Christians preached and how they lived, kept him at home on Sundays.

In the spring of 1954, standing in front of the pastor, the Rev. A. E. Crumady, I added my name to the roll and joined St. Paul. The sound of God's voice became clearer once I returned to civilian life. I could hear His call. It tugged on my heart strings. It kept me awake at night.

I immersed myself in church activities. St. Paul Baptist Church activities became my social and religious life. In the coming years, I became a church deacon. I taught Sunday school and eventually became the Sunday school superintendent. Those acts of service provided training for my spiritual calling, to be a minister. That gave me some satisfaction as to working toward the realization of becoming a minister.

God called me. I yearned to respond to fulfill the call. To answer yes, just as Jeannetta had said yes to my marriage proposal.

Chapter: 27
WEDDING NIGHT

When I returned to Jacksonville, I moved in with my older brother George, who worked at the Post Office following his discharge from the Army after World War II. However, my experience as an MP didn't seem to matter much to anyone. All I could find was work as a laborer on construction sites. I planned to take advantage of the GI Bill and enroll in one of the colleges in Jacksonville that accepted Black students. Ambition burned in my chest. I wanted to make something of myself. But first I had to get married. Jeannetta and I had decided we would get married in Jacksonville, then discuss returning to live in California. We set the date for Friday, May 7.

• • • • • • • • • • • • • • •

Since Jeannetta had just graduated from high school and I was just out of the Army, and both of our families were not well off, we couldn't afford a lavish wedding. We couldn't even afford to rent a hall or marry in church. So, we arranged for Pastor Crumady to conduct the ceremony at her parents' home.

A friend, Benny Nickerson, was supposed to be my best man. He was supposed to drive me to Jeannetta's house on South Myrtle Avenue. As Friday afternoon turned into evening, Benny was a no-show. Somehow, he been waylaid. I was late for my own wedding. I was standing around, nervously looking through the window to see if he had arrived, when the phone rang. It was Rose Latimer, Jeannetta's mother. My future mother-in-law sounded anxious. She almost seemed on the verge of tears. At weddings, usually it's the bride who keeps the groom waiting, not the other way around. My young bride was ready, but I was absent.

"Are you coming?" she asked. The question floored me. How could she ask that question when I had waited so long for this day to come? I wanted to marry Jeannetta more than I desired anything in life.

Mothers are protective of their daughters. Rose Latimer somehow imagined that I had cold feet and had changed my mind about marrying Jeannetta. I had spent the last three years seeing a world outside Jacksonville. I had experienced the freedom of life in California. I had seen the Hollywood sign on top of the hill overlooking Los Angeles. Had those caramel-colored California girls turned my head? Was I still willing to get married? Was I ready for marriage?

Desperate not to keep my bride waiting any longer, I called a friend from around the corner and asked him to take me. When I pulled onto South Myrtle Avenue, I was an hour late.

For her part, Jeannetta was ready for marriage although she was only 17. She had been waiting for this day for more than three years. She knew the kind of wife she wanted to be and the kind of husband she didn't want — one who beat on his wife. Across the street from where she grew lived a man named George, and every weekend he was beating his wife.

"I was wondering if that's what goes on in a marriage," Jeannetta told me. "I didn't want that to happen. What I saw with George, it seemed like every weekend he was beating his wife. I didn't want that. I was looking for a good life, a happy life."

When I arrived at the house on South Myrtle Avenue, I walked inside. I was flush with embarrassment. Sweat bathed my forehead. I was nervous, but none of that mattered the minute I set eyes on Jeannetta. She wore a knee-length white dress and a veil, which I later learned she received from her aunt. Her beauty left me transfixed, rooted to the spot as I stood before the Rev. Crumady, our pastor, as he waited to officiate our wedding ceremony. Her beauty, what caught my eyes in the crowded Stanton High auditorium three years before, electrified me. She was my first and only love, my bride. When I looked at Jeannetta, the pent-up desire of the previous three years seemed to overflow in my heart.

Her daddy, O. D. Latimer, gave her away. He stood proud and erect in his white suit next to her. Her younger sister Carol was the bridesmaid. I cannot forget the euphoria of calling Jeannetta my wife after all the letters and the distance between us when I served in the Army.

After the ceremony, I was so excited, I walked around the house in a daze. Our wedding was a small gathering. My mother was the only member of my family in attendance.

After the refreshments were done, I walked out the door alone, ready to return to the apartment I shared with my brother and his wife.

Minutes later, as I was about to climb into the backseat of a taxicab to drive me home, I saw Jeannetta standing at the curb. I thought she had come outside to say goodbye.

"Good night," I said to Jeannetta. "I'll see you tomorrow."

At my words the smile disappeared from her face, a moment of panic seemed to cloud her face.

I was 21. I had spent the previous three years in the Army, I had seen and heard matters I had no right to hear, but I was still very naive about the world. My father had never offered his advice on what it meant to be a husband. I had no idea about how I should behave on my wedding night. I was about to leave my bride to go home with her mother, while I went back to my single room. Although Jeannetta was four years younger than me and lived a sheltered life, she knew husbands and wives should spend their wedding night together.

As I opened the door to get in the cab, Jeannetta stepped off the curb, reached out her hand and grabbed my arm.

"I am coming with you," she said in the quiet way I had grown to appreciate. With those five words she slipped into the backseat and snuggled beside me as we drove the 10 minutes to the room my older brother, George, rented us.

Our honeymoon was a 10-cent cab fare across town to my older brother's two-bedroom apartment not far from Edward Waters College. He rented me a room for a modest fee, and that's where we began our life together. Years later, when George's drinking took its toll, he fell on hard times. The Post Office fired him because of his alcoholism. He lost his wife. When he was down on his luck and needed a job, I offered him one at the gas station I owned. Whatever I could do to help my brother, I would.

We lived with my brother in his two-bedroom apartment for a short time. The place wasn't large enough for two families, especially as Jeannetta was expecting our first child, Rosemary. Afterward, we moved in with my parents on Grothe Street.

I had come home to Jacksonville determined to take my bride back to California. That never happened. Concerns for my parents won out. I needed to be close to them. We stayed in Jacksonville for the next two decades. We never even visited California.

Chapter 28:
CIVILIAN WORK

For one year after my military discharge and return to Jacksonville, I could find nothing but laboring jobs. At the University Hospital, I worked as an orderly. Being a hospital orderly was one of the nastiest jobs imaginable. It involved moving dead bodies. Anything others didn't want to do, you did it.

I wasn't accustomed to being around dead bodies. If someone died on the operating table, they called the orderly to take them down to the morgue. If the doctor was nice, he would help you put the body on the slab. You gain a deep sense of appreciation for life when you go through something like that.

But things turned bad in a hurry.

I thought I was making $1 an hour. When I saw my first paycheck, I realized they were paying me 75 cents an hour. When I asked, the woman in the personnel office insisted I agreed to work for 75 cents an hour. It seemed criminal to do such dirty work for so little.

"I'm refuse to work for 75 cents," I told her. "I quit."

"Aren't going to give me two weeks' notice?" she asked.

I said, "No. I am giving you notice now. I quit."

I couldn't work for 75 cents an hour. I walked down the stairs and walked home.

After I quit that job, I worked as laborer that paid me $1 an hour mixing mortar in the hot sun. I needed a job, so I didn't complain.

A friend worked as a brick mason. He paid me $1 an hour. If he had a job on 20th Street, I had to pay him to ride in his truck. Somehow, I felt exploited. He was going to work. I worked with him. He was my friend. We went to school together. But he charged me. A brick mason made good money. But laborers didn't.

Chapter 29:
MAXWELL HOUSE COFFEE

After I quit wiping patients' behinds and was working as a laborer for $1 an hour, a friend told me Maxwell House Coffee was hiring, so I rode my bicycle down to put in an application. The day I got there they were actually interviewing. I interviewed well and they hired me on the spot.

My supervisor was a white man named Merrill Bromly. He was a fine man with a very gentle nature. He wouldn't harm a mouse. He was in charge where the coffee came down and went into jars in the assembly line. You had thirty or forty jars you brought in the store. Forty or fifty white women kept the jars moving. My job as a tow motor operator was to supply that line with the bottles. They came in containers, twenty to forty per box. They would be stacked in the warehouse. My job was to keep the line supplied. In that section were all white women. There were no Black women in that department. Black men worked all over the plant, including in the area where the coffee was being made.

Ed Balance was the general manager. He set the tone for hiring Black men and offering scholarships for Blacks to go to school. Balance hired Black electricians. He hired young Black men and put them in high positions. He had a reputation for his philanthropy and for being a humanitarian.

My financial situation changed considerably after I was hired at the Maxwell House Coffee Company factory in Jacksonville. The factory was first built in 1910 on Bay Street by Joel Cheek, founder of the Cheek-Neal Coffee Company. The coffee was named in honor of the Maxwell House Hotel in Nashville, which first served the morning beverage. The factory at 735 East Bay Street where I worked was built in 1924 to accommodate the rapid growth of what would become America's most popular coffee brand.

It was owned by General Foods, the massive conglomerate. My role was to drive the forklift to carry the cans into the factory where they were filled with the ground coffee. I loved my job. My bosses loved me. I worked in air-conditioned comfort. After laboring under the hot Florida sun pushing a wheelbarrow all day, working at Maxwell House felt like a dream. I was set for life. I was prepared to grow old with the scent of fresh ground coffee in my nostrils. I was a lifer.

Each day I arrived at home, I couldn't contain my excitement about my job. The pay was good. I made about $200 a month. It allowed Jeannetta, our baby daughter Rosemary, and I to live more comfortably than before. The working conditions were beyond my wildest dreams.

But in moments of clarity, deep down inside I yearned for something more. The calling to be a preacher tugged at my heart and soul. As I attended classes at Walker Business College, my instructors opened a world of possibilities that lay before me. A college education could set my family on a path of comfort and success for generations to come. Those dreams would not come true with me working on a factory floor. I had to reach for more. Ambition poured through my heart as I worked each day. There was a better future for me. I was prepared to grab it with both hands.

Chapter 30:
THE ADVERTISEMENT

On May 7, 1955, the big news in Jacksonville was that the 22-story South Central Home Office building of the Prudential Insurance Co. of America opened on the south Jacksonville waterfront. It was the largest office building in Florida and marked the city's arrival of its skyline, reported Florida Times Union that day. The paper also reported that city, county and state law enforcement officials met to devise a plan to clean up the dumps, dives and juke joints as part of Mayor Haydon Burns' plan to eliminate the blight of taverns on Bay, Main and Ocean streets.

One day that spring, I saw an advertisement in the Negro section of the Times Union, the city's daily newspaper where my father worked nights as a janitor for years. The ad said the city was looking to hire Negro police officers. There was going to be a test specifically for Negroes.

At the time, I was working at the Maxwell House Coffee factory. I enjoyed my work and harbored ideas of a long career with the company. But at the same time, I had begun taking classes at Walker Vocational and dreamed of making something of myself beyond employment at a coffee factory. I was ambitious. I wanted to go further than my mother and father who were barely literate and had to struggle to make ends meet all their lives.

When I saw the advertisement, my heart leapt for joy. I had been a policeman in the Army. I had law enforcement training. I knew how to wield a baton and shoot a pistol. I had done investigative work and knew how to safely guard dangerous prisoners. I was aware of the presence of Negro officers who patrolled our neighborhoods and the downtown Black business section people called the Gold Coast, because there was so much money, legal and illegal, flowing from one hand to the next. I admired the way Negro police officers carried themselves. They were nothing like the white policemen who patrolled our neighborhoods as if they were a foreign occupying army.

When I saw the ad, I knew nothing stood in my way to get accepted. In order to qualify, I had to have an eighth-grade education. I could easily top that. I had graduated from Stanton High with my diploma. My background was spotless. I had never had even a traffic or parking ticket. I had never had any trouble with the law. I had earned an honorable discharge from the Army. At 22, I was well within the age range to wear the badge.

My only concern was physical. At five feet nine, I was tall enough. But I worried about my weight. Police officers were required to weigh at least 155 pounds. I was barely 155 soaking wet. I was a skinny guy. No amount of eating had made me any stouter.

· · · · · · · · · · · · · · · ·

Being a Negro officer seemed to be the perfect fit for me. I would have to do some of the same things to become an officer as I did when I went through the training in the Army. In addition, having been a military policeman, I brought certain skills. I could conduct investigations and interrogations. I had been trained in firearm use and safety. Military experience translated well to civilian police work. That's why many police departments sought ex-military policemen or soldiers because of their sense of discipline and training. It gave us an advantage when it came to civilian life. We knew how to take and follow orders and respect the chain of command.

Chapter 31:
THE TEST

On the day of the Negro exam, about thirty or forty of us showed up to take the test at a room at Jacksonville City Hall. We all walked in to face the white proctors supervising the three-hour written exam. The questions involved basic police work, law and police procedure. My experience as an MP and an investigator worked to my advantage.

The test for Negro police officers required knowledge of police work. I, or anyone for that matter, couldn't expect to just walk in off the street and pass the test without preparation. There were police questions with no reference to race. You had to know your police procedural. If I am pursuing a criminal and he crossed the state line into Georgia, I could not bring him back to Florida without permission from Georgia. If I lost sight of him, I could not arrest him. I could only arrest someone if I am in hot pursuit. If I lost sight of him, I lost all authority to arrest him in terms of the offense he was committing. I was not in hot pursuit. I can't see you commit an offense in one place and lose you and see you someplace else and arrest you. You can only arrest someone who is committing an offense in your sight. Otherwise, you must get an arrest warrant. You are arresting the suspect based on the warrant. Any police officer can then make the arrest.

After three hours, I walked out of City Hall confident I had aced the test. I had been confident about exams before and failed. But that day in 1955, I was supremely confident about what I had done. None of the questions stumped me. I answered everything on the paper in my neat penmanship.

As a veteran, civilian exams are tailored to us. In order to pass, I had to score at least 70 points. Once I reached that score, I received five or seven points for being a military veteran. Those extra points would come in handy if I had the same score as another aspiring police officer who was not a veteran, and we were vying for the last spot.

Prior to taking the police exam, I was subjected to a preliminary police background which made me eligible to take the test. In 1952, Chief Police Cannon had introduced psychiatric tests for those applying to the fire and police departments. I also passed that test with flying colors. There were no disqualifying factors to prevent me from taking the exam. If there were, I wouldn't have been able to take the exam.

· · · · · · · · · · · · · · · ·

The biggest hurdle to me becoming a Negro Jacksonville police officer was physical. I had to meet the height and weight requirements before I could take the test. My biggest problem was my weight. I was a tall, skinny guy. I had the height. To qualify for the police department, I had to weigh at least one hundred and fifty-five pounds. I am eating bananas and drinking a lot every day leading up to the weigh-in. My normal weight was 150 pounds. The day of the weigh-in, I qualified with two pounds to spare. I weighed one hundred and fifty-seven pounds.

The results came back in four to six weeks. That was the longest wait of my life. Each day I returned home to Jeannetta and my baby daughter, Rosemary. I checked the mailbox. A letter had arrived in the mail. I was one of 14 recruits who passed the written exam. I had passed the psychological exam. I had passed the medical physical. I was ready to do something meaningful with my life.

I had a decent job, but working in a coffee factory was not my career goal. I needed a better job. Being a Negro police officer came with pay and prestige. Being a Negro policeman also came with a pension and authority. My name would be known throughout the Black neighborhoods, in our bars and in our churches. Among a population of 50,000 Negroes, 20 of them were designated as officers of the law, representatives of the city. That put me in a select group. Once I received a letter confirming I had passed the test, the next hurdle was the Police Academy. I was 22 years old and felt that, after my experience in the Army, I could do anything that came my way.

Fourteen Negro recruits passed the test and were admitted to the Police Academy. Like the two earlier groups of Black recruits, we were not allowed to train at the Jacksonville Police Academy. We were relegated to train at Wilder Community Center. It was not that we didn't like the Wilder Center. It was an integral part of Black communal life in Jacksonville. It provided for familiar surroundings. However, it reminded us of our inferior status as Negro officers, who were issued used uniforms and hand-me-down pistols and who were not allowed to arrest white residents. Other than the location of the training, the rigor and intensity was equal to that of the white officers.

The civil service announcement had made it abundantly clear that we were to serve the Negro community only, but hearing it spoken out loud was jarring. The duties and responsibilities of a policeman were enthusiastically explained by a most deliberate captain of our training division. The second week of our training, he made it clear that we had no authority to arrest white offenders. It was the police director's matter-of-fact manner that bothered me most about our limited police power.

Our police training required us to be physically agile and to handle firearms. We had to be able to perform on the range. That meant hitting the targets with regularity. Of the 14 Negro recruits in my cohort, all but one graduated from the police academy. Among our cohorts, the only candidate to flunk out couldn't shoot straight. He never learned to hit the target on the range.

· · · · · · · · · · · · · · · ·

With the addition of our group, the Negro police precinct almost doubled in strength. Six officers were hired in 1950, eight officers hired in 1953 and 13 officers hired in 1955. We were now 27 Negro officers. That number was as many as had been on the force in 1899 when Negro officers were kicked out of the department following the passage of House Bill 4 by the Florida Legislature. Our presence was celebrated and treated as a novelty in the city's history. Our assignment was simple — patrol the Negro business and residential community. It was viewed as an experiment to appease Black activists and to assuage Black anger. What I have come to understand was that the Negro police officer on the streets of Jacksonville was part of a much larger struggle, one that had begun in earnest more than a century ago. I was not just a Negro police officer. In putting on the uniform, I would become a foot soldier in the long, meandering struggle for power and equality. African Americans could not have one without the other. Policing and power went hand in hand. The presence or absence of Black policemen patrolling the streets of Southern cities mirrored our political status. A close examination of American history reinforced that truism.

BOOK V:
POLICING AND POWER

Chapter 32:
ARRESTING THE PRESIDENT

Black men wearing a police uniform mirrored the rise of Black political power. Throughout our history, we wore the uniform and assumed legal authority whenever we were allowed to take our rightful place in America's body politic. On the contrary, we were robbed of the opportunity to protect and serve during the long periods when Southern legislatures systematically deprived us of our legal and constitutional rights.

During Reconstruction, in the heady days after the Civil War, America took concrete steps — Black men sat in Congress and in legislatures throughout the South, and Black policemen patrolled the streets. They exercised considerable authority. And unlike decades later when Negro police officers were barred from arresting whites, Black police officers had no such restrictions. They served with honor and courage. I am a spiritual descendant of those officers.

One of those officers was William Henry West. West was born into slavery in Prince George's County, Maryland in 1842. After the Civil War erupted, West fought in Company K, 30th U.S. Colored Infantry which was formed in 1863. He survived the Battle of the Crater, which occurred on July 30, 1864, and was part of the Siege of Petersburg.

A year later, after the war ended, America struggled to decide the fate of millions of the formerly enslaved, my ancestors. Reconstruction, a northern remedy to correct centuries of Southern racial oppression, was one solution.

On August 1, 1871, West was appointed to the Metropolitan police department. He was one of two Negro policemen employed by the District of Columbia, a city which even then had a significant population of Black people. By then, the White House was occupied by Ulysses S. Grant, a former general in the victorious Union cause. The inept Andrew Johnson, who succeeded Abraham Lincoln after his assassination, had been hounded out of the power.

West was known for being gentlemanly. He was also fond of good, fast horses. He was also fearless. He didn't shrink when faced with the choice between his duty and overlooking wrongdoing. One day, West was working on patrol near 13th and M Streets Northwest when he encountered President Grant speeding in a carriage drawn by two horses. The police department had received reports of horse drawn carriages speeding in that area. After a mother and her young child had reportedly been run over and seriously injured by a speeding horse and carriage, West was dispatched to the scene. Washington Evening Star reported that as West was talking to witnesses, a group of speeding carriages came toward him. West put up his hand to stop the scofflaws, among them the occupant of 1600 Pennsylvania Avenue.

"Well, officer," the commander-in-chief said impatiently, "what do you want with me?"

West was respectful but didn't shirk from his duty.

"I want to inform you, Mr. President, that you are violating the law by speeding along this street. Your fast driving, sir, has set the example for a lot of other gentlemen."

After President Grant apologized, West let him off with a warning for excessive speeding.

The encounter with a Negro law enforcement officer would not have come as a shock to the Civil War military hero turned politician. Black police officers had been patrolling the cobblestone streets of the nation's capital for almost a decade.

Grant, however, didn't heed West's warning. The next evening, the Black policeman saw the unrepentant Grant again speeding in his horse and buggy. Grant was traveling so fast, it took him a block before he could rein in the horses and bring them to a stop.

The affable former general played the innocent card.

"Do you think, officer, that I was violating the speed laws?" he asked.

"Yes, I do, Mr. President," West replied.

Grant's excuse was that he didn't realize he was speeding.

"I am very sorry, Mr. President, to have to do it, for you are the chief of the nation and I am nothing but a policeman," West reportedly told Grant, "But duty is duty, sir, and I will have to place you under arrest."

The former Union general and his speeding friends who were also detained, were taken to the police station. He was ordered to post a $20 bond and released. He and the others were scheduled to return for trial the next day.

The Washington Star newspaper reported that "32 ladies of the most refined character and surroundings" voluntarily came into court and testified against the drivers, who bitterly contested the charges. Grant was not among them. He didn't appear in court. President Grant later commended West for performing his duty.

"Let no guilty man escape, if it can be avoided. No personal consideration should stand in the way of performing a public duty."

This is the only known incident of an incumbent United States president being arrested. This largely unknown incident reported in the September 27, 1908 edition of the Washington Evening Star, reflects the standing of Black officers during Reconstruction. West retired that year after 35 years in the department.

William H. West is largely forgotten except among Reconstruction era historians. But his actions symbolized the courage and commitment to duty exemplified by Negro policemen trying to undo the scars of centuries of American bondage and racial oppression, and his spirit lives on. Even though I didn't know his story when I wore the uniform, in a way I felt imbued with his mantle. When I patrolled the streets of Jacksonville, I had the respect of those whom I had sworn to serve and protect. My presence on the street made them feel safer. They didn't have to worry about being brutalized by disrespectful white police officers. I was not just an officer. I was a symbol — a symbol of Black Jacksonville residents taking their rightful place in the service of their city, my city.

Chapter 33:
POLICING AND POWER

William Henry West's status as a Negro policeman reflects the place and time in which he lived. The District of Columbia was populated by a sizable Black population, long before the Civil War. After the Confederacy was defeated, Reconstruction opened the door, ever so briefly, for the formerly enslaved to assume their rightful place in American society. During Reconstruction, Union soldiers occupied the vanquished South. Blacks united with white Republicans to gain power. For the first time in American history, we were elected to American legislatures, city commissions, town councils, sheriff's offices, the United States Congress — the House of Representatives and the U.S. Senate. Hiram Rhodes Revels was the first African American U.S. Senator following his election by the Mississippi State Legislature. The second, Blanche Bruce, another Black Republican, also hailed from Mississippi.

Black political power rides shotgun with the Black policeman. The presence of Negro policemen is perhaps the best reflection of the earliest emergence of Black political power in the American South. It is no coincidence that Black police power and Black political power rode in tandem. When I examine American history, I see that whenever and wherever African Americans exercised political power, they also exercise law enforcement authority.

In 1872, two years after ratification of the Fifteenth Amendment, Chicago, a city founded by a Black man, hired its first Black policeman. There's no mistaking the timing. This was a golden age for Black people in our country's history. This was during Reconstruction, in the years immediately following the Civil War. The defeat of the Confederacy, and the abolition of chattel slavery, with the Antebellum South in ruins, set the stage for my ancestors to finding their footing and their voice. Black power had been unleashed after two and a half centuries of bondage. Blacks were elected to the U.S. House of Representatives and the U.S. Senate in numbers never imagined for the formerly enslaved. Black police officers, constables and Black sheriffs took their place alongside Black legislators in those heady years after President Lincoln's Emancipation Proclamation and passage of the Thirteenth, then the Fourteenth and the Fifteenth Amendments.

The Thirteenth Amendment abolished slavery; the Fourteenth granted citizenship to my ancestors after the Supreme Court's shameful Dredd Scott decision of 1849 stripped citizenship from even free men of color. The Fifteenth Amendment in 1870 enshrined my ancestors' right to vote and with it the right to hold elective office.

No African American held a federal elective office before the ratification of the Fifteenth Amendment. After Revels and Bruce left office, it would be almost a century before an African American was elected to the United States Senate.

But we know what happened in the years to come. American has rarely kept faith with its citizens of color. Courts, Congress, state legislatures and non-state actors have denied us rights enshrined in the U.S. Constitution, a document we hold sacred. We believed in those documents when others didn't, even when they were written to exclude us. The gains of the post-Civil War years would be undone by the Compromise of 1877. Our freedom and our power disappeared after Congress settled the disputed election of 1876 with a deal that gave Rutherford B. Hayes the presidency over Democrat Samuel J. Tilden in exchange for withdrawing federal troops from places like South Carolina, Florida and Louisiana. In those states, Republican state governments could not survive without the support of federal troops. White Republicans soon followed the federal troops opening the door for Redeemer Democrats. This was the beginning of a dark period in our history.

Chapter 34:
THE POWERLESS AND THE PUNISHED

"It was not a question of crime but rather of color that settled a Negro's conviction on any charge." — W. E. B. Dubois *Souls of Black Folk*

Once federal troops left the South, Black Republicans lost power. African American U.S. Senators Hiram Revels and Blanche Bruce were not returned to the U.S. Senate as white Democrats in the Mississippi Legislature adopted a new constitution that disenfranchised Black voters. Throughout the South, the Black populace was subjected to domestic terrorism to intimidate them from voting. The Black codes became law in the former Confederate states. Hard-fought gains of the post slavery era disappeared within a generation. Racial segregation became the law of the land in the Southern states of Alabama, Arkansas, Florida, Georgia, South Carolina, North Carolina, Mississippi, and Louisiana and Texas.

In 1896, following a challenge by Homer Plessy, a New Orleans resident who was mostly white but had some Black ancestry, the United States Supreme Court, in its *Plessy v. Ferguson* ruling, upheld racial segregation in public facilities. As the nation's highest court had done nearly half a century earlier in the Dred Scott case, it set back the cause of Black progress for generations. In a 7-to-1 vote, the court ruled that it was constitutional to have separate public facilities for Blacks and whites if the facilities were equal. In doing so, the court all but nullified the Fourteenth Amendment, which had ostensibly established the legal equality of the formerly enslaved and their former masters. The decision deferred to racist white Southern legislatures when it came to delegating police powers, laws that affected the daily lives of Blacks and whites. Jim Crow became a way of life. America had once again reminded us that rights given can always be revoked.

By 1905, Black men were robbed of the vote by every state legislature in the Solid South. It would take more than half a century for another African American to be elected to represent the South in Congress.

The lack of political power stood in sharp contrast to the size of the African American population in the South. In 1910, before the Great Migration began in earnest, 90 percent of the nation's 8.8 million African Americans lived in the South. But of those, fewer than half a million were registered to vote. Polls taxes, literacy tests and sheer intimidation from groups like the Ku Klux Klan served to prevent Black voter participation. The reversal of political fortunes meant that we had very little say in municipal hiring decisions.

The absence of Black voters on the rolls meant we were absent in the jury deliberation room where our fates were often unjustly decided. All-white juries sentenced Black men, both the innocent and the guilty. The lack of political power, the persistence of all-white juries, meant that "Black men are often tried not by their peers, but by men who would rather punish ten innocent Negroes than let one guilty Negro go free," Dubois wrote.

Meanwhile, jury nullification became a way of life to acquit white men accused of atrocities against Black men and women. Lynching sent a message to both Blacks and whites. The grizzly public spectacles served to keep us in our place, compliant and subservient.

The lack of Black political power in the South was paralleled by our vulnerability to extrajudicial punishment. Between 1882 and 1968, the NAACP recorded 3,446 Black men were lynched across America. Of those, 79 percent happened in the South. Mississippi, Georgia and Texas, states known for the legal execution of Black men, led the way. While Florida had fewer men lynched — 212, my home state had the highest rate of lynching Blacks per capita. For every 1,250 Blacks in Florida, one was lynched between 1882 and 1930, one study found. That rate was seven times higher than in North Carolina and nearly double the rate of our next-door neighbor, Georgia.

• • • • • • • • • • • • • • • •

My hometown was not immune to the fever of cruelty and terror. The Equal Justice Initiative documented seven lynchings in Jacksonville between the late 1800s and 1950. On the night of September 8, 1919, John Morine and Bowman Cook were dragged from Duval County Jail and lynched by a mob of angry white men. Both had been arrested on murder charges after a white businessman, the brother of a justice of the peace, was killed in a fight downtown.

Cook and Morine had the double misfortune of being held in the same place where another inmate accused of molesting a 12-year-old white girl was being held. A mob of about 50 armed white men assaulted the jail to lynch the accused child molester, only to find that he had been moved out of town to protect him from being lynched. Seeing the target of their anger was beyond its grasp, the mob took the two Black suspects. Cook and Morine were driven to the outskirts of the city and shot repeatedly. The mob tied ropes around their necks. No one was ever charged in their killing.

On August 23, 1923, Benjamin Hart, who cut wood at a logging camp, was lynched in the area near Kings Road and 12th Street in Jacksonville by a group of men, some of whom claimed to be sheriff's deputies. The men converged on the camp after a white woman said a Black man peeped into her window. Hart was picked out from the four Black men who were found sleeping at the camp. His bullet-riddled body was found with his hands manacled. No one was ever charged for the killing of this innocent Black man.

Chapter 35:
FEW BLACK POLICE OFFICERS

Before 1921, Negroes walked the police beat in only about 10 Southern cities — Baltimore, Knoxville, Memphis, Wheeling, West Virginia, Tampa, Florida, Galveston, Austin and Houston, Texas. By 1924, Washington, Louisville and Beaumont, Texas, added Negro policemen. Still, progress was slow as Jim Crow remained the law of the South. In 1940, fewer than 50 Negro policemen were employed in the states of the former Confederacy, according to then-Florida State University Professor Elliott M. Rudwick.

According to the 1940 Census, 75 percent of the 13 million Black Americans called the South home. The states with the largest Black populations — Mississippi, South Carolina, Louisiana, Georgia and Alabama didn't have one Negro policeman patrolling the street. South Carolina, with a population of more than 700,000 Black people who made up more than 43 percent of the population, had not one Black police officer.

Negro neighborhoods were poorly patrolled. White police officers rarely appeared in Negro neighborhoods. And when they did, their treatment of Blacks was often harsh and brutal. While their presence, though infrequent, was problematic, their absence meant that our neighborhoods, segregated, separated and impoverished, were at the mercy of criminals. Black neighborhoods lacked police protection. They paid taxes but lacked representation. This lack of police protection, combined with white police brutality, for Black leaders within Florida, reflected their lack of political clout and their inability to affect change that would improve the lives of the people who looked up to them. The absence of police protection, especially Black police protection, was galling on two fronts. It sent the message that whites did not believe we had the moral fabric to exercise the authority of law enforcement. And in their eyes we weren't smart enough and we weren't competent enough to safeguard our own communities; we couldn't be trusted with authority.

White Southerners convinced themselves that we could never be good policemen. Bred on the milk of racial superiority, Southerners couldn't stomach the sight of a Negro in uniform. After all, they lynched Negroes who served their country honorably for the temerity of wearing the uniform in public. Worst of all, white men remain haunted by visions of miscegenation — Black men being able to exercise power over white women. White men found it unthinkable that a Black man like me would stop and arrest a white woman in public. For generations, Black men like me were lynched for merely looking at a white woman.

They kept looking for excuses why police departments remained all white across more the 90 percent of cities across the 13 states that comprised the defeated Confederacy.

Another excuse for maintaining the color barrier in law enforcement was that white officers' morale would suffer if cities hired Black officers. White officers would quit rather than work alongside Black officers, they claimed. Cities like Greensboro, North Carolina, and Atlanta offered up the poor white officer morale excuse for refusing to hire Negro officers, Rudwick found. Some politicians even warned that "the fabric of Southern tradition would be torn away" if Negroes were allowed to be police officers.

The absence of Black police officers on the streets of Southern cities reflected the lack of Black political power. Due to poll taxes — a voting fee, which was a classic Jim Crow era concoction to keep Blacks from voting, voters were required to pay their poll tax before they could cast a ballot. Meanwhile, poor whites were exempt from the poll tax because of "grandfather clauses," which exempted them from the poll taxes because their grandfathers had voted in previous elections. Many unschooled rural and urban Blacks were also disenfranchised by literacy tests, threats of violence and other voter suppression tactics.

······················

Until after the Second World War, there were fewer than 250,000 Black voters across the 13 Southern states. Of those Black voters, many voted in meaningless general elections but were unable to wield any political power in state legislators and city councils. With the end of the Second World War, the return of Black veterans who had fought Nazism overseas saw greater activism and a surge in the number of Negro voters. Understandably, men who fought for democracy abroad were not content to return home and be disenfranchised.

Meanwhile on the home front, Black civic groups lobbied liberal whites to gain access to the levers of power. The rise of the Negro police officer paralleled the rise of Black political power and participation. Civic groups argued that, given the harsh and intemperate nature of white police patrols in Black neighborhoods, it made more sense. It would be more cost-effective to assign Negro officers to patrol Negro neighborhoods. These Negro officers would not patrol white neighborhoods, and so the prospect of white suspects being arrested by Black officers was greatly reduced.

According to one survey conducted by the New South publication in 1945, 134 Negro men and women worked for police departments in the South. That number might be deceptive since it included school guards, who were not sworn law enforcement officers. By 1950, the number of Black policemen had increased by more than threefold to 425. This included the six recently hired in my hometown, Jacksonville, for the Negro Precinct, Substation 3. And by 1954 the number had risen to 800, but that number included 87 women school guards, who were not sworn officers.

Even in cities with Negro officers, the strength didn't reflect the size of the Black population they were asked to patrol and protect. In places like Norfolk, Virginia, there were eight officers for 80,000 Negroes in 1959.

In Dallas, Texas, six Negro officers were responsible for policing 130,000 Blacks. These officers were recruited as a response to pressure campaigns by Negro and biracial associations. Once the pressure ended, the hiring ended. In1945, there were 27 police agencies with Negro policemen. In 1954, there were 165 agencies that employed Negro policemen.

The hiring of Black officers was not always welcomed by some segments of the Black community, researchers found. It's a fact I saw for myself as a patrolman. Some "lower class" Negroes resented Negro policemen and often would request a white police officer. It was not uncommon for such types to try to discredit Black officers with white officers, as Andrew Ball learned in his study of three Florida municipalities that hired Negro officers.

· · · · · · · · · · · · · · · ·

White Southerners feared that Negro policemen would arrest white people, especially white women. This was the reason for opposing the hiring of Black officers or for restricting their numbers and their authority and jurisdiction to segregated districts.

In a survey of agencies across the South, in about one third of cities, a Negro officers could arrest a suspect regardless of color. In some cities, Negroes had to call white officers to arrest white perps.

In Jacksonville, Negro officers couldn't arrest whites who committed misdemeanors but could arrest felony suspects.

The increase in Negro policemen coincided with Negro political participation. Four times as many Blacks voted in 1950 as in 1940. During this period there were almost eight times more Negro policemen. The increases were not sustained from 1954 to 1959 in the years after *Brown v. Board of Education*. Negro officers were better educated than our white counterparts.

Upward mobility was frustratingly absent. Promotions were slow. Negro officers were denied tests. Hence, there were few Black sergeants and even fewer Black lieutenants and captains.

Even as they wore the uniform, Negro officers faced workplace indignities. They were not allowed in the headquarters. They weren't trained in the same academy or in the same classrooms. In the 1930s, Negro officers in Louisville were not allowed to wear police uniforms while off duty on their way home.

• • • • • • • • • • • • • • • •

James Andrew Ball did his master's theses on the experience of three Florida cities — Belle Glade, West Palm Beach and Tallahassee in hiring Negro police officers in the early 1950s. Ball learned that in Belle Glade, Florida, a rural community near Lake Okeechobee, Negro leaders felt Negro policemen would not deal as harshly with members of their own race while white officials felt that Blacks would be hesitant in bringing civil rights charges against a Negro policeman. Another reason generally accepted by both Negroes and whites, was that Negro policemen should be able to interact more effectively with members of their own race, particularly in securing information. In Belle Glade, Florida, a city commission candidate pledged to back the hiring of Negro policemen. He won the election against an incumbent in 1950.

Chapter 36:
THE HISTORY OF BLACK POLICE OFFICERS IN JACKSONVILLE

On Sunday, July 16, 1950, three days before I would celebrate my 18th birthday when I would no longer need my parents' permission to join the Army, Jacksonville prepared for a major milestone that would have a significant impact on my life. Not far from where I lived with my parents and siblings, a ceremony was being held. The choice of Sunday was odd. It was on the Sabbath and the day of religious observance in our deeply religious North Florida community that Mayor W. Haydon Burns swore in six police officers who would form a Negro Precinct.

When Henry Harley, Edward Hickson, Alvin James, Beamon Kendall, Marion Massey and Charlie Sea took the oath to protect and serve, it marked the first time in 61 years that Black men were allowed to wear the police uniform and patrol the streets of Jacksonville.

Those pioneers of law enforcement were hailed, ignorantly I must say, by many as the first Black Jacksonville policemen. But what I didn't know at the time, and most of my friends and neighbors were grossly unaware of, was that Jacksonville policing was once synonymous with Black police officers. In 1950, the white power structure preferred not to acknowledge that Blacks possessed a proud history of law enforcement service on the streets of Jacksonville. But that history had been whitewashed in the reign of terror following the enlightenment of Reconstruction. It had been erased from our collective memory by the harshness of Jim Crow segregation. A racial amnesia had set in for generations. The only history we were taught was the sanitized version designed to keep us in our place. But the great Black awakening following the end of World War II had begun. America, white America, could not deny us our rightful place in society for much longer.

On that blessed Sunday, the long night of darkness was over. Our community had long lobbied and petitioned for black officers to patrol our streets and our neighborhoods. We were tired of being disrespected by white officers. We paid taxes but received no protection. Our neighborhoods were at the mercy of the criminal element — young men and rabble-rousers, dice throwers, street walkers and pimps. It was hard for respectable families to walk unmolested on the sidewalk. White police officers only showed up after trouble happened. And when they did, their condescension and paternalism was hard to stomach. It felt like a case of double victimization. The criminal element stole our safety and property, and the white police officers stole our dignity. Hiring Negro police officers in American cities, like the appointment of Negro MPs years earlier, was a stepping stone in our struggle for equal protection under the law.

· · · · · · · · · · · · · · · ·

It was also a moment to remind ourselves of the rich tradition of African Americans in law enforcement, not only in Jacksonville but across the South. You wouldn't have known it, based on the Duval County Sheriff Dale Carson's 34-page Annual Report in recognition of America's Bicentennial celebrations. Black law enforcement officers received scant mention in the report's timeline, which dates the Jacksonville Police Department to the founding of Duval County in 1822 — "1889. For a number of years prior to this time the Police Department was comprised primarily of Blacks. The Florida Legislature passed House Bill No. 4, which in effect, eliminated the integrated police force and provided an all-white police force — chief, first lieutenant, first sergeant, 24 patrolmen and four extra men."

The next mention refers to historic events 61 years later:

"Police department began hiring Black police officers again."

The third mention of Blacks in Duval County/City of Jacksonville law enforcement history is relegated to a section under the heading, "Reign of the Carpetbaggers."

This document, published more than 100 years after the abolition of slavery and the affirmation of our rights as American citizens, couches the progress of Blacks and Republicans in the years following freedom in language of the Confederacy.

The operation of the Police Department under the new charter of 1888 was led by Chief of Police James Hoey. At the time, the City of Jacksonville Police Department was comprised primarily of Blacks, the report stated.

"In 1889, House Bill No. 4 was passed by the Florida Legislature giving the governor power to abolish all offices in the City of Jacksonville and to make new appointments to fill them. The newly appointed Board of Police Commissioners appointed an entirely new police force."

Sheriff Carson's annual report leaves so much unwritten, unsaid, and unacknowledged. The omissions in the report are egregious. It is a classic whitewashing of our history, the kind of whitewashing that inspires me to tell this story. That short passage encapsulates how Jim Crow operated and how whites systematically used the legitimate levers of power to illegitimately disenfranchise and dispossess Blacks.

What the annual report omits is that the governor in question was Francis P. Fleming, a Jacksonville native and a Democrat. To be a Southern Democrat in 1888 was to be a segregationist and white supremist. Fleming's pedigree and credentials were impeccable. He enlisted in the Confederate Army and rose to the rank of first lieutenant. So wedded was Fleming to the Confederate cause that even after he was injured in combat, he returned home and raised new volunteers for a company that fought at the Battle of Natural Bridge near St. Marks, Florida, on March 5, 1865. During the war, Fleming fought under Generals John Magruder, Joseph Johnston, John Bell Hood and Robert E. Lee.

It was no surprise, then, that the man dubbed Florida's second worst governor would act to remove Blacks and their white Republican allies from power in Jacksonville and have them replaced with whites. Being an avowed Confederate, Fleming would have chafed at the federal troops occupying his hometown. He would have been even more hostile to the presence of former slaves in positions of authority as police officers in the two decades before he ran for the governor's mansion.

Carson's report also omits Jacksonville's rich history of Blacks during Reconstruction. Thankfully, those details are filled in by The Jacksonville Historical Society in telling my pioneering history in law enforcement. In that article, the writer stopped for a few moments to remind readers that I was standing on the shoulders of giants, long before Charles Sea and others donned the uniform, Black men had served with honor. They served until America's reactionary, racist DNA closed the door to them based solely on the color of their skin.

As much as folks like to pretend that slavery and the Civil War happened such a long time ago, the events of that time shaped my life and the Jacksonville of my boyhood and adulthood.

During and after the Civil War, Jacksonville was consistently occupied by Union and Federal forces until 1869. But Black men wore the police uniform even before that time. In 1863, while war still raged between North and South, a Black man, Officer William Johnson, was sworn in with the Jacksonville Police Department. Seven years later, on April 12, 1870, when Johnson responded to a call, he encountered "a very strong and intoxicated" man. The suspect picked up Johnson and threw him to the ground, fatally injuring him. Johnson died two days later. He was only 35. Johnson's name is etched on the National Law Enforcement Officers Memorial in Washington, D.C., as the first Black American officer to be killed in the line of duty.

But even as Blacks in Jacksonville were mourning the loss of one of their own in April 1870, they had reasons to celebrate. That month, Jacksonville held elections that resulted in victories for Republicans and Black Freedmen. Dave Pettis became the first African-America elected to the office of the Board of Police Commissioners. Five Black police officers, two Black jailors and two Black constables were also voted into office.

George H. Mays was Jacksonville's first Black police sergeant. In 1878, Mays became the second Black Town Marshal. The name of the first Black town marshal has been lost to history. A town marshal represented the police force. Before the Civil War, the marshal had the authority to deputize any resident of Jacksonville to aid him whenever force was needed. All men were required to volunteer for the civic night patrol.

In 1887, a new city charter changed the title of "Captain of Police" to "Chief of Police." That change in the charter also drastically altered the demographics of the city. The new Jacksonville city charter abolished the towns of LaVilla and Fairfield, and annexed them along with their Black residents. This resulted in an integrated government. It meant Blacks tasted power in Jacksonville. Black citizens filled the positions of five of the aldermen and the municipal judge. By December 1887, among the ranks of the police department, 15 of the 24 policemen, two police sergeants and the Chairman of the Board of Police Commissioners were Black.

· · · · · · · · · · · · · · · ·

Our history is rife with progress and reaction, Black improvement, and white backlash. Not surprisingly, the previously white dominated city administration refused to accept the 1887 election results. Unfortunately, timing is everything. At that time, Jacksonville was in the grip of a worsening yellow fever epidemic. By July 1888, a third of the city's population was stricken. Jacksonville was placed under lock down; authorities imposed a quarantine and a strict curfew. No one could enter or leave the river city.

What happened next was a playbook that would be repeated throughout the South for generations of Jim Crow rule. White Democrats and conservatives accused the newly elected Black and white Republican city officials of incompetence.

• • • • • • • • • • • • • • • •

All politics is local. But as we have seen in Florida, power can be exercised from a distance, namely Tallahassee, to change circumstances on the ground in places like Jacksonville. Democrats and conservatives had just the right man in the governor's mansion when on May 16, 1889, the Legislature passed House Bill No. 4. It gave die-hard Confederate supporter Governor Fleming the authority to abolish the elected town government and appoint officials of his own choosing. Fleming didn't waste much time. At the stroke of a pen, Black Police Commissioners no longer walked the corridors of Jacksonville City Hall; Black police officers vanished from the streets of Jacksonville. It would be another six decades before they returned.

Chapter 37:
BLACK PERIL AND WHITE POLICING

In retrospect, as I look back at that crucial time in my life, in the 50s as I became a man and came to understand the society in which I was raised, I often struggled for the language to describe my plight. My search for that language brought me to Gunnar Myrdal's *An American Dilemma Vol II.* Myrdal's foreign, European perspective and sociological training allowed him, like the Frenchman Alexis de Tocqueville, author of *Democracy in America,* a century earlier, to see and understand my country in the ways that we Americans, Black and white, often fail to do.

The police system under Jim Crow, Myrdal found, was a natural evolution of policing during slavery. It explicitly served the interest of monitoring Negro slaves and free Negroes. Whites, despite their prevailing myths of the happy slaves, lived in constant dread of insurrection, the Swede argued.

Policemen in the South were by tradition watchdogs of all Negroes, slave or free, innocent or guilty.

All public officials in the South were white. Whites believed that Negroes should be barred from positions of public authority at every level. In my hometown, when the governor adopted that law House Bill 4, Blacks disappeared from office, elected or otherwise for more than half a century. That was no truer than in the instance of police officers. At one point most of Jacksonville police officers were Black. But that memory was entirely erased, until only a few living people remembered the days of Black police officers.

During my childhood and early adulthood, the white policeman was the Blackman's most important, most frequent point of official contact. The white policeman was the personification of civic order, white supremacy and white authority to the Negro community. He was the law with a badge and a revolver, Myrdal wrote. His word was final; he was the state's witness in court; his word was unimpeachable; it must be accepted without question.

White officers arrested us, white jurors convicted us, white judges sentenced us, and white prison guards locked the keys to our jail cells.

"For Negroes to break the rules against one white person is to break the caste rules against all the white community, and pose a threat to all white persons," Myrdal wrote.

Even small infractions of the rules must be punished. The white policeman was delegated the authority to punish. He was allowed to punish us for breaking the rules of social norms. To empower and enable the police to do that job, it meant that the justice system gave the white policeman lots of leeway to act on its behalf, even if punishment fell outside legal boundaries. In other words, white policemen were allowed to break the law to maintain the social order — Jim Crow's caste system. To question his authority was to question the society in which we lived. To weaken his authority was to weaken Jim Crow. Such cracks could not be allowed.

Thus, the white policeman's word had to be taken over a Negro's, even if the facts showed otherwise. This, Myrdal explained, was a case of social necessity. The prevailing Jim Crow wisdom was that it would undermine the policeman's authority if he was not supported 110 percent. We were arrested for real and imagined violations of the caste rules — if we laughed at the wrong time, if we appeared sullen in the presence of whites, if we stood our ground in the face of unfairness or injustice.

Myrdal described Jim Crow as creating an air of "consistent illegality" that frustrated our quest for justice. But that was not surprising. Every day, in thousands of ways big and small, America told us we had no rights that white folks were obligated to respect.

Bus conductors and bus drivers were the defenders of social inequality. Under the written and unwritten code of the Jim Crow South, my siblings and I could be arrested for just about anything. Many arrests occurred on street cars and buses where I could be arrested for demanding the right change from the conductor or for refusing to give up my seat in the correct section of the car to a white person. I could be arrested for being in the white section of town after dark; I could be arrested for being disrespectful to a police officer or speaking in a way considered to be sassing a police officer.

A sort of police power was delegated to every white person. White people were part of an unspoken conspiracy to keep Blacks in their place. The courts and the police were co-conspirators in upholding the caste, Myrdal wrote. They were vigilant watchdogs against social equality.

In Jacksonville, like elsewhere in the South, we were discriminated against by the police, by the courts and in private dealings with white folks. We were at their mercy. We were poor, powerless to stop them politically, and socially were the untouchables, considered inferior and occupied the bottom of the social pyramid.

Part of the explanation of why the Negro got more legal justice in the North, Myrdal argued, was the fact that Negroes were able to vote in the North. Consequently, they possessed a share in the ultimate control of the legal system. In the South, we lacked voting power. We were subjected to the whims of whites at every stage of the legal system, from arrests to adjudication to incarceration.

"The police system in the South to a great extent served the explicit purpose of supervising Negro slaves and free Negroes, and of hindering slaves from escape. They were given the widest license to seize, whip and punish Negroes and generally to act as agents of the masters. The police in the South were by tradition watchdogs of all Negroes, slave or free, criminal or innocent," Myrdal wrote.

We lived under the constant fear of personal threats of physical and fiscal harm as a result of disagreements with whites. In the South, a century after the Dred Scott decision, we possessed no rights that whites in the South could not ignore with impunity. In the Southern cities like Jacksonville, our lives and property were practically subject to the whims of any white person who wished to take advantage of me or to punish me for any real or fancied wrongdoing, just like the white man who pulled me over when I was driving Coach Small's car that day when I was in high school. On the other hand, a white man could steal from a Black man or mistreat him anywhere without fear of reprisal, because the Negro cannot claim the protection of the police or courts. Seeking personal vengeance on the part of the offended Black man usually resulted in "organized retaliation in the form of bodily injury including lynching, house burning or banishment," Myrdal found. Many young Black men involuntarily joined the Great Migration in haste as they fled for their lives. Perhaps the saddest commentary about the plight of the Black man under Jim Crow was that the only check on the white mistreatment of Negroes was a rather vague and unformulated feeling on the part of the Southern public opinion that "a white man should not be mean to a Negro, except when he deserves it," Myrdal wrote.

At the same time, every Black man needed the insurance of a friendly white man to vouch for him, to speak on his behalf in the event of trouble.

His life could be forfeit downtown, if he had no one to step forward and say, "That's my Nigger." Those three words uttered from the lips of a white man could mean the difference between life and death, incarceration and freedom. It was the code under which we lived and, too often, died.

Violence could occur at any time. It was the fear of this random violence as much as the violence itself, which created the injustice and insecurity. The chance nature of violence for us Blacks was a societal hazard, which thanks to the color of our skin, we had no way of avoiding.

· · · · · · · · · · · · · · · ·

The real function of the police in many Southern Negro communities seemed to be limited to rounding up vagrants, crapshooters, non-cooperating prostitutes, and drunks. These occasional arresting excursions served several purposes. They kept both petty criminals and law-abiding Negroes intimidated. They maintained the flow of cash to police headquarters, both from illegal sources and from court fines. Rarely did it serve to preserve order, Myrdal found.

Police service to our communities was both limited and lazy. White officers usually cruised around in their radio cars. They preferred to stay on the main thoroughfares, where there were businesses. They essentially left our neighborhoods unprotected, vulnerable to the chaos and whims of those for whom illegality was a way of life.

Not surprisingly, we wanted to have Negro police officers because we were tired of the brutality of white policemen who patrolled our neighborhoods. We paid taxes like the white folks. We got little in return. Getting public service jobs was a way for us to flex our political muscle. But more importantly, we paid taxes and we deserved adequate police protection. White officers riding around in patrol cars infrequently in our neighborhoods ceded the streets to the worst elements.

This was a problem not just in Jacksonville, Florida and throughout the South, but the entire country.

· · · · · · · · · · · · · · · ·

In 1930, in America, a country of more than 122 million people, there were 1,297 Negro policemen, 521 detectives, marshals, sheriffs, constables, probation and truant officers in public services. Of those, only 18 percent worked in the South, including Washington, D.C. In the next decade, the number of Negro police officers increased slightly as cities saw the hiring of Negro officers as a cure for rising crime. For the white power structure, Negro policemen meant fewer civil rights complaints against white police officers. Negro officers knew their way around their neighborhood, knew their communities and could arrest Black suspects without always having to display overwhelming force. The Negro policeman was respected because he was better educated than the white officers and he was chosen, like Jackie Robinson, to be an example for his race.

White aversion to hiring Negro officers seemed to be greater the larger the Black population was. Alabama, Georgia, Louisiana, Mississippi, and South Carolina, states with more than one third Black population, had not one Negro officer. These states accounted for 40 percent of America's Black population. Only two states with more than 25 percent Negro population had Negro policemen in 1940. North Carolina had one Negro officer who worked in Princeville, a predominantly Black suburb of Tarboro, located in the eastern section of the state. At the time, Florida had five Negro officers. Three Negro officers worked in Daytona Beach and one each in the southwest Florida cities of Sarasota and Fort Myers.

The antipathy between Black and white, white policemen and Black residents was evidence in the bloodshed. For much of the early twentieth century, white police officers killing Blacks and vice versa were a uniquely American phenomenon. Between 1920 and 1932 of the 479 Negroes in the South killed by whites, 260 or 54.5 percent were killed by law enforcement officers. Of the 47 Negroes outside the South killed by whites, 32 or 68.1 percent were killed by officers.

Of the 473 whites killed in the South by Negroes between 1920 and 1932, 173 or 36.6 percent were law enforcement officers. Of 63 whites killed by Blacks outside the South, 18 or 28.6 percent were officers.

Over the past nine decades, the racial bloodletting has not slowed. But in the early 1950s, we desperately hoped that hiring Black police officers would at least stem the tide.

BOOK VI:
THE ROAD TO THE NEGRO PRECINCT

Chapter 38:
HAYDON BURNS

When I returned to my hometown, Jacksonville remained in the grip of Mayor W. Haydon Burns, the former public relations consultant and appliance salesman who was first elected in 1949. Back then, Burns, a newcomer to politics, won by openly courting the city's Black voters. As the St. John's River inevitably runs to the Atlantic Ocean, the alliance between Burns and Jacksonville's Black community, segregated and racially oppressed, was a confluence of political opportunism and political aspiration. Blacks in Jacksonville, like those in cities across the South, had been agitating for Negro police officers for decades. Negro officers were seen as the answer to the problem of white police brutality and the lack of police protection in segregated Black neighborhoods and business districts. Like the introduction of Black MPs in Columbia, South Carolina years earlier, the presence of Black policemen on the streets of Jacksonville was part of the Black struggle for equality and civil rights. Burns promised Negro police officers and a swimming pool if Negroes backed his mayoral bid.

• • • • • • • • • • • • • • •

William Haydon Burns was born in Chicago on St. Patrick's Day 1912. Ten years later his family moved to Jacksonville where Burns attended Andrew Jackson High School. His father, Harry Haydon Burns, served on the Duval County Commission.

The young man's parents were well off enough to send him to Babson College, a small private business school in Wellesley, Massachusetts, that focused on entrepreneurship. When he returned to Jacksonville without earning a degree, Burns, a born entrepreneur, sold appliances and operated a plumbing and electric company, a flight school, and a greeting card company. After the United States entered World War II following the attack on Pearl Harbor in December 1941, Burns joined the Navy and served as an aeronautical salvage specialist assigned to the Office of the Secretary of the Navy.

After the war, Burns returned to his hometown and set up shop with a public relations and business consulting firm and continued to sell appliances. That business experience turned out to be the perfect training for his next career move, when as a political neophyte he entered the race for Jacksonville Mayor in 1949. Burns touted his ability to control Jacksonville's racial conflicts. To back up his boast, as mayor he even deputized fire fighters to help strengthen the police force to fight integration.

Burns was a committed segregationist who courted the city's restive Black population for their support. He opposed racial integration while offering Blacks a few scraps. Although some white politicians were hesitant to openly court the Negro vote directly for fear of retaliation from the white community, Burns astutely recognized that the Negro vote in Jacksonville was a vital source of political capital for those seeking public office. He promised the Negro community and its leadership that he would build a swimming pool for Negroes and hire Negro police officers in exchange for their vote. Although Blacks made up about forty percent of the city's population in the early 1940s, their political clout was far less. In 1946, blacks were twenty-one percent of Jacksonville's registered voters. A year later, there were twelve thousand Black Democrats as FDR's New Deal policies enticed traditionally Republican-leaning African Americans away from the party of Abraham Lincoln. The city's Black leaders conducted voter registration efforts to increase the numbers in an effort to influence the outcome of at-large elections. Thanks to Judge Waring and other progressive members of the judiciary, the private Democratic primaries quickly became a relic of the past.

Burns' public pronouncement that he would build a swimming pool and hire Negro policemen did not release him from having to "get straight" with the Negro community. The term "getting straight" meant that he had to pay local Negro political hacks a fee for delivering the vote.

These political hacks were well known in the Negro community and among the white politicians who sought and paid for their services. The conditions used by these hacks were questionable and suspect at times, but since they were unofficially working for those responsible for monitoring the voting laws, nothing was ever made of it. It was not unusual to permit public violations of any laws in the Negro community which would not have been allowed to exist in the white community.

The most attractive and appealing schemes used by these hacks were fish fries in some impoverished areas of the city. It was rumored that the fish fry sandwiches often came with a five- or ten-dollar bill along with the hush puppies — a bribe used to influence the vote. The popular and respected political hacks hired hundreds of people during the campaign season to canvas door-to-door, speaking directly to potential voters, who would be given a card containing the names and offices of those candidates that were recommended. Politicians did not hesitate to spend their money hiring these political hacks rather than buying a one-page advertisement in the colored edition of the Florida Times-Union.

People in the Negro community looked forward to campaign season as they were hired by political hacks to put flyers with groceries in mailboxes and take them door to door. There were no rules against politicians paying people for their vote. It was an accepted practice even though it was corrupt and comparable to Bolita, which was against the law, but overlooked because it provided a living for many in the community.

In some instances, political hacks went to church on Sunday and put extra money in the collection plate or even in the pocket of the pastor to "encourage" the congregation to vote a certain way. These political hacks were corrupt campaign managers who had earned a reputation as being somebody who could deliver the vote.

These were members of the community who basically profited by using their influence among their own people. It's one thing to support somebody out of respect, and it is completely another to do it for personal gain. Those who did the latter were traitors in the Negro community who were paid by politicians, and sometimes given a job for their services in bringing in the vote. These hacks didn't bring their political skills to help the Black candidates, who unsuccessfully tried to break up the white monopoly on municipal power beginning in 1951.

"Getting straight" with the Negro community was a well-known fact of life for politicians, and it wasn't all bad. The political operatives didn't put all the money in their own pocket — they had to go out and spend some of it to hire people to bring in the vote. Of course, they refused to support some white politicians because of their poor reputation with the Black community. Burns was different. Burns didn't demonize Blacks, but was considered a segregationist because he supported the status quo and discouraged any moves toward integration. He had no baggage with the Negro community. He managed to keep his promises, but he could not have been elected without the political operatives.

During the Burns mayoral campaign, the work of the political hacks was decisive. Burns won an unexpected victory over the incumbent C. Frank Whitehead for Mayor of Jacksonville. The Negro vote unquestionably made the difference.

In 1945 C. Frank Whitehead had challenged and defeated a far more entrenched incumbent, John T. Alsop Jr., who had occupied Jacksonville City Hall for 18 years. Now, Whitehead faced the wily Burns. Burns defeated Whitehead in the Democratic primary. In the general election, Burns fended off a challenge from businessman William Ashley, a Democrat who ran as a political independent. He didn't stand much of a chance. Burns won handily.

Burns proved to be a born salesman who could sell his ideas and his vision for our city. He promoted Jacksonville all over the world and offered tax incentives in his successful campaign to lure large companies to his hometown. He produced a slide show, "The Jacksonville Story," which he showed in Israel, the Soviet Union, and at the Hague, as well as across America. Insurance companies such as Prudential Insurance moved from the Northeast and set up shop in Jacksonville. Soon the River City was known as the insurance capital of the South. But very little of this progress benefited us, the Black residents. We still lived off scraps, economically and politically.

・・・・・・・・・・・・・・・

Burns' campaign pledges to provide recreational facilities for Negroes and to hire Black police officers did not prove hollow. In fulfilling the latter promise, Burns made a historic step in the life of our city. Without knowing it, he belatedly tried to address one of the fundamental shortcomings of life under Jim Crow and correct wrongs made six decades earlier.

Chapter 39:
MAYOR BURNS'S HISTORIC ROLE IN PRECINCT 3

How the newly elected Mayor W. Haydon Burns, aware of the racial and political fallout that might result, went cautiously about fulfilling his campaign promises to the Negro community is a story worth recounting. The Jefferson Street Swimming Pool was built with some city offices beneath it, including the office for a Negro Precinct, serving a dual purpose.

Soon after taking office, Burns was instrumental in the adoption of a new city charter that created a five-member commission to serve as the executive branch of the city government. The police and fire departments, along with some lesser but essential departments, were placed directly under the authority of the mayor. Jacksonville teamed with cities across the South to evaluate the effectiveness of Negro officers in those cities. A strong recommendation came from cities such as Savannah, where Black officers were introduced in May 1947.

As the new year progressed, it was clear the Jacksonville establishment was ready for the experiment of Negro police officers. The initiative picked up editorial support from the Jacksonville Journal Newspaper, an afternoon publication then owned by the Perry family. On Saturday, February 4, 1950, the Journal came out in support of Negro police officers on the streets of the city's Black neighborhood and business district.

> ### NEGRO POLICE FOR JACKSONVILLE
> Most noteworthy thing about the city commission's plan to hire Negro policemen is not that the step is being taken, but rather that it was not taken long ago.
>
> The issue of appointing members of the Negro race to our law

enforcement staff is a highly controversial one politically, and probably it is for that reason that it has been sidestepped all these years. There is ample historical ground for this political "touchiness," but still it does not make a sound approach to problems of law enforcement. The only real issue involved is whether or not the employment of Negro police, whose activities will be confined exclusively to members of their own race and to Negro neighborhoods, can bring about better enforcement in Jacksonville.

We believe it will do so. To face the facts honestly, some of our colored districts are hotbeds of petty crime, of rackets, of assaults, and of general lawlessness and disrespect for law.

It is true that a white policeman can patrol a Negro neighborhood to make an arrest, to break up a fight, or to investigate a robbery. But always there is a barrier he is not permitted to cross. In a white neighborhood he may be looked upon as a symbol of law and order, and as such he is welcomed for the protection he gives; in a colored neighborhood, he may be feared as an intruder.

Because this situation exists, a force of Negro policemen can do much to improve conditions among our colored population. Law-abiding and peace-loving citizens will cooperate with him. He should come to be looked up to as an ideal, thus inspiring respect for the law, and at the same time, his intimate knowledge of the people and their ways should help him in actual police work.

Negro policemen have worked out well in many other Southern cities, and there is no reason why they should not prove an invaluable addition to our local force.

• • • • • • • • • • • • • • • •

Under the careful supervision of Mayor Burns, Jacksonville's Chief of Police Sherman Cannon wrote a letter of request that was submitted to the City Commission on May 2, 1950:

Gentlemen:

After due consideration, I feel that this department needs and can use to advantage at least six Negro policemen to be used in the Negro section of the City of Jacksonville. Accordingly, I recommend that a Negro division be set up in the police department and that there be created therein the separate class of Negro policemen. Further, I also recommend that the civil service board be requested to establish and furnish us with an eligibility list for the class of Negro policemen in the police department Negro division.

Yours very truly,
Sherman Cannon
Chief of Police

Cannon, a graduate of the FBI National Police Academy, was appointed chief in 1947. In the two years before Burns arrived on the scene, Chief Cannon had moved to reorganize the Jacksonville Police Department. He assigned assistant chiefs of police to handle personnel and complaints, records, procurement, budgets, and building maintenance. He hired civilians to replace and free up uniformed officers from handling fingerprinting, clerical duties, and communications. In 1953, Chief Cannon also introduced a five-day, forty-hour week for department employees.

After this letter was read out loud to the commission, a motion was made to accept the Chief's request and then it was seconded, but a heated discussion followed. Two of the commissioners protested that they had not been given proper notice of this recommendation and were not prepared to vote in favor of it.

They made pointed inquiries regarding the duties of the new Negro officers.

Would they have anything to do with traffic?

Would they have authority to arrest white people?

Would the Negro officers be trained at the same time and place as white officers?

How would they be promoted?

Three of the five Commissioners finally voted to accept Chief Cannon's recommendation while two abstained with the understanding that many of their unanswered questions and concerns would be settled by the Civil Service Board.

Mayor Burns cautiously directed Chief Cannon in designing boundaries and limitations for the newly created Negro division within the Jacksonville Police Department. The resolution was passed by the City Commission to hire six Negro police officers.

The process was placed in the hands of the Civil Service Department to establish the criteria for hiring. The City of Jacksonville had a large pool of qualified applicants since, as a racial group, there was widespread under-employment. Several members of the Civil Service Department and political community insisted that the Negro applicants have higher standards of employment than white applicants for entry level positions in the police department. Normally, the minimum educational requirement for police officers was having completed the eighth grade.

Prior to 1950, employment opportunities for young Negro men were limited to the U.S. Post Office or the military. For those few who were privileged to graduate from college, they could become doctors, dentists, nurses, lawyers, teachers, or college professors. The most profound effect on the Negro community, in addition to establishing a new economic class of police officers, was the direct and consistent order that was established in the community — an order that had been woefully neglected by the Jacksonville Police Department prior to that time.

Six Negro officers were selected from the pool of 45 applicants. I don't know how many of the 45 applicants passed the Negro officer's exam. Each was subjected to a criminal background check. They couldn't have any criminal convictions. There was also a physical exam. They also had to meet height and weight requirements.

The first six Negro officers were Edward Hickson Sr., Henry Harley, Charlie Sea, Beamon Kendall, Alvin R. James and Marion Massey. They paved the way for future officers in Substation 3, Negro Precinct, Jacksonville Police Department.

The half dozen officers were respectable men. A black and white photograph of that group showed them standing tall and lithe. There was not one overweight or chubby officer among them. That was because the experiment for Negro policemen was so important neither the Black community nor white politicians who endorsed the project could afford failure. So Black clergymen and doctors and dentists sought out the most suitable eligible Black men in the community.

Some were Army veterans of World War II. Others, unlike their white counterparts, had sought to educate themselves beyond the eighth grade. They all had completed high school. One of the potential recruits had a college degree and was capable of taking his place in the highest echelons of Jacksonville City leadership if not barred for the color of his skin.

Jacksonville's first Negro police officers since 1890 were sworn in by Burns in a low-key ceremony at City Hall on Saturday, June 10, 1950.

Still, there was some apprehension by members of the Negro community that the chosen six police recruits would not successfully complete the police requirements to become police officers. The Negro recruits completed police training at the Wilder Park Recreation Center instead of the Police Academy.

Wilder Park was named for Charles B. Wilder. In 1927, Jacksonville Public Library opened the Wilder Park Library for Black residents. Located at Third Street and Lee Street in the heart of the Black Sugar Hill neighborhood, the library was built to serve the growing Black population of Jacksonville. In 1930, descendants of Charles Wilder donated thirty acres for what would become by far the largest public park for Negroes in Jacksonville.

Wilder Park was reachable by the Davis Street streetcar line. I could walk to it from our home on King Road. At Wilder Park, boys could run on the track, play baseball on the well-maintained diamond or go inside and read at the library. The Wilder Park Community Center, located at Third Street and Mount Herman Street, was built in 1938. During my boyhood, it was a beehive of educational and social activities. The Mummies Club even sponsored Saturday night at the recreational center, which of course, judging by my lifelong inability to dance, I never attended.

• • • • • • • • • • • • • • • •

The white police instructors were the same ones who trained white officers at the department Training Academy, but the policy was not to use the same training facility as that used for white officers. They ventured into the heart of our neighborhood to train our Negro officers. I could imagine the excitement that greeted the men as they got off the streetcar or walked or rode their bicycles to the makeshift training academy.

The Saturday swearing in ceremony was followed by more than four months of police academy training at the Wilder Park Recreation Center, and finally, the long-awaited graduation day arrived. A newspaper article in the Florida Times-Union ran on November 10, 1950, with the headline, "Six Policemen Graduate at Impressive Ceremony Friday."

Gathered for the services of graduation were practically all the dignitaries of city government headed by Mayor Burns, who gave the new charge to the officers and presented their certificates of graduation. The article noted that "More than 5,000 persons gathered in and around the Wilder Recreation Center during the afternoon rites which saw these six outstanding young policemen inducted into office as members of Jacksonville's Police Department."

I was a high school junior when these men were hired onto the police force. They visited Stanton High School in June 1950, and I was deeply impressed by them. They were handsome. They possessed an air of dignified authority. Each demanded respect.

Much later, I got to know more about each of them as colleagues. They were educated, responsible citizens who represented the Negro community well. Each of these men was exceptional, and yet they experienced indignities and racism beyond description.

• • • • • • • • • • • • • • • •

It was accepted that the Negro precinct would be under the supervision of white officers. The first supervisor was a rookie, Sgt. W. L. Bates, who often spoke of his utter disdain for having been assigned to the "Nigger Precinct." As the most recently promoted sergeant, Bates didn't have an option when he was assigned to Substation 3. A man of average height (5'10"), he was openly aggressive and resentful. No doubt he was placed on the defensive because of an inferiority complex. Most of the Negro patrolmen at Substation 3 were taller and better educated than he was.

Sergeants George Branch and A. B. Gilbreath were later assigned to Substation 3. Sgt. Branch had several brothers and nephews on the force who held major positions and rank in the department. He was a large, unpretentious man from South Georgia, who felt at ease and comfortable around the Negro officers. Sgt. A. B. Gilbreath was a soft-spoken, good-natured veteran police sergeant with a sensitive and likable manner. He was slow to speak and a deep thinker. He had a sincere liking for people, and respected the officers who worked with him.

Despite the inequities, such as consistently receiving second-hand uniforms and equipment, these first six officers of the Negro Precinct were destined to bring some order and protection to the businesses and entertainment sections of the Negro community in Jacksonville.

When the city first hired Black policemen, they walked Ashley and Davis streets. When they got to the east side, if there were any white businesses, they started on the west side of the street.

Black residential neighborhoods were delineated by certain streets. White areas were white and Black areas were black. Around 27th and Main Street was white, but if you went to 25th and Main, that was Black. There was no question about Black and white neighborhoods. All of this was well defined by the authority that authorized the Negro police officer. There was little chance of us being dispatched to a white residence. Few whites lived among us. Perhaps there was a white store owner who lived above the store located in a Black neighborhood. Most of those were Jewish European immigrants who settled in the Black community for trade purposes when Jews were discriminated against, long before they were considered white.

The Ashley and Davis Street sections were the main areas where the Negro hoodlums, dice shooters, drug pushers and prostitutes were in control. White officers routinely rode through these areas, but seldom gave much attention to the criminal activities underway. These activities frightened away many of the citizens who wanted to visit the business and entertainment establishments in that location. A dramatic change occurred in the minds and hearts of the Negro citizens of Jacksonville, particularly the business owners, when police officers of the Negro division went to work on the evening shift in November 1950.

Stanton, our one Negro high school, was located at Broad and Ashley Streets in the heart of the business and entertainment section of the city. In that day, everybody walked to school, so it was necessary to pass through that section on the way home. The new police force made a definite impact on the safety of students going to and from high school.

• • • • • • • • • • • • • • • •

Mayor Burns was consistent in hiring Negro officers prior to the next city election. Black police officers were Burns' political payoff for the Black vote in Jacksonville. They had delivered before, and in turn were rewarded with Negro officers. It didn't matter that the Black officers were barred from the Main Police Headquarters. It didn't matter that they were forced to patrol on foot and were not permitted use of the patrol cars. It didn't matter that they were issued used, torn uniforms and hand-me-down pistols. Black officers patrolled the streets. They became symbols of our increasing political leverage in a system that had long denied us a voice or a seat at the table.

The city hired eight more Negro police officers in 1953. Those officers were George Bradley, Robert George, Solomon Weston, Augustus Jones, Johnnie Doe, Freddie Mack, Joseph Seldon and Milton Newson.

I got to know some of the officers quite well. There were some characters among them. Weston was a sergeant in the U.S. Army and fought in the Italian theater during World War II. He was a graduate of Florida A&M College. After he was discharged from the Service, Weston married Edith Higginbotham in 1947, and his son Hal was born two years later. Weston applied to the police department, school board and Post Office. Struggling to make ends meet, Weston took the first job that came along. Weston was among the first batch of Negro sergeants. In 1964, he and a fellow Negro officer were promoted to lieutenant as a political ploy, as Burns was running for governor. After Burns was elected to the governor's mansion, he rescinded the promotion. Hal Weston said his father never returned the lieutenant's bar. It's now hung on the wall of Hal's funeral home in Jacksonville. In 1975, months after I left the department for Tallahassee, Weston retired and filed to run against Carson in the upcoming election. His son Hal said his dad lost because he took the Black vote for granted, which allowed Carson to run up big numbers even in the predominantly Black precincts. Despite that setback, Weston went on to have a successful career as a paralegal in the State Attorney's Office. He lived long enough to see Nat Glover, one of his fellow Black officers, get elected as the first Black sheriff in Florida in 1995. Weston died in 2008 at age 88.

· · · · · · · · · · · · · · · ·

Because they did not have a building for the first officers hired, they had been placed in one of the various changing rooms below the swimming pool. When the eight additional officers were hired, another changing room under the pool was added to the precinct. There had been no public access whatsoever to these offices. Officers took no calls or complaints at the Substation. All the calls for assistance were directed to headquarters downtown. The first six officers were driven to their beat and dropped off by their supervisors. They then walked the beat until they were picked up and taken back to the pool, where their vehicles were parked.

Once the eight new officers were hired, the walking beats were expanded. The precinct got one police vehicle. That expanded the patrol area to include more of the business community sections. It was still bordered by certain streets. Officers could not patrol in their vehicle, so they still walked their beats.

A swimming pool for Negroes was built at 4th street and Jefferson Street in the heart of the Negro community, and a dedication service was held on April 9, 1951. That occasion, in addition to the hiring of Negro officers, cemented the political alliance between Mayor Burns and a fledgling Negro political community that sustained what was to be the longest consecutive serving mayoralty in Jacksonville.

THE EARLY DAYS...

Charles played football at Jacksonville's Stanton High School.

Charles and Football Coach James "Bubbling" Small

MILITARY DAYS...

Charles Scriven's formal military portrait

Charles was assigned as an MP to an all-Black unit. Military Police served as law enforcement on military installations.

Jacksonville's first Negro Police Officers in the twentieth century

JACKSONVILL'S EARLY BLACK-IN-BLUE

Jacksonville's Negro Police Officers outside Precinct No. 3

KNEELING (left to right) Jesse Jackon, Edward Hickson, Clarence Barton, Marion Massey, Edward Jefferson, William Harris, Walter Solomon, Frank Hampton, and Solomon Weston

STANDING (left to right) Sgt. A. B. Gilbreath, Capt. W. L. Bates, Alvin R. James, Charles J. Scriven, George Henry, Freddie Mack, Obie Bowan, Henry Harley, Tommy Mays, Milton Newson, Joseph Seldon, Lewis C. Williams, Robert Jenkins, Robert George, Sidney Gaines, Johnny Doe, Augustus Jones, Charlie Sea, George Bradley, Beamon Kendall, and Sgt. George Branch

THE NEGRO PRECINCT

Charlie Sea was promoted to Sergeant in 1958. He was the first Jacksonville African American police officer killed in the line of duty since William Johnson in 1870. Sea was only 33.

The first Police Athletic League in 1957

POLICING AND COMMUNITY RELATIONS...

Neighborhood Jamboree sponsored by the Jacksonville Police Benevolent Association in 1958

The Benevolettes, the organization for Black policemen's wives

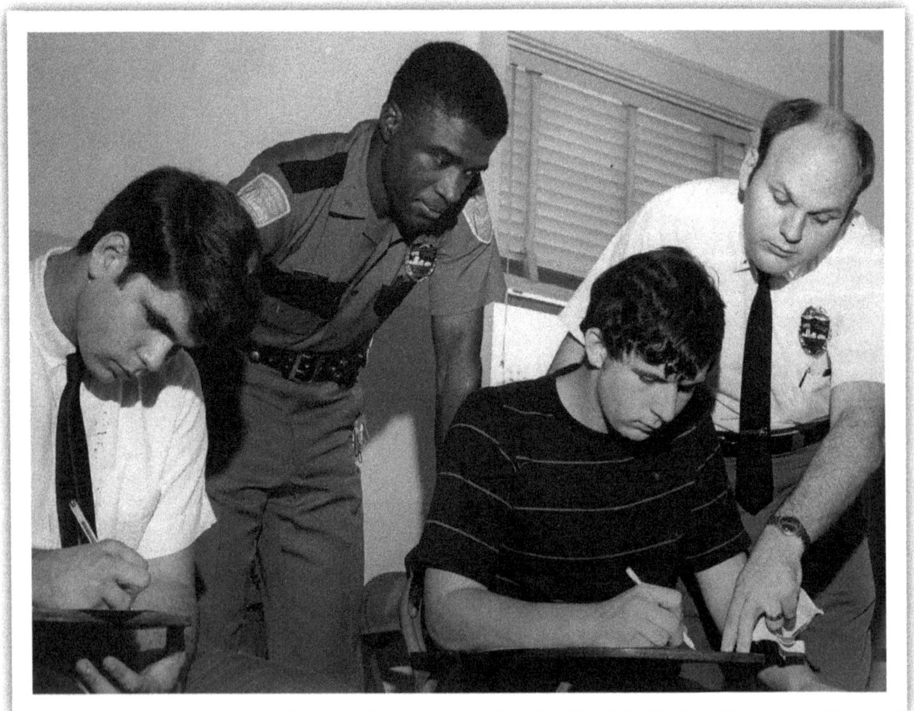

Sgt. Scriven with Lt. John Goode, the first Director of Police Youth Affairs, counseling students

Boylan Haven High School Patrol (all girls school)

Charles Scriven's promotion to Lieutenant with his wife, Jeannetta at his side

Martin P. Garris defied the sterotypes with his ability to love beyond the prejudices of the times. He fought for Black officers to join the Police Officers' Union and stood side by side with Blacks in that effort.

Charles and Jeannetta with Martin and his wife

Martin was an ordained Baptist Minister. He loved people, both Blacks and whites. He was for integration. He lived what he preached.

MARTIN P. GARRIS

Charles and Martin Garris celebrating with friends

Parole Commission swearing-in

Commissioners Maurice Crockett and Charles J. Scriven

Parole Commissioners (left to right) Maurice Crockett, Anna Bell Mitchell, Jack Blanton, Ray Howard, Roy Russell, Charles Scriven

PAROLE AND PROBATION COMMISSION

Governor Rubin Askew and Charles Scriven, Chairman of the Parole and Probation Commission

Reverand Charles Scriven is the Volunteer Recipient of the 2011 Capital Regional Medical Center's First Humanitarian Award.

RECOGNITION

Lanse and Tyler with Charles and Jeannetta PBA Awards

The Fraternal Order of Polie held a Dinner in Charles's Honor.

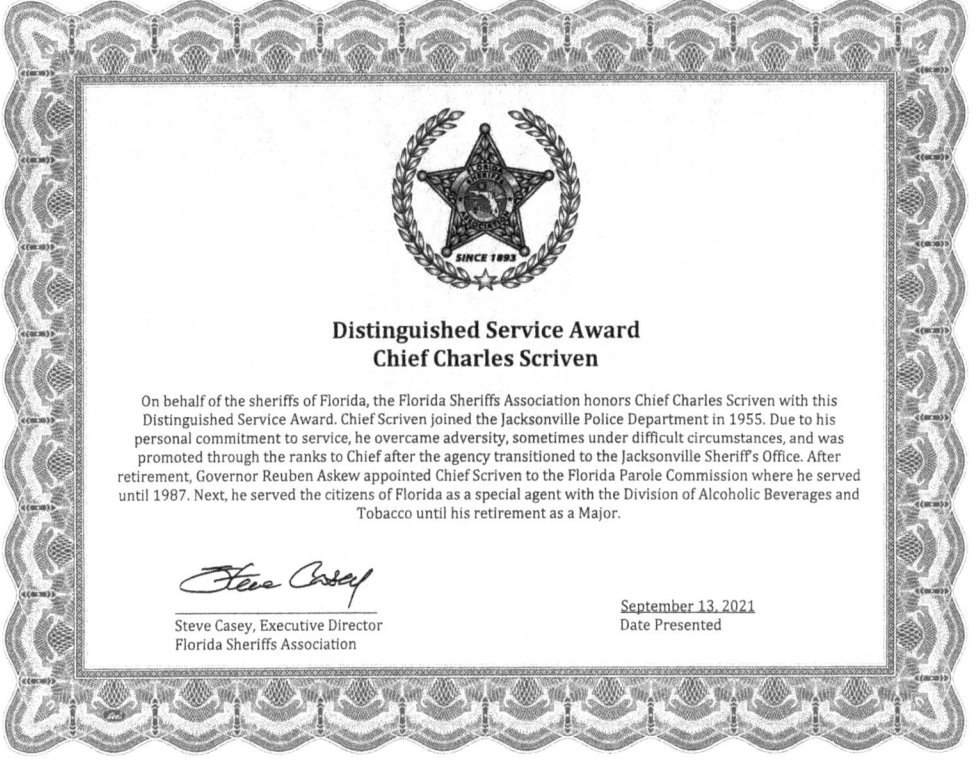

Thank You Charles for sharing your journey with others and me. The transparency of your life's story is quite refreshing and inspiring. Your perseverance and overcoming of racial hatred and discrimination is a daunting task for anyone. Doing it without harboring resentment, hatred, and revenge in your heart is admirable. It truly causes those who read your story to take inventory of their own lives.

Returning to your life's calling of preaching the gospel was inevitable as evidenced by your years of serving others in a chosen professon of criminal justice. However, putting others before self is a calling of the heart, not the demands of a profession. You answered the call and served well! Your reward therefore is assured.

"Whatever you do, work at it with all your heart, as working for the Lord, not for human masters, since you know that you will receive an inheritance from the Lord as a reward. It is the Lord Christ you are serving."
Colossians 3:23-24

God Bless you as you continue to be a blessing to others.

Your friend, Calvin Ross
   Former Secretary Florida Dept. of Juvenile Justice, Former Chief of Police for the City of Miami, Former Chief of Police for Florida A&M University

The old neighborhood in northwest Jacksonville

THE SCRIVEN FAMILY

The Scrivens, Charles and Jeannetta, with their first-born child, daughter Rosemary

Charles in uniform with Baby Rose

Daughter Rosemary graduates with a Master's Degree in Education.

The Scriven family – Lansing Scriven, Rosemary Hairston, Jeannetta Scriven, Charles Scriven and Leonard Scriven

Charles became a Minister of Christ.

GUIDING HIS FLOCKS

The congregation of the First African Baptist Church in St. Marys

Minister Scriven and members of the Corinth Christian Fellowship

Charles Scriven, a man of God

Chapter 40:
BECOMING A NEGRO POLICE OFFICER

My cohort was the last one to be trained at the Wilder Park Community Center. Wilder Park and our Sugar Hill neighborhood suffered a fate like so many urban Black neighborhoods, not just across the South, but throughout America. Even as I was undergoing police academy training, the die had been cast, and the future of Wilder Park and Community Center had been decided in Tallahassee. Earlier that year, during the 1955 legislative session, the Florida Legislature created the Jacksonville Expressway Authority. This new independent agency decided that Wilder Park, the most treasured public space for Blacks in Jacksonville, would better serve the interest of white Jacksonville and economic progress. Wilder Park was erased to make room to facilitate traffic between the St. Johns River and the Trout River. The JEA demolished the Wilder Community Center in 1958 to construct Interstate 95, the north-south thoroughfare that would transform automobile travel on the eastern seaboard.

At the time of my police training, Substation #3 was also housed in the Wilder Park Civic Club Building. No doubt in anticipation of the demolition that was soon to follow, the substation was moved to the Blodgett Homes Housing Project, located at 1201 N. Davis Street. Our class consisted of fourteen men, thirteen of whom completed the academy. The Negro Precinct was manned by twenty-seven Negro officers along with our white supervisors.

As Black officers, we were required to be under the leadership of white supervisors. We were not allowed to arrest whites. We did not investigate traffic accidents between whites and Blacks and between whites. All twenty-seven officers were assigned walking beats; patrol cars were for white officers only.

Even though we possessed limited power, the mere fact we wore the Jacksonville Police Department uniform was revolutionary. Prior to that, Blacks were totally absent from city jobs except the sanitation department. But we were looking to escape the violence that was coming from the white policemen. In order to do that, we had to get Black policemen to get away from that violence. But first we had to be exceptional to get in the door, and to stay in, we had to be exceptional. We had to still appear subservient, or we got a reputation, like Charles Scriven, that you were a smart Nigger. But I couldn't be any other way. I had served in the Army. I had lived outside Jacksonville, and I had enjoyed life beyond the South. I spent more than a year in California beyond the clutches of Jim Crow segregation. I had seen and performed professional police work. I didn't share many of the psychological handicaps of some of my fellow officers who preceded me in 1950 and 1953. My whole attitude toward being a Negro policeman was different. Many of my colleagues were burdened by questions of inferiority. Where they saw obstacles, I saw opportunities. That's one thing that held them back. I always believed you can keep a man down if he thinks that's where he belongs. So, even after the door is opened, he remains in the same place because he has lost his desire to be free.

As soon as I donned the used and faded police uniform, my life took on a new shine. My name became a celebrity. By being in the city where I was born and reared, I had a name already. My father, L. J. Scriven, was the kerosene man. After I passed the test, I assumed the title, Officer Scriven.

When I completed the police academy, I got a $7.50 raise after my probation period ended. We might have been making $100 or $120 a month. By then, the twenty percent disparity in pay between Blacks and whites had been settled. I was delighted to be paid that much. It was more than my father had ever made in his life. Back then, I could buy a loaf of bread for five cents. I could catch a cab for ten cents. I could go to the movies and see three features for twenty-five cents. If I was going to take Jeannetta to the Strand, I had to dress right. I couldn't go in there like I just got off from the sawmill. I had to look my best.

・・・・・・・・・・・・・・・・

At the Substation, we convened every day before going on patrol and we returned there before going off duty and heading home. Unlike some police departments in the South, in Jacksonville Negro police officers were allowed to wear our uniforms home. That was a constant source of pride, for me, my wife, my parents, and for the whole Negro neighborhood.

My pride soared and so did my ambition. I wanted to be a police officer and to rise as high as I could in police work. I was driven to be the best. I refused to be average. I enrolled in Walker Business College in the evening to further my Stanton education. Sometimes during the day, if I could sneak off to the college and take a class, I would do it.

The motivation came from my father. He was always struggling to make ends meet. I got that kind of inspiration from seeing him working at least two jobs all his adult life. It started when he would take me to work with him to clean up the printing floor at the Times Union. He bought an old truck to sell kerosene and wood. He was basically illiterate until he attended adult night school when he was in his thirties. I learned from his example of constantly striving to be better.

When I was growing up, we rented a house. Eventually, my father was able to save up enough money to buy a lot on Goethe Street, and a few years later he was able to build on that lot, to have a family home. He was always an entrepreneur. Instead of building a house for just himself, my mother, my younger sister Jean, and brother James, my father built a duplex so he could collect rent to pay his mortgage. That house in still stands in the Durkeeville neighborhood today.

That was my example.

Sometimes people are held captive by their condition and the community where they lived. They don't see themselves rising and getting above their station. I saw my father rise above with his education and going to school. I learned that I could do the same thing. When I got on the force, there were many who were on the force as a patrolman five years. They had adjusted to that level of attainment as a patrolman. I was already looking beyond merely being a patrolman.

Chapter 41:
THE ROOKIE

Upon graduation we were issued our uniforms. I was taken aback by the trousers that I received. They were patched and worn around the hems. It was also apparent that the equipment provided for the new Negro police officers had been exchanged before they were issued. I received an old gun and old bullets from my supervisor of the Substation.

Bates was promoted to lieutenant after I joined the Negro division. He still spoke with disdain for having been assigned to the "Nigger" Precinct. His lips curled downward as he spoke the words. He did nothing to hide his dissatisfaction. The department policy was that the rookie sergeant had no choice where he would be assigned. He also was quick to say that the least desired assignment he received had become a quick and sure way to be promoted since he was the only supervisor in Substation 3.

After I graduated number one in the recruit class, Lt. "W. B." informed me, "I always put my best men on the worst beat." I was assigned to work the Ashley and Davis Street area. My first walking partner was one of the first officers hired in 1950. A. R. James was a big man with a small heart. He was six-foot, six inches and about two hundred and sixty pounds, but he had a very nervous disposition. He jumped at shadows.

As a rookie, I had assumed that I had to arrest criminals and deter crime, so I eagerly looked for signs of illegal activity. I had a lot to learn. For instance, there were the numbers (Bolita) sellers. My partner knew that you looked the other way for sellers who were "connected" downtown.

I was curious and did not look the other way. I later learned that some of these sellers and their backers for the numbers business would send a token of appreciation downtown to the police officers for their "blindness." It was not a crime where anyone was hurt, and it provided a livelihood for many people in the Negro community. The numbers were legal in Cuba, and today's Lottery is the equivalent, but in those days Bolita was illegal.

After being naively over-zealous, I couldn't ignore the dice throwers and the other petty criminals. I was reassigned. I was moved to a beat with no business and less activity. Except for a restaurant, a confectionary, and a dry cleaners, most of my beat was residential. I don't really know how I agitated Lt. W. B., but he put me in Sgt. A. B.'s squad and assigned me to the midnight shift on the east side, walking the beat alone.

Fortunately, Sgt. A. B. was a fine, personable man, and as he drove me to the newly created solo midnight beat on the east side, he said to me, "The lieutenant wants to get rid of you, but I asked him to let me have you. Just walk the beat and don't do anything but what you have to do."

Night after night, I walked the beat alone. I learned to see and not to see some things. That made the difference during my probationary period when I could have been terminated without recourse. Once the probationary period was completed, an officer had a right to appeal termination.

My personal experience of walking the east side alone was challenging. The Florida Avenue beat was like Ashley Street in some ways. This was a place where most of the Negro businesses, the pool halls, the restaurants, beer joints, beauty shops and churches were located. When I worked the evening shift, I had a chance to meet some store owners and members of the general community who were glad to see a Negro police officer walking the east side beat. I often saw the white police patrol car riding through the area. We did not have any kind of professional or personal contact with each other, but I assumed they would be there to back me up if needed.

I worked from 11 p.m. to 7 a.m. I soon learned to like the beat, and valued the relationships I had developed with the residents I met. I was later placed back on the west side after one of my brother officers screwed up and was placed on the east side beat for his delinquency. He had lied about a break-in, and he let a burglary suspect escape after the man was caught breaking into a store. The incident was called "arrestee escape."

After the officer took the suspect into custody, he opened the car door in a way that the door stood between him and the suspect. There's a proper way to handle a suspect in custody. I knew that from my time as an MP. You get out of the car, then you open the back door and say, "Come on, get out." The fellow was already running when he emerged from the back seat. Normally, you will get between the door and block that person. He didn't do that. We haven't seen that suspect since that day. For all I know, he's still running.

Strangely, when that same officer and I came on together, I told myself, "He will never make it on the force."

My prediction proved to be tragically correct. When he was off duty, the officer was known to carouse with another man's wife. One day, when he was with the woman, living on the edge cost him his life. He tried to beat a train by driving through a crossing as the engine approached. He didn't make it. Neither did she.

• • • • • • • • • • • • • • • •

Being a Negro police officer brought a certain celebrity. That was not surprising since Jacksonville was home to a large Black community. The twenty-seven officers essentially represented law and order for thousands of Black residents. We were accorded a special kind of recognition. Wherever we went in public or to church gatherings, we were recognized.

It was a special feeling to walk into a church and take a seat. Then from the pulpit, the pastor or deacon would call my name. "Mr. Charles Scriven, one of the latest members appointed to the Jacksonville Police Department."

I was recognized because of what I represented. It felt good to be recognized. I occupied a coveted position that, until a few years earlier, was unattainable to members of my race.

Most of the officers assigned to Substation 3 were exceptional. They stood tall. They were men of integrity. They bore a sense of pride and dedication to their work, and commitment to serving the Negro community. But there were some who were afraid of their own shadow and avoided confrontation. We all knew who they were by their name and disposition and were extra careful when we were assigned to work with them.

Experience also made the difference in law enforcement. Older officers knew better than the young officers. The lack of experience made them less effective.

The physical size of a police officer also made a difference. I had a short partner, and many times after we got called to a scene, he inevitably would get into a fight. He thought people tried to take advantage of him because he was short. His height didn't make any difference to the people he encountered; it was all in his mind.

• • • • • • • • • • • • • • • •

Police work is unpredictable. When you responded to a call, there was no telling what to expect. On what appeared to be a routine day, my partner and I were dispatched to an address in response to an abandoned child. When we arrived, an elderly woman told us that a mother who she knew only from the local bar she frequented had asked her to keep this child for a couple of hours. She said that it had been over a week since she was caring for the boy. The woman had not come back for her child, nor had she called to check on the young boy. She said she was struggling to take care of herself and was unable to care for this child. I told the elderly woman to call us should the absent mother contact her to pick up her child. As I left that address, I took the boy into custody.

The boy appeared to be six or seven years old. He was taken to the juvenile center. I then asked and received permission from the court to keep this homeless child until the mother called for him. In my investigation, I learned that the mother would leave the child with anyone for a temporary period when she was at a bar. They had no idea where she lived or worked. This behavior pattern was noticeable, but this time she did not come back to pick up the child. My heart and soul went out to this boy. I took him home with me and explained to my wife, Jeannetta, what I had done. She did not object to what we thought would be a temporary stay for an abandoned boy. I was surprised at the reaction of some of my friends when I told them about what I had done. They commented about things like, "You don't know where that boy came from or anything about him." The only thing I knew was that he was a homeless child and needed a place to stay.

Jeannetta had hesitantly agreed to let him stay with us temporarily. It did not help matters when he peed in the bed the first night he was with us. The poor boy was traumatized by his mother's abandonment. I remember vividly taking him to town with me on an errand one day. I asked him to stay in the car while I went in the store briefly.

When I returned, he was crying hysterically.

"What's wrong?" I asked him.

"I thought you had left me," he muttered through his sobs.

I could not begin to imagine the traumatic childhood this six-year-old had been through, so I wanted desperately to provide a place for him. We had Rosemary and Lanse, but I had enough room in our recently purchased home on Eighth and Venus Streets. But Jeannetta objected to the idea of our keeping him and I did not want to cause any difficulty in our home.

Jeannetta observed that we had already adopted a daughter, Reenee. She was a student in Jeannetta's elementary school class when her foster parents had died. I still felt that we had enough room in our home to take in another child. All we needed was more room in our hearts for a homeless and abandoned child. Later, it occurred to me that Jeannetta might have thought he was my outside child. She might have suspected that I was surreptitiously trying to include him in the family. For peace's sake, I never broached that issue with her.

The boy, Phillip, stayed with us for a short time, and I felt a different kind of joy to be able to help him. I was finally able to find a couple who was childless and who had adopted a girl and also wanted a boy. I arranged with the court and the new parents to take Phillip on a particular day. When that day came, Jeannetta took the day off from school to ensure the transaction involving Phillip was completed. I cried the first tears I cried as the adopted father physically had to take this little six-year-old screaming boy from my arms. My heart was breaking as I let him go. In the short time we shared, we developed an attachment. I loved him as my own son. During the years that followed, I kept up with Phillip, who went into the military. Sadly, he died of AIDS in his middle-twenties. I went to his funeral service, and that too is an experience I will never forget.

· · · · · · · · · · · · · · ·

Another memorable event was when one of the two white sergeants assigned to the precinct was caught in an act of "hanky-panky" at the precinct station with a Black woman. A patrolman, who had stopped by the precinct at the time when it was usually vacant, unexpectedly stumbled upon the intertwined couple. The white sergeant was immediately reassigned to main headquarters, but Substation 3 would never be the same again.

Lieutenant Bates then started a clumsy investigation as to the apparent behavior of the sergeant and who might have known of his taste for Black women. Some of us Negro officers knew the sergeant loved Black women but didn't say anything. That was information one kept under wraps. It was useful to have and strategic not to share. But Kindall, one of the first senior Black officers from the class of 1950, let his dissatisfaction be known. That upset Lt. Bates because he felt Kindal should have let him know.

In retaliation, Lt. Bates placed him in charge of the Negro school safety patrol and crossing guards. This position of the Negro School Safety Patrol was newly created. He took a senior officer and put him in this newly created, non-enforcement position — supervising school crossing guards and the student safety patrol. It was considered a major demotion.

Being assigned to a patrol car and being on a beat was a position to be valued. but that newly created position was considered demeaning. It all stemmed from the white sergeant and the black woman being caught in the precinct. The white sergeant was never reprimanded, nor was he suspended.

He was simply reassigned. It was a reminder that the racial rules were being rigidly enforced. The price of breaking them was far less costly for whites than for us Black folks.

Chapter 42:
POLICING WHILE BLACK

By law and by policy, we were forbidden from any situation that would require any interaction with white residents. If that interaction was unavoidable, I was expected to call my white sergeant and wait for him to come to the scene of the incident. Our manual stated that we were prohibited from going to the aid of a white officer, but he could come to assist us. There had to be little or no contact with the white community. That was the social, civic and political makeup of Jacksonville. That was part of the deal to establish a division exclusively for Negroes, and would allow the return of Black police officers to Jacksonville's streets for the first time in the twentieth century.

If I had an encounter with a white person on a police matter, I had to call my white sergeant, and he would interact with the white person. In Jacksonville that was the unwritten rule. In many parts of the South, that rule was spelled out. Black police officers didn't arrest white suspects.

Once I arrived on an accident scene and I saw it was a white person, I called dispatch and notified them, "This involves a white citizen." If a sergeant suspects a white person is involved, he would just show up at the scene.

The system was so set up if I stopped somebody for speeding and the driver turned out to be white, the sergeant could write them a ticket. It was the same as if the sergeant had stopped them. In court, the judge didn't look upon the arresting officer if he was Black. Whatever the white officer said, that was what the judge accepted.

• • • • • • • • • • • • • • • •

In Jacksonville, a white person knew when they went to court that the judge sitting up there on the bench would not hear the accusation directly from me or any other Negro officer. I would tell the white sergeant who would relay the information to the judge that my Negro officer said this or that. That was sufficient.

There's a thing called prima facie evidence — first impression. That's what counted in court.

I had to be very careful arresting somebody. If I told the judge a man did something, and he didn't do it, the judge still believed me. One thing about authority, you must be careful how you use it. You won't remember harm you did to another person, but they will. I didn't want somebody to spend time in jail or at the prison farm because of my mistake.

If they were disrespectful to me in anyway, I could hint to the judge, and that would be another $250 fine or another month on the prison farm.

• • • • • • • • • • • • • • • •

As Negro officers, we were very delicate in dealing with white women whenever such encounters became unavoidable. Even if she was guilty of breaking the law, she was still white. Even when the white sergeant came, he was very differential in how he treated white women. Black women got no such treatment. Court staff put Black women in the same holding pen for Black men, but white women got very different treatment. They were allowed to sit in the courtroom, while Black women were confined in the same holding area as Black men. That was so demeaning. I considered this every time I made an arrest, knowing how the person was going to be treated in jail. Other officers knew, but they didn't care one way or the other. White women had a special status.

One day, two Black officers pulled over a white woman and all the merchants came out to see if they were going to take her to jail. When I went to the scene, the Negro officers said they wanted to put her in jail.

"Why do you want to arrest her?" I asked.

"She said 'You niggers wouldn't have stopped me if I wasn't a white woman,'" one of the officers replied. She had run a red light. That was a traffic violation.

They let her provoke them by using the word Nigger. Under normal situation, they would just write a ticket and let her go. I was a supervisor. Once you call the supervisor to the scene, the supervisor must resolve the matter. The officers were upset. That was all the more reason I wanted to act responsibly, even if she had called me a "Nigger" supervisor.

One of those two Black officers was a newly hired officer named Nathanial Glover. Three decades later, Glover would be the first Black Sheriff elected in Florida since Reconstruction

If I had made the decision to arrest her, I would have to call headquarters to have white officers take her into custody. She violated the traffic laws by running a red light. But there was no law against her calling them a nigger.

· · · · · · · · · · · · · · · ·

Jacksonville needed Black officers because Jim Crow law enforcement, with all-white police departments, was a failure. White officers could not effectively police the Black community. They didn't know my community. They didn't know my people in my community. Policing works in terms of intelligence and knowledge of the people being policed. Under Jim Crow, JPD officers didn't need to know and understand the communities they are assigned to serve. Their goal was not effective policing but exercising authority by any means necessary.

In our segregated society, a white man possessed authority from just being white. I remember while working the east side beat, I encountered a belligerent Black man who told me I couldn't arrest him. He woofed and strutted around like a Bad John. But when a white officer showed up, he immediately stood at attention. He was instantly docile. I could hardly hear him speak above a whisper. The Black community was afraid of the white police officer. He could beat up anybody whenever he wished. We knew of his brutality. The white officer's presence was enough to keep the peace. My supervisor, Bates, made extra money moonlighting providing security at the Negro theaters. He just pulled up a chair near the ticket office to keep order.

A white officer's lack of knowledge meant he couldn't be effective. Not only did white police officers not know the Black community, but they didn't want to understand it. To understand us was to see us as humans, as equals deserving of respect. To do so would violate his charge as the enforcer of white supremacy. He was sworn to uphold the existing system of inequality. To do otherwise was considered racial betrayal. It meant risking being called a "Nigger lover," the worst epithet in the white world. Also, the worst white officers were assigned to our neighborhoods as a punishment. That exacerbated our lack of police protection.

The white officers' lack of Black social and cultural knowledge led to untold tragedy for us. When a white officer sees two Black men in animated conversation, he thinks they are arguing. In his mind, these two Negroes are about to start a fight, when they are just being loud and animated. That's how Black friends behave among friends. Too often a baseless call to JPD headquarters resulted in an unnecessary arrest in the Black neighborhood. For generations, Blacks argued that white officers can't effectively serve residents with whom they are unfamiliar socially, culturally and economically. This unfamiliarity led to many false arrests, acts of police brutality and unwarranted deaths. Not surprisingly, the hiring of Black policemen in Jacksonville brought some sanity to policing the Black community. We knew our community. We knew the people and they knew us. We knew how to resolve minor incidents without carting off men and women to jail.

Chapter 43:
CHAOS THEORY

White officers caused more chaos in the Black community than criminals. Property damage was a problem. Blacks stole from Blacks. It was one thing to police for property crimes, but we also wanted protection from the white officers who came into the community to investigate these complaints. We knew when we called a white officer, we expected him to be less courteous. He wouldn't behave the same way in the white community as he would in a Black community. How much damage was caused by white officers who came into our neighborhood and called our grown Black men "boy" and grown women "girl"? My neighbors were never Mr. or Mrs. Jones when the white officer made out his report at police headquarters.

When you call 911, criminals have already taken your money. Now the white police officers come and take away your dignity as a person. They won't treat you with respect. They prefer to call Black people "Auntie" and "Uncle."

By calling you by your first name, you can't get that back. It was William Shakespeare who once wrote, "He who robs me of my gold or silver robs me, but he who takes my dignity and good name, it does not enrich him but makes me poor." You are taking something from me that doesn't help you, but it takes my person, my essence as a person. It takes my dignity away. It does something to the community and to the members of that community. You can replace a TV, but how do you replace the dignity of the person you insulted when you came to investigate the crime of which I was the victim? It was like being victimized twice.

Blacks stealing from Blacks was commonplace. But what the white officers did was much worse, much more insidious. It destroyed trust; it sowed cynicism; it eroded the value of those who looked to law enforcement to alleviate the lawlessness that pervaded our neighborhoods. It meant we were being taxed without receiving the equal protection and services to which we were entitled. The white officer came into the Black community with a baton and a pistol at the ready. He was the victim of his own background. And we were often the victim of his ignorance, bigotry, and violence.

In fact, the white policeman could, with impunity, assault a Black man or give him less police service and still report high crime among the Black community. High crime was caused by less service. Black communities had higher crime rates because the white establishment believed that Blacks were more prone to crime. High crime was allowed to fester by a more permissive law enforcement approach in Black communities. There are activities allowed to go on in Black communities that are not tolerated in white communities. Notice how "No Trespassing" signs often proliferate in poor neighborhoods?

Law enforcement attitude toward policing in the Black community is based on the white devaluation of the Black community. If you think nothing of a community you serve, then your service is going to be poor. If you don't have respect for the community you serve, how much service are you willing to give?

On the other hand, as a Negro officer, I lived in the community. I knew the sacrifice families made to keep a roof over their heads. I knew their struggle. Those neighbors were my neighbors. Their property and their dignity were what I considered as I served them. Their daughters were my daughters. I treated their sons as my own. I sought to keep them out of juvenile lockup for minor offenses. That made a big difference. A deprived and underserved community needed more compassion and sympathy than the majority community. Crime is crime. But we knew that many things that were commonplace in the Black community would never be permitted in the white community. As a Black community, we knew we couldn't challenge it and call attention to some of these improprieties. We were not taught that in police academy. The reason they were not taught that because it was not part of their community experience.

A lot of the Black man's experience goes back to how he was treated in slavery. When the other whites slept, the white policeman was watching the Black community. That's why he wasn't penalized even when he broke the law. Because he was the law. He was there to watch us, not to protect us. If he made a mistake and penalized us for alleged bad behavior, they said that was just good policing. A doctor buries his mistakes. The patient died of other complications. Policemen cover up their mistakes.

• • • • • • • • • • • • • • • •

As a Black police officer, I knew that the group who preyed on the community, who did the robbing, the mugging and the prostitution, were who I had to fear. They no longer controlled the streets. Those who once controlled the streets now had somebody whose sole job was to keep the streets safe and decent. Families could not walk down the street without fear or the nuisance of hearing foul language or avoiding dice throwers and street fights.

Husbands could take their wives out to dinner in the downtown business area without having to worry about the riffraff on the sidewalks. When they got out of the theater at nine or ten o'clock and walked to their car, they had less worry about being mugged or strong armed at gunpoint. The Black precinct brought a strong sense to the community and the entire community where Blacks lived. Business owners were glad to see us. When I walked into their establishment and to eat, people came over and told me they felt safe with me eating nearby. It was a real coming-out for the Black community. The Negro policeman was good for business. Any businesses that contemplated coming into any city considered two things — crime and schools. When Jacksonville hired Negro officers, conditions improved in the Black community.

Chapter 44:
CHARLIE SEA

One of the first group of Black men to join the Jacksonville Police Department was Charlie Sea. A black and white photograph of the six men shows Sea standing tall and proud. A grainy photo on a Downed Officers Memorial shows Sea as a stocky man with a face that belongs to a man who is unafraid of tough times. Sea was quiet and dignified. An introvert, Sea was one of those smart Negroes who kept to himself, and yet he earned the respect of his fellow officers. Officer Sea was the first president of the Negro Police Saving Club. I met Charlie when I joined the department in 1955 as a member of the largest and last cohort of Negro officers to expand Substation 3.

For almost a decade, Negro officers had walked the streets of Black Jacksonville risking their lives to maintain order but without the hope of promotion. When I joined the department, I had the same rank as officers who had joined the JPD five years earlier. Mayor Burns kept his promise to hire Negro police officers. Promoting us was not part of the bargain. To make matters worse, we were not allowed to join the police union, the Fraternal Order of Police (FOP). The FOP negotiated on our behalf without our consent. We didn't have a say in the matter. Our fate and our future seemed tied to Mayor Burns' political aspirations, whether he was running for reelection or testing the waters for a run at the governor's mansion in Tallahassee. Other departments in South Florida had Negro sergeants and lieutenants in their ranks.

Eventually, Burns and the Civil Service Commission announced a sergeant's test for Negro officers. Sea was the only Black officer to pass the sergeants' test in 1957.

In the coming years, as Burns' political profile grew and he positioned himself to run for statewide political office, the city offered the sergeants' test. Other Black officers passed the test, but they had to wait to be promoted. Eventually, after several attempts, I would pass the test. But I had to stand in line, like the others, and wait to obtain those three stripes on my sleeve.

Sea and three others, Edward Hickson, Beamon Kendall, and Solomon Weston, were promoted to Sergeant in 1958. It meant that for the first time in decades, Jacksonville had Black police officers in supervisory roles. By then, the department had issued us patrol cars, so we could ride around with the sergeants. One sergeant was more laid back, while the other was more hands-on. Having Black sergeants gave me hope that I would one day be promoted. I saw career opportunities that I hadn't seen before. The patrolman from last week was now your sergeant. You rode together and patrolled together. He had moved up. I could move up too. The community was proud of having Black sergeants, and we were too. The Black sergeants' exam was our ladder to climb.

• • • • • • • • • • • • • • •

At this point, the Negro Precinct had 27 officers including six from the 1950 cohort, eight from 1953, and thirteen from my class in 1955. In our unit, we knew who was brave and who was a hothead, who could be trusted to have your back and who was afraid of their own shadow. One of those officers was on patrol with Sgt. Sea on the fateful Sunday morning of May 24, 1959. Sea and his partner were driving in a patrol car when they responded to a call about a disturbance just after midnight at Duval Street and Myrtle Avenue in the LaVilla section of Jacksonville. When they arrived on the scene, the two officers got out of their vehicle and walked toward the backyard in the 300 block of North Myrtle Avenue where they spotted a suspect. The two approached the suspect at the rear of a porch at 313 North Myrtle Avenue when Sgt. Sea tried to question him.

They walked into an alley and asked what was going on. The suspect refused to answer and slid off the porch trying to escape. As he fled, he fired his pistol at Sgt. Sea and his partner. Sea was struck and mortally wounded. As Sea fell, his partner reportedly gave chase, firing off a few shots in a vain attempt to stop the suspect.

Sea was only 33. He was the first Jacksonville African American police officer killed in the line of duty since William Johnson in 1870.

From what we heard at the Negro Precinct, after the suspect shot Sea, his partner on patrol apparently turned and ran and later shot blindly back into the alley. I understand two police officers being killed, but I couldn't understand one officer being killed and the assailant getting away. Typically the second officer either gets shot or shoots the suspect. Neither happened. We knew the other officer was a coward. The suspect escaped.

Usually, whenever a police officer is shot and killed in the line of duty, a blue mist descends over the law enforcement. Officers are rampant in their desire to apprehend the suspect. Anyone driving around on the road cannot help noticing the high visibility of blue lights flashing and police cars driving to and fro in a frenzy. That Sunday morning was not quite like that. The death of a Negro officer didn't create much of a stir, especially among the white officers at police headquarters.

There was no high intensity manhunt for the suspect. White officers would ask us, "Have you caught the killer yet?"

We were Negro officers in life and in death. One's culture and color made a difference in one's professional career. Detectives identified the suspect, who apparently left town in a hurry. The furor soon subsided, and people moved on. Unfortunately for the suspect, a Jacksonville resident who sold Mary Kay cosmetics was visiting South Florida when she recognized him from one of the posters that were distributed around her Black neighborhood back home in Duval County.

She tipped off the Jacksonville authorities and soon the suspect was behind bars. Often, cop killers could face the death chamber. But this suspect was sentenced to life in prison.

Chapter 45:
SCHOOL PATROL

I was a member of the Jacksonville Negro Precinct for four years when tragedy struck Charlie Sea. We mourned deeply for Charlie Sea. He was one of the first Negro officers hired in 1950 and was highly respected. He stood tall among us. He was a nice guy, but he did not stand for nonsense. The tragedy of Charlie's death in 1959 opened opportunities for other members of the Negro Precinct.

• • • • • • • • • • • • • • •

When the Jacksonville Police Department promoted three sergeants in the Negro Division in 1958, I was number five on the list. After Sea was killed in 1959, the person who was next in line to fall into that rotation was Sgt. L. C. Williams. He went into the patrol division which meant rotating 11 p.m. to 7 a.m., 7 a.m. to 3 p.m., and 3 p.m. to 11 p.m., and he had to supervise a group of men on each of these watches. This meant that when I was promoted to Sergeant in 1960, they had the position of School Safety Police Director and supervisor of school crossing guards available. It had been a demeaning position for the officer before me, but it was a promotion for me, and it was the best thing that could have happened. Instead of being in the patrol division, I was home every evening and not out wrestling dangerous thugs around the clock. That afforded me an opportunity to work more in prevention with the younger Black kids in school. My career was not developed as a policeman on the street, but instead I had a chance to deal with kids where they could look up and see me and say, "Oh, I want to be like Sgt. Scriven." That's how my career developed.

About that same time, Chief of Police Luther Reynolds called a meeting of all the sergeants in his office. When we walked into his office, all the white sergeants sat on the front row. The Black sergeants left a row between themselves and the white sergeants and sat behind them, and I sat behind the last row of Black sergeants. The Chief of Police gave us his usual spiel about what a good job we were doing, encouraging us to keep it up. He smoked a cigar the whole time he was conducting the meeting. Before the meeting was over, I asked him a question.

"Chief, when I came on the force in 1955, we had a policy that said Black officers could not arrest white offenders. I want to know what the policy is now?"

Everybody was squirming in their chairs and Reynolds kept chewing on his cigar for quite a while. He looked at me and said, "Well, I'll get back with you later."

When I went back to my assignment, the director of the section in which I was working, the captain, chided me. He said, "You know that if you have somebody you want arrested, all you've got to do is call me." We all knew the policy was that if you had to arrest a white person, you were to call your white supervisor.

It soon got around the department that Charles Scriven had asked the forbidden question. My fellow sergeants chided me for bringing that up. They'd ask me, "Have you gotten your answer yet?" I never did get an answer from Reynolds.

• • • • • • • • • • • • • • • •

After several failed attempts, I passed the sergeants' exam. I was committed to educating myself. Right after I joined the Jacksonville police department, I began taking classes at the Walker Vocational and Commercial College. That went on for two years before I started a degree program at Edward Waters College.

When Sgt. Charlie Sea was killed in 1959, I was on the list of Negro officers to be promoted to sergeant. My name rotated and I wasn't promoted. There were more senior Negro officers ahead of me.

When one officer broke one of the many unwritten rules, it set in motion an opportunity that would alter the direction of my law enforcement career. During most of the first decade of the Negro Precinct, we were supervised by white sergeants. For whites, supervising Blacks was not a plum assignment, and in the Jacksonville Police Department it was no different. The task was assigned to the most junior white sergeant in the department. It was his prize for getting promoted. One sergeant had a fondness for Black women. That led to a tryst in the precinct, and he got caught. If this had been a Negro police officer getting caught with a white woman, that officer could have been lynched. No such punishment awaited the white sergeant. He didn't receive a reprimand. That didn't sit well with my Negro officers and me. We were outraged at the hypocrisy and disrespect. Most of us talked among ourselves, but one among us felt compelled to speak up, Patrolman Beamon Kendall. When the white sergeant got caught having an affair with a Black woman in the precinct building, Kendall spoke up vehemently about it. In retaliation, the supervisor of the precinct demoted Kendall, who was among the first Black officers on the force. He was reassigned to supervise the school patrol in charge of crossing guards and the student safety patrol, a non-enforcement position.

Every department has a punishment assignment. When I ran afoul of my superiors years earlier, I was punished by being put on the midnight shift walking alone in Black neighborhoods. Being assigned to the Black school patrol was the punishment for Kendall. When they moved him out of the patrol division to supervise the school crossing guard, that was a demotion. His peers knew it, and he knew it. I knew it. Kendall was one of the first Black officers and here he was supervising school crossing guards.

After Charlie Sea was killed, however, the white lieutenant couldn't keep that senior officer in that job supervising school crossing guards. He was one of the senior Black officers in that job. The officer who had been assigned to school patrol was moved back into the supervisory rotation.

But they had to find someone else for that job. When he got ready to take Kendall out of the doghouse, he put me in there.

I was known as a smart Nigger. I was the least liked officer in the precinct. I was making trouble. I bucked the system. I refused to act like a dumb Black man. I was attending classes. I aspired to be a preacher. I carried myself differently. I was not pompous, but I was a proud Black man. I refused to shuck and jive. In the view of the white sergeant who supervised the Negro Police Precinct, I was among the most disposable. I was sent off to supervise black crossing guards at the black schools.

He put me there as punishment. It was one thing to put me in a place for punishment and another to see the potential of the position. You shouldn't want to put one of your senior officers supervising safety patrol. That's a punishment. It hurt them, but not me. Once I got into that position, if he had wanted to punish me, he would have to take me out of there kicking and screaming.

In order to hurt a man, you are going to have to do something to him to make him feel like he's punished. I was the youngest of all the Negro officers. I was being placed in a supervisory role even though I didn't have any officers under me. What was supposed to be a put-down turned out to be the best job I ever had.

As the supervisor of the Safety Patrol, I oversaw the crossing guards and the safety patrol program for each Black school in Jacksonville. I trained and supervised the school children with flags as well as the crossing guards who ensured they walked safely across the busiest intersections in the city. We also had school crossing guards, mostly ladies, who were stationed at heavily traveled intersections where they would supervise kids crossing at traffic lights. The boys and girls from the school would be near them as well. I supervised a mixture of retirees who worked two to four hours a day, for which they were paid by the Duval County School District. It was easy work. If they lived within a block of the intersection where they worked, they could work in the mornings from seven to nine o'clock and then walk home when the kids were in school. When school let out the kids in the afternoon, the crossing guards returned with their signs to make sure the youngsters walked home safely. It was nice part-time work. I always had a surplus of workers. The most difficult part of the job was giving adequate attention to the entire city where Black children lived and walked to school. I would take a specific time to work a section of the city where people might typically exceed the speed limit in a particular school zone.

One morning, I stopped a female motorist for speeding. As I walked up to her vehicle, the woman was trembling. I said, "Everything was fine." That encounter reminded me of how much authority I had with my badge and my uniform. Some people are naturally frightened of the police. If they commit a violation, they don't know how you're going to react when you approach. When I realized she was afraid of me, I said, "Settle down. Go on, just drive more slowly." She was trembling and crying as she drove away that morning.

• • • • • • • • • • • • • • • •

Being supervisor of the School Patrol turned out to be one of the best jobs I ever had. Since I only worked the day shift, I was home every night. I was off every weekend. I didn't have any rotating shifts from 7 a.m. to 3 p.m., 3 p.m. to 11 p.m. or 11 p.m. to 7 a.m. I didn't have any nervous, anxious riding partners to worry about.

On the job, I was not fighting with thugs. A patrolman would normally feel uncomfortable when getting a call to a robbery or trouble. Blood and violence and chaos are often part of his daily routine. Since I was a supervisor of the School Patrol, my days were divorced from that chaos. The position allowed me to attend Edward Waters College uninterrupted by rotating shifts. I could attend classes in the evenings. Occasionally, I could take a class during the day when things slowed down between the morning drop off and evening pickups.

When I was a patrol officer, I saw blood from time to time. But in charge of the School Patrol, I was like the Negro precinct's goodwill ambassador. I visited schools and made speeches, I supervised crossing guards. Everybody liked me. What position had more influence with the families of these kids who are going to school?

I built a constituency. By having a non-enforcement position, I could do more public relations. I could reach kids and show them another side of law enforcement. I was visiting schools, meeting the principals, teachers and students and instructing them on traffic safety. "Hey, Officer Friendly," they called out to me. I met influential people, businesspeople whose opinions mattered at City Hall. They are saw me not as an officer enforcing the law, but as a law enforcement officer teaching kids about law enforcement and showing them how to be safe on the street.

The highest honor was being a Negro policeman walking the beat in the Black neighborhood and driving a patrol car. How do you punish me? Put me in on non-enforcement duty. Being in charge of what was called the "schoolboy patrol" was not considered a prestigious assignment. But I always believed it's not the job, but the man doing the job. You could put a man in a small position, and he can let it be small. I was not that kind of man. When I was put in a small position, I enlarged the position and the position enlarged me.

The crowning event was taking the boys and girls on the train up to Washington, D.C., for the annual jamboree sponsored by the American Automobile Association each summer. When we boarded the Amtrak train, it was the highlight of the year for me and those school patrol students. We toured the Washington museums and memorials. We toured Mount Vernon, George Washington's homestead. The young people had a coveted experience.

• • • • • • • • • • • • • • •

More importantly, that position got me what I wanted, promotion to sergeant in 1960. Each summer when I took the group of students to Washington for the convention, we were accompanied by a white captain, lieutenant, and sergeant. I was still a patrolman.

A Negro advisor to Mayor Burns was pretty sharp. At some point, he told Burns that it didn't look right having a white captain, lieutenant and sergeant, but a Black patrolman when the Negro school patrol goes to Washington.

That same night at the convention, the mayor's office called the police chief and told him to make me a sergeant. I had passed the sergeants' test. I was top of the black sergeants' list. I was qualified for the promotion. It made for good politics and good public relations for the mayor and the Jacksonville Police Department. There was no provision earlier stating the safety patrol supervisor had to have the title of sergeant. They gave me the title. It suited the mayor's position in terms of having a sergeant in charge.

The department had a sergeant for each rotating shift. However, when they made me sergeant, I had no supervision of Negro officers. I had an identification of being supervisor of the School Safety Patrol and school crossing guard.

The night before it appeared in the newspaper, Police Chief Luther A. Reynolds called me and told me I was going to be promoted.

· · · · · · · · · · · · · · · ·

Being a member of the Negro precinct and the Jacksonville Police Department enabled me to buy a house and support my family. Jeannetta taught elementary school. We were children of Jim Crow. We both attended all-Black, segregated schools before the *Brown v. Board of Education* case made "separate but equal" illegal. Being in the public schools as a police officer and head of the School Patrol, I was reminded every day of my own education and of all we lacked when I was a student. I knew the inferiority of the schools. What was I going to do? I visited them every day as part of my work. Keeping order in Black schools was a full-time job. It competed with the task of educating Black students. I saw a lot of disruption. I often broke up five fights one day and four fights the day before.

· · · · · · · · · · · · · · · ·

If you went to a school where the boiler went out every winter, and you were sent home because there was no heat, that school was inferior. Jeanetta taught school. She saw the hardship and despair first-hand. It touched her heart. When one of her students, Reenee, lost both of her foster parents, we adopted her and raised her along with our daughter Rosemary, the same as if she was of our flesh and blood.

We didn't get the books and equipment in black schools, and had double sessions. Where whites went to school for six hours a day, we went four hours because of the double sessions. The morning session was from 8 a.m. to 12 noon and the evening session from 1 p.m. to 4 p.m. If you are spending six hours a day in school and I am spending four, you don't have to be a college graduate to see the difference.

Our daughter, Rosemary, was born the first year of our marriage. Our first son, Lanse, was born seven years later. Our youngest son, Leonard, was born seven years later. By the time our daughter was old enough to attend school, we were still getting on our feet financially. She attended public schools all the way to Stanton High. We made a different choice for Lansing, who we named for a prominent Black dentist who served in the U.S. Army in Jacksonville. Lanse attended Episcopal School from kindergarten all the way through high school.

Lanse loved basketball and was captain of the basketball team. He thought he was good enough to play successfully at one of the Jacksonville public high schools, but sports was not his prime focus. Education was. Episcopal School was founded in 1966 like many of the schools in the South that were founded as a white response to the Supreme Court's *Brown v. Board of Education* decision. The school cost about $400 or $500 a month, but we wanted Lanse to have a quality education. If it meant working extra and making a sacrifice, that's what we did. We did the same thing with our younger son years later after we moved to Tallahassee, the state capital.

The stakes were high. I wanted my son to have what I didn't. I wanted the best for him. With sacrifice I could afford the best education my money could buy. Episcopal School had an average class size of seventeen students. It had a ratio of ten students per teacher. It had a 100 percent college placement rate for its students.

By comparison, even the best Negro public schools were very poor. We sacrificed so he could go to a private school. He might have been one of five Blacks at Episcopal School. I had to pay a nice healthy fee. When Lansing finished high school, he was able to get into Duke University. He wouldn't have been able to do that going to a Black school considering the poor quality of education. My wife and I decided we were going to send him to private school so he could get a better education. It paid untold dividends. After Duke he went to Florida State College of Law. Lanse would go on to clerk for Judge Hatchett, the first Black Florida Supreme Court Justice and later federal district judge. He would become the president of the Hillsborough Bar Association. Later, his wife, whom he met at Duke, would be appointed the first female African American federal judge in the Middle District of Florida. Those educational choices available to my son became possible only because I made a lifelong commitment to good education.

BOOK VII:
LEARNING DOESN'T STOP

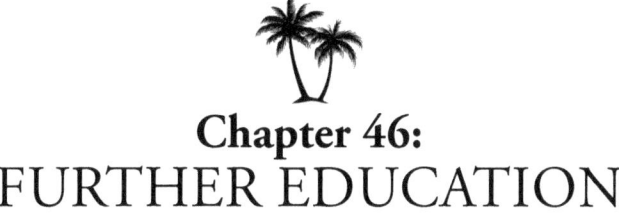

Chapter 46:
FURTHER EDUCATION

My experience at Stanton High School and my service with the military left me with a hunger to better myself. Seeing my father L. J. Scriven scrape to make a living infused me with ambition to go further in life. My father was practically illiterate until he was an adult and went back to night classes. My mother worked at home and didn't have the educational background to do much else.

When I returned from military service in 1954, I didn't come home to Jacksonville empty-handed. With my honorable discharge, I was eligible to take advantage of the GI Bill. Back in 1944, President Roosevelt and Congress put into law the Servicemen's Readjustment Act, which provided a range of housing, educational and other benefits for veterans.

Taking advantage of the GI Bill in 1955 after joining the Jacksonville Police Department's Negro Precinct, I enrolled for classes at the Walker Vocational and Commercial College in Jacksonville. Walker was founded in 1917 when Richard Wendell Walker and his wife Dr. Julia Walker opened the school at 412 West Broad Street. The college eventually moved to Ninth Street and Myrtle Avenue in the heart of the city's downtown Black community.

Walker College served as a transitional bridge for veterans returning to civilian life during 1920 through 1970, and to local citizens in the community. The school offered courses in secretarial training, office machines, bookkeeping, accounting, and insurance. The College also trained men and women in the trades. Students learned upholstering, tailoring, dressmaking, radio and television repairs. These trades could earn Black men and women a decent living. A photograph from the Florida Memory project shows well-dressed Walker female and male students in a typewriting class. Some students were standing while others sat and typed on manual typewriters under the watchful eye of a teacher in a crowded classroom.

I was not great with my hands. I was never going to be a tailor or shoemaker, but as a young police officer, I believed in myself. I was confident in my ability and my intelligence. Even though the way to promotion and advancement in the Negro Precinct was not yet clear, I believed that I needed to be prepared when the time came.

Scheduling classes between the changes in my rotating shifts, I attended Walker College for two years. In 1959, I transferred to Edward Waters College, one of the oldest schools created to educate Black students. As a Black man in Jacksonville, my higher education options were limited. Jacksonville University, a private two-year-school, was all-white. Florida A&M University, the school of choice for many of my former Stanton classmates, was also out of the question. It would have required me to pick up my family and move to Tallahassee. As young police officer just getting financially established, that option was not realistic. So, I entered Edward Waters College.

Edward Waters College evolved from the first school in Florida created for the education of Blacks after the Civil War. Established in 1866 in Live Oak, Florida, by the African Methodist Episcopal Church, the school's mission was to educate the former enslaved and their children to reap the benefits of freedom during Reconstruction. Based on the success of Blacks in law enforcement in Jacksonville and North Florida, in the years leading up to 1900, Edward Waters College and Stanton did an amazing job.

I began taking classes part time with my eyes on a degree. By then, the urge to preach and become a pastor had returned. I felt being a pastor was my calling I could no longer ignore. I had to pursue it. My schedule as a policeman changed frequently so I took one class at a time with my eyes on my goal.

Chapter 47:
A STUDENT OF PHI BETA SIGMA FOUNDER, LEONARD MORSE

Never let your schooling get in the way of your education, Mark Twain is rumored to have said. I attended Edward Waters College for school, but on its campus, I crossed paths with three men who inspired me and gave me a real education.

Among them was English professor John Ease. Then there was the president of Edward Waters College, President William. B Stewart. Being in his presence made you want to strive to rise above your station in life. President Stewart was a very distinguished man who led EWC from 1951 until ill-health forced his retirement in 1972. President Stewart inspired me as well. Under Stewart's leadership Edward Waters was accredited as a junior college and had restored its four-year curriculum in 1960. But the person who impressed and impacted my life the most was Leonard Morse.

I began taking classes at Edward Waters in 1958. Soon afterward, in religion class, I met Dr. Morse, who had been the college president a quarter century earlier. Morse was born January 12, 1891, to a distinguished family in Boston, Massachusetts. As a young boy, Morse showed early promise. He attended elementary and secondary schools in New Bedford, Massachusetts. At graduation, Morse was the valedictorian of his integrated high school.

A short time later, he ventured south to enroll at Howard University in 1912. While at Howard, Morse was one of the founders of the Phi Beta Sigma Fraternity. A student of Greek, Morse came up with the fraternity's name, wrote the first constitution and was the chapter's first president. A young man of boundless energy, Morse was not just busy with the fraternity. He tutored other students in languages and history, was director of social services, and president of the young men's Progressive Club during his third and final year at the "Mecca." What's more impressive is that with all those social activities, Morse graduated from Howard in three years with two degrees, an AB and a B. Ed. degree. He was the first person to accomplish that academic feat.

His lifelong academic journey took Morse to Ohio, where he earned a Bachelor of Divinity at Wilberforce University followed by a Master's from Northwestern in Evanston, Illinois. He went on to earn Doctor of Metaphysics and Doctor of Psychology degrees from the College of Metaphysics in Indianapolis, Indiana. A man of the Word, Morse was elected presiding elder in the AME Church and was elected president of what was then Edward Waters College in 1933.

When I first met him, Morse was dean of Theology and head of the Department of Religious Studies. I was attending Edward Waters part-time and aspired to be a minister. At that time, Morse was regarded as the last living founder of Phi Beta Sigma Fraternity. He inspired me to become a Sigma man. I pledged Sigma in 1958. Morse founded Sigma chapters across Florida. Having a chapter at Edward Waters with one of the founders, we were envied. There was no other historical Black fraternity with a living member back in the 1960s. Morse was it.

Dean Morse lived about eight or ten miles from Edward Waters. Once I got to be around him, it was worth altering my schedule to pick him up and drop him off in the morning and afternoon. Dean Morse taught a philosophy course in the evening. We met at 6 o'clock. It was really like tutoring, because I was the only student, and because of Dean Morse's status, they let him keep the course with one student. It took me some time to appreciate what an opportunity I had to be tutored by Leonard F. Morse, founder of Phi Beta Sigma. A lot of students avoided him because of his toughness.

Even after the semester was over and I passed Morse's philosophy course, I found a way to spend time with him by offering to drive him to EWC each morning. I would pick him up and take him to the college, and in the evening, I would come to pick him up and drive him home. I didn't have to do that, but it gave me a reason to be around him and to soak up his wisdom. I could not get enough of it. And he embraced me. He adopted me as a son. We had a special relationship. I got to know him and his wife very well. I became a member of the family. He had two sons and three daughters. I am still in touch with the grandchildren.

Dean Morse had a two-story library in his house, where he lived with his wife, Gertrude. When he died in May 1961, his family gave me his library. Some of the books had his name written in them. He was the dearest man to my heart. Other than my father, Morse had the most significant impact on my life as a person and as a man. He gave me something that my dad could not give because of his time and place in life. My father was illiterate. Morse came along and he bridged that threshold, because where he took me and where he pointed me, my father couldn't. That was not his makeup. My father gave me the integrity and the desire for hard work, but Morse represented a place and time in my life that came about through his own accomplishments. He helped me to see a whole new horizon, another world, an academic world, that he had gone through. That would have been a dream for my father. He didn't finish the 8th grade until he was well into his 30s.

Dean Morse made the difference in my life in terms of challenging me to be an intellectual and not just to be someone involved in what we called "nigger mess." He wanted me to be a top student. It was an honor and pleasure to go to his house. If he wasn't ready, I would sit and listen while he dressed and put in his teeth. He would tell me about the time when gun powder was invented. He was just brilliant. Of course, I didn't realize what an adventure being around so much wisdom was.

Beyond his sharp mind and encyclopedic knowledge, Dean Morse was an individualist in a society that rewarded conformity. Many people try to conform with the people around them in order to fit it in. Morse would not. He was always himself, whether at home or at work. He didn't try to be like you in order for you to like him. He understood what it meant to be an individual. I learned good study habits from being around him. You never heard him say anything he didn't believe. He was a brilliant man, but he was not a diplomat. He could have gone higher in the AME Church, even elected to be a bishop if he was willing to play political games. Dr. Morse didn't suffer fools gladly and he didn't pretend. He didn't hold back. He was brutally honest, but he wasn't rude. But if the Bishop was dishonest or unethical, he would tell him so. Morse was not a boot-licker. He stood by his principles at the expense of self-promotion. If he thought something, he said it. That limited his stature and influence in social and religious settings. I wanted to be like Leonard Morse. I don't know if I had the capacity to be a rebel in society like he did, but I yearned to be more like him.

Dean Morse didn't abide by the rules of Jim Crow, either. Sometimes, he would walk from the college to the bus stop. Buses and all public transportation were segregated. We were still relegated to the back of the bus — everyone except Dean Morse. He would get in the bus and sit right behind the driver. One day, he sat next to a woman who was sitting behind the driver.

She looked at Morse and said, "I am white." She expected Morse to get up and move to the back of the bus. Instead, he replied, "I had nothing to do with that. You have to blame your parents."

That was Dean Morse. Losing him in 1961 was very painful. I found in him a second father, a role model, a person of stature I could emulate. As a man, I found a hero, a superman in Dean Morse. When Jeannetta gave birth to our second son in the late sixties, I named him Leonard in honor of Dean Morse.

Chapter 48:
SHERIFF DALE CARSON

My fate was inextricably linked with the shifting tides and fortunes of Duval County and Jacksonville law enforcement. In 1933, the year after I was born, Rex Sweat was first elected Duval County Sheriff. Sweat had been appointed Road Inspector and head of the Traffic Department before he won the office of Duval County's top lawman. Sweat despised organized crime and during his five terms fought to keep the mafia out of Duval County. He believed in the death penalty. During his tenure, he pulled the lever nine times to carry out the death penalty on those convicted of murder in Duval County.

The Duval County Road Patrol was controlled by Sheriff Sweat from 1932 until 1956, when he was defeated by a political newcomer, William Alpheus "Al" Cahill, an insurance executive, following a heated and personal campaign.

While Cahill turned out to be an effective campaigner, law enforcement was not his strong suit. He had taken over the role of Duval County's top law enforcement officer while lawlessness was running rampant. Sweat had run the Sheriff's Office for three decades. For 34 years, nothing moved without Sweat's permission. With his departure, criminals stepped into the breach. Widespread bribery and illegal liquor sales and gambling, the hallmarks of the organized crime that Rex Sweat had successfully fought for three decades, were rampant along the Beach communities outside the Jacksonville city limits where the Sheriff's deputies patrolled. Jacksonville was also a Navy town bustling with servicemen. Navy shore patrols paid to keep an eye on servicemen couldn't ignore the criminality they saw.

In 1958, Navy shore patrol officials tipped off Governor LeRoy Collins' office to widespread bribery, illegal liquor sales, and gambling under Cahill's watch. The former businessman was also incompetent when it came to enforcing the law.

Collins had a well-earned reputation for his work on women's rights, education, highway safety, labor, health, and welfare. Prior to being elected Florida's 33rd governor in 1954, Collins, a Tallahassee native, had been voted as the Florida Senate's Most Valuable Senator and had been repeatedly lauded by his colleagues. Faced with allegations of Cahill's misdeeds and incompetence, Collins suspended him for neglecting his duty and gross incompetence. Cahill wore the sheriff's badge for all of one year and three weeks.

Collins' next move would influence the course of my law enforcement career. In 1958, he appointed Jacksonville-based FBI agent Dale Carson to replace Cahill. The FBI had a Jacksonville field office from 1924 to 1937, when it was consolidated into the Miami Division. During World War II, Jacksonville agents played a key role in apprehending Nazi saboteurs who were dropped off by German submarines, came ashore at Ponte Vedra Beach and buried explosives on the beach. The Jacksonville Field Division Office was established on February 3, 1958 in the U.S. Post Office building downtown, and F. A. Frohbose, Jr. was the special agent in charge.

• • • • • • • • • • • • • • •

Carson was born January 16, 1922, in Amsterdam, Ohio, a small town of just over 1,000 residents about equal distance from Pittsburgh, Pennsylvania and Akron, Ohio, founded by a Dutchman in 1823 at the junction of Lick Run and Yellow Creek, which runs into the Ohio River. One of the several still-standing original homes in Amsterdam was owned by the Carsons. In 1919, Amsterdam was the scene of the deadly Y&O mine which claimed 20 lives. Carson attended the high school that was constructed in 1926.

He served in the U.S. Army in World War II and was decorated. Returning to civilian life, Carson worked as a police officer in Columbus, Ohio. While in uniform, he attended classes at Ohio State University where he earned a bachelor's in criminology. Around that time, (1946?), he married his childhood sweetheart, Doris Newell, who was born in Carrollton, Ohio, a village named for Charles Carroll, the last surviving signer of the Declaration of Independence. Located about 13 miles northwest of Amsterdam, Carrollton, the county seat, had just over 2,000 residents when Doris was born in 1925.

She graduated top of her class at Ohio State University Medical School. Dale Carson's law enforcement career began in the City of Columbus Police Department working as a detective with the Baltimore & Ohio (B&O) Railroad, where he worked for two years before he entered the FBI Academy at

Quantico, Virginia in 1951. He was later assigned to Jacksonville. Carson, who had the clean-cut features and coiffured hairdo of a movie star, was a family man, with two sons and a daughter. His wife Doris began practicing medicine in 1952 and would be known in Jacksonville as a brilliant obstetrician and gynecologist. In the coming years, Dr. Carson rose to become president of the Baptist Medical Center Medical Staff, the only female physician to serve in that role. She would become an advocate for Planned Parenthood and for people with disabilities. In later years as she fought bravely against multiple sclerosis.

In 1958, Carson was a fairly inexperienced 36-year-old agent stationed in Jacksonville. Initially, Collins was set to appoint John Riley Smith, a senior FBI agent in Jacksonville office, but Smith was set to retire in a few years. At the time, Dale Carson was the junior FBI agent, and D. K. Brown was the special agent in charge of the Jacksonville Office. Carson was junior to both Brown and Smith, and was scheduled to be rotated out of Jacksonville and reassigned to another FBI Office in another city. Since his wife's medical practice was established, Carson was reluctant to move.

According to reports at the time, Smith contacted Governor Collins and recommended Carson for the sheriff position. After Smith retired from the FBI, he became the third in command in the Sheriff's Office, as director of services.

D. K. Brown, who served six months as Jacksonville Police Chief before consolidation, was appointed under-sheriff as part of Carson's command staff in the consolidated agency. Three former FBI agents in Jacksonville became the top law enforcement officers in Duval County and Jacksonville. They brought a professionalism and ethics to the troubled, all-white Sheriff's Department. As the winds of change blew through Jacksonville, our paths and career would merge.

• • • • • • • • • • • • • • •

Carson had a sense of humor. He used little things that indicated his bias, but it was always subtle. One of his favorite jokes came with a racial tint.

"I saw a bunch of people in a barrel. They were pulling together. It was the first time I saw Blacks pulling together," he joked. Carson was very different from the old White-boy sheriffs that wore the badge across the Jim Crow South. As a graduate of the FBI Training Academy, whatever his racial proclivities, he emerged from Quantico with a deep sense of integrity about law enforcement. J. Edgar Hoover's selection process meant FBI agents were a special breed. Many wannabe G-Men didn't get in. Carson was very soft spoken and very deliberate in his speech and actions. He was cautious as well as politically shrewd. When he was appointed Sheriff in 1958, the road patrol was entirely white. There were no uniformed Black officers. The few Black men in the Duval County Sheriff's Office served summonses and other paperwork to the county's Negro residents. It would be a decade before that changed.

His integrity, however, was unquestioned. I was around him a lot. If there was corruption in the Sheriff's Office, Carson didn't know about it.

He brought a professionalism to an all-white, troubled Sheriff's Office. In the years after he took over as Duval County's top lawman, Carson's officers and the FBI investigated corruption in the Jacksonville Police Department, which was rife with rumors of payoffs and ignoring illegal activities.

A decade after Carson was appointed sheriff, he became chief executive of the consolidated Jacksonville Police Department and Duval County Sheriff's Office, known as the Jacksonville Sheriff's Office. He developed a national reputation and became a finalist, shortlisted to become FBI director to succeed the retiring Clarence Kelly in 1977. By then, I had left Jacksonville for a new challenge in Tallahassee. But in the intervening years, I had the opportunity to observe Carson closely. He appreciated my work as God's Little Helper and an ambassador to Jacksonville's Negro community. In time, he rewarded my service with history-making promotions.

Duval County voters re-elected Carson sheriff seven times before he retired in 1986. In retirement he played golf every week and taught Sunday school at Riverside Presbyterian Church. He died of congestive heart failure at his wife's beloved Baptist Medical Center on May 27, 2000. Carson was 78.

Chapter 49:
A PASTOR WITH A PISTOL

I had only been on the police force for about two years when the desire to be a minister of Christ again possessed me. I tried all I could to ignore this urgent demand upon my life, which would mean a change in my career. When I couldn't remain silent about it anymore, I then told Jeannetta about the overwhelming desire that had taken possession of me.

"I want to quit the police force and go to seminary," I told her. "I feel God is calling me to preach."

I was sincere in my desire, certain in my belief, zealous in my willingness to obey God's call. But Jeannetta had a different point of view. What she heard me say was that I wanted to leave my good job with the Jacksonville Police Department, take the little money we had saved in the years since we got married, and go to a theological seminary. Although difficult legally and politically, being a Negro policeman had gained celebrity status. It offered me social status as well as an income to live better. The ministry, unless I was pastoring a First Church with status, offered no guarantees of a decent income. Here I was, holding one of the most coveted Black positions in the city, having an income that allowed me to afford a home and pay a mortgage without any major difficulty, and I was telling my wife I wanted to take a vow of poverty and leave the force.

At the same time, we had a daughter.

"Are you going to take the money we've saved and do something like that?" Jeannetta asked.

People in the community looked up to preachers who had larger fellowships, had decent houses, and were able to feed their families and have a nice car. That was not the young preacher coming up; that was after years of hard work, of having a title and an education. One doesn't get that by osmosis. There's a lot of time between going to seminary and pastoring the

First Church in Atlanta. There's lot of hardship along the way.

I could see where Jeannetta was coming from. I had a real job. A good home. We were comfortable financially. I reasoned that if I responded to the call and I entered a seminary, I might have to leave home and get a job. The Lord had not laid the call to preach on her heart, but on mine. I've heard ministers say they had a call to go do something, and the wife said I didn't get that call. It wasn't your call, it was mine.

"I didn't know I was marrying a preacher," Jeannetta said.

She didn't. She got two for one. A preacher and a policeman.

She hadn't anticipated what was coming in terms of my dedication to the ministry. The degree of sacrifice depends on one's willingness to accept what you want and what you expect to gain. Some people want to go to church, but it's raining. They don't want to get wet.

I loved Jeannetta. Other than my mother, she was the only woman I had ever loved. Although, she was a few years younger than me, she possessed a maturity beyond her years. Her words struck at me. Her voice cut through all the other voices in my head. I was in a good job.

I had begun my education. Our family was getting on its feet financially. I could serve God as a police officer when I answered calls and saw the pain and despair of many of my fellow Black residents of Jacksonville. I decided to stay on the force and become a minister for Christ in a police uniform. It wasn't shared with my wife. But it was what the Lord wanted me to do.

・・・・・・・・・・・・・・・・

Choosing to carry a baton and a Bible was one of the best decisions I have ever made. I had become a deacon in the St. Paul Baptist Church under the pastorate of the Rev. A. E. Crumady. I was superintendent of the Sunday School, but that still did not satisfy my desire to answer the call of Christ to preach.

As a military policeman, I had seen temptations and worldly desires derail my earlier call to be a minister of Christ, but now as a mature man, having been forgiven by Christ, I was ready to accept the challenge of being a policeman and minister of God simultaneously.

I gave my first sermon at the St. Paul Baptist Church in June 1961. The Rev. C. S. James was the interim minister at the time. Pastor Crumady, who married Jeannetta and me, had died that April. I preached my first sermon to a sanctuary filled with almost 200 congregants who came to hear the policeman/preacher.

It didn't take long for me to understand why the Lord wanted me to be bi-vocational — a policeman and a preacher. As a police officer, I had an audience you didn't see on Sunday morning. The audience I had was on the streets of Jacksonville. That's where I ministered. That's where I got my reputation for being "God's Little Helper." I was known as the preacher policeman who carried a gun. Sometimes people would ask me if I was armed.

"I am not carrying a gun for my safety. I'm carrying it for yours," I sometimes replied.

Some preachers and citizens found it fascinating.

There are people I helped because my position brought me in touch with them. They were not the ones you saw sitting in church on Sunday morning. Some were drunks, prostitutes, drug addicts and dice throwers. Although, they didn't get up and occupy the church pews, they were still part of humanity. They were still God's children even though they were declared official sinners by the court system and by the community and given derisive names. But they are loved just as much by God as those who aren't on the fringes of society.

When people who commit a crime, you don't always have to arrest them. Some people are needy. They steal because they need money to pay their rent or to buy food to take home. You can help. If I could do something to keep them out of court, I would.

. . . .

My biggest influence was on the department itself. The police officers respected me. Whenever I appeared and I was part of something, it was going to be right because Sgt. Scriven is here.

I was received fairly well as a minister by my fellow police officers. In fact, I sometimes felt a little uncomfortable when their conversation changed noticeably at my unexpected appearance. They expected and demanded more out of me than they expected and demanded of themselves, but I had the respect of my fellow officers. If they were being loud and profane as I approached, their voices dropped, their conversation changed. They often came to me with questions about ethics or morality. If they were recruiting other officers for a scheme of dubious morality, they knew not to try to rope me in.

My call to the ministry put more pressure on me than the average police officer. My role was spiritual as well as legal. I saw the people I was called to serve as a member of the body of Christ as well as a citizen of my city. The husband who had abused his wife when he came home drunk was more than simply somebody to be arrested, but somebody who needed Christ in his life. In some instances, I was not just putting somebody in jail, I was taking the time to counsel and give food and or clothing. Once, I gave a child my credit card on a cold day and asked her to tell her mother to buy her a coat and bring the card back to me on Monday. My fellow officers teased me, saying "You won't see that card again!" But sure enough, the card was returned to me on Monday morning by that same little girl on her way to school, wearing a new warm coat.

The understanding of my fellow officers didn't extend to the lieutenant in charge, however. I went to work one day and told the lieutenant in charge that I had been invited to speak at a local junior high school chapel service at 10 a.m. He said, in a very pointed and uncompromising tone, that I would have to "preach on my own time."

· · · · · · · · · · · · · · · ·

After Lt. W. B. said I had to preach on my own time, that's what I did. He was talking, I guess, about sermons on Sunday morning with a congregation of saints and sinners. I had a much larger thought in mind of taking each opportunity to minister for Christ in or out of uniform as a preaching moment.

The first challenge that I faced was to convince other ministers that I was a repentant sinner and was sincere in my devotion to the call of Christ. Other preachers were skeptical about me. They questioned my sincerity, but once I got beyond that barrier, I became the person they would call for advice. They would call me on special occasions because they felt I had something to say. I represented an area in government that was closed. I could walk in, but they could not because of my position in government. If they had a parishioner in jail and wanted to see them, I said, "Come let's go." They couldn't go in by themselves, but they could go in with me. I could talk to the judge because of my position on the force. I could even talk to the arresting officer. If Charles Scriven said he's alright, the officer might give the suspect a break.

Many times, preachers would call me, "I want to talk to you not as a preacher but as a policeman." I had the status within the community. My role as a police officer was important when bad things happened.

I knew that my having to carry a pistol would make some of them uncomfortable but that was a part of my uniform. I tried to have them understand that the deadly weapon I carried was not for my personal protection, but for and to be used on behalf of the members of the community that I served. Some of the brothers received me hesitantly as a budding member of the ministerial community and others stayed a measurable distance from the preacher who "carried a gun."

I continued attending the ministerial meetings of the clergy each Monday at 11 a.m. at different churches on a rotating schedule. The regularity of my visits and the corporate exchange between us was working. They began to see and hear me as a minister who was employed with the City of Jacksonville Police Department. They also saw me as a resource, a person who knew how to help one of their sheep who might have some difficulty with the law. If they got arrested, I might be able to put in a good word for them or speak on their behalf at sentencing.

I learned that my personal interaction with them on a consistent basis removed some doubts about my character for good or ill. I carried a pistol while in uniform, but soon members of the fellowship began to ignore it.

I remember distinctly on one occasion that a member of the ministerial brotherhood simulated patting me down in a playful manner to see if I was armed while in civilian clothing. I was unarmed. I was not carrying a weapon at the time. It was a standing policy of the police department to always have your pistol with you wherever you were on or off official duty, but I often ignored that policy because of the ease and comfort that the persons around me seemed to have felt when it was obvious that I did not have a pistol.

The clergymen of the community began to be more cordial and receptive of this redeemed man who had become a minister and wore a police uniform. I began to receive invitations to bring "the message of the day" on special occasions at some of the local churches. After all, being a policeman and a preacher was a bit unusual. You could never tell when you might need one or the other or both at the same time — a guardian of the soul and a protector of the body.

After I began preaching, I became acquainted with the Reverend H. L. Patterson, an insurance agent who worked for the Afro-American Life Insurance Company and was minister of the First African Baptist Church of St. Marys, Georgia.

First African Baptist is affectionately known as "The Mother Church" because of the many offshoot churches in Camden County, Georgia started by former members. It was founded in 1863 even as the Civil War still raged, with many of its 45 members still enslaved. Pastors Rev. U.L. Houston and Rev. J. M. Sims held services in a building in downtown St. Mary's.

In 1905, the congregation built a permanent sanctuary on the corner of Wheeler Street and Ashley Street. When the Rev. Patterson assumed the helm in 1957, he joined an unbroken line of strong pastors that stretched back to the last years of slavery. Paterson took out a loan to renovate the fifty-year-old sanctuary.

Rev. Patterson often invited me to preach in his absence. I drove about 40 miles from Jacksonville with Jeannetta, daughters, Rosemary and Reenee, and son, Lanse. In October 1966, when the Reverend Patterson was called to become pastor of a church in Saint Augustine, the officers and members of First African Baptist Church invited me to become their minister.

I joyously and humbly accepted the pastorate of this small fellowship. They wanted me, this rookie minister, for their pastor. Each minister needs to feel a sense of approval for his commitment to the call of Christ. This validation or reassurance of Christ often is received when an established body of believers calls you to be their pastor. You also have an additional status among the other clergy when you have the title of pastor and preacher/policeman.

I assumed full responsibility for being a minister of Christ and did not, on any occasion, miss the opportunity to let it be known that I was also a policeman. I took every opportunity to invite my fellow police officers to worship with me at the church I pastored in the town on the banks of the St. Marys River northeast of Jacksonville.

Chapter 50:
MARTIN P. GARRIS

Growing up in Jacksonville under Jim Crow could have, except for the grace of God, created in me an intense hatred for white folks. You cannot hate a man and you can still hurt him. Contrary to what some people say, the opposite of love is not hate but indifference. Hate requires a more active, deliberate emotion. But indifference is accompanied by an immorality that dehumanizes the object of that indifference. You are just as guilty when you ignore or condone an evil act as if you had committed it yourself.

To hear a person say "I don't care about Black people," was as painful as the hate. In many instances, the white community showed its attitude towards us not by outright hate but by indifference. There was a prevailing lack of empathy for the plight of Black folks. They had no feeling for us at all. There is something to converting a man who has feelings, but the man who says that he doesn't care, that is something else.

• • • • • • • • • • • • • • • •

In the 1950s American South, equal friendships between Negroes and whites were hard if not nearly impossible to find. Often, our relationships were sown with mistrust buried under centuries of myths and stereotypes. As I worked as a Negro police officer and struggled to make my way in a profession that had long been closed to Black men, one white man defied the stereotypes. That white man, unlike the legions of others who pretend, found a way to live out the true love Christians preach and teach in a way that surpassed every expectation.

In 1960, other officers in the Negro Precinct began talking about a white Christian gentleman on the Jacksonville police force. Since I was an aspiring minister, they urged me to meet him. The other Black officers who met him, got to know him and were very impressed. They talked about this white officer who loved Black officers and loved Black people. They said he hugged Black women in public. They said he would talk about Dr. Martin Luther King and other Black leaders, and that was long before it was fashionable to do so. He loved Dr. King so much that some of the Black officers got tired of hearing him talk about what a great man Dr. King was. Some of them tried to avoid him because they didn't want to hear the latest announcement about Dr. King. This was after the protests in Montgomery and Birmingham, when Dr. King was still a very polarizing figure, three years before the March on Washington, before King's "I Have a Dream" speech and before he won the Nobel Peace Prize. He also loved to quote Mahatma Gandhi, who had inspired Dr. King's non-violent approach. This white officer went into the Black community preaching at Black churches because of his relationship with Black people. There was no question about his love for people and for Christ. He possessed an ability to love beyond the prejudicial conditions under which we lived. That officer was Martin P. Garris, IV.

• • • • • • • • • • • • • • •

Martin was a few years younger than me. He was born on June 16, 1936, in Jacksonville and served in the United States Army. During the mid-1950s, Martin was stationed in occupied Germany. After he left the Service, Martin joined the Jacksonville Police Department in 1960.

By then, I was a sergeant in charge of the school patrol. Martin was stationed at the main police headquarters. White officers didn't come to the Davis Street precinct unless they absolutely had to. But Martin was different. He enjoyed being around Black folks. He was an ordained Baptist minister. Baptists, more than any other white Protestant denomination, didn't like racial mixing. They had long provided a moral and scriptural framework for establishing and maintaining Jim Crow segregation. But Martin preached in Black churches at a time when white Baptist preachers didn't rush into Black church pulpits. Martin was a different kind of Baptist preacher.

I first met Martin at the Negro Precinct on Davis Street. He was anxious to meet me, having heard about me. My reputation preceded me. I was the policeman who wanted to be a preacher. He shared my strong Christian faith.

We became immediate friends. I would invite him to my home. Jeannetta would prepare dinner for Martin and his wife. The next time Martin and his wife would invite us to dinner at his house. We went out socially together. At that time, that was not done. A respectable white man and his white wife didn't go out to dinner publicly together with a Black couple. After all, this was Jacksonville. The lunch counters in downtown Jacksonville were still segregated.

There are some people who dare the community in which they live to challenge them publicly to their face. Martin was that kind of person. If you were a Christian, and he was a Christian, he would challenge you as a white man to live out your faith. He just didn't live his faith within the Black community. He lived it within the community where he worked and where he lived. I had unquestioned confidence in whatever he said and whatever he wanted to do.

• • • • • • • • • • • • • • • •

I quickly learned that my fellow Black officers were not exaggerating about Martin's admiration for Dr. King. You couldn't speak to him for five minutes before he would mention something Dr. King said in one of his speeches.

I have never had a man embrace me and love me the way he did. If I needed help to pick up my son, Lanse, from school, Martin would volunteer. That's the way he was.

Martin loved people. Many people who you meet would shake your hand, but Martin would shake your hand and embrace you. He didn't just talk about loving people. He lived it.

Even those who didn't like him, respected him for his love and devotion for doing the right thing

He loved all people. He loved Black people. He loved white people. He was for integration. He lived what he preached. There were whites who loved Black folks, but they loved us conditionally. Martin's love was unconditional. Some whites can associate with Black people and yet they are uncomfortable around them, thus Black people felt uncomfortable, but not around Martin.

Around Black men you would expect him to be a certain way. When he was around white people, he acted the same way with me. If he didn't, I would have felt the difference. But there was never an opportunity to do so. He was true to himself. His life was an indictment of Jim Crow. His life was a testimony.

He could put his arms around your shoulder, whether you are male or female, and in no way would you feel demeaned. He didn't patronize or act flirtatious. When we were together it was not unusual for a Black woman to greet him, and he would embrace her and kiss her on the cheek. That was Marvin. That was before it was socially acceptable for a Southern white man to behave that way with a Black woman in public, and in a way it still isn't.

Martin was very conscious of what he was doing. He wanted people to see a white man interact differently with Black folks. Some people would do things unconsciously because they saw the advantage of what it meant. He was conscious enough to know the difference in race relations and acted accordingly. At the same time, he knew there were white officers who would resent him. His consciousness and his work ethic were those of a Christian man. He was aware what needed to be done and needed to be done publicly, so he did it.

••••••••••••••••

Everybody in the white community knew him when he started preaching. Since he would come to my house for dinner, and I would visit him for dinner, we became very close. He was free to come and go in the Black community. He made a big difference because he was different.

Martin was bigger than the other whites around him. Even those who didn't like him respected him for his love and devotion for doing the right thing. He did what he could to influence the situation, but the bias was too much for him to overcome. His community didn't embrace him and his ideas. To a great extent, he was fighting on both fronts. Here's a man who treated people as if they counted.

Martin was maladjusted in that he did not accept the time he lived in. Martin saw where man could be. Martin had lunch with me, a Black man, when it was not common for a white man to do so publicly.

His relationship with me was a very open and daring one. It was expected of me to be, if not militant, then to be dissatisfied with the status quo. But it was not expected of him to tell white officers that they should do certain things.

••••••••••••••••

I felt the brunt of discriminatory practice that was exercised in the city, state, and nation. Martin let his religious understanding of Christ transcend the white community in which he lived. No matter how much you believe something, you must respect a man who says one thing and lives it. The members of the Black community saw this in him. The white police officers saw this sincerity.

A big part of his love and dedication to doing the right thing was reflected in the way he fought for me and other Black officers to join the police officers' union, the Fraternal Order of Police. After he joined the Jacksonville Police Department in 1960, Martin quickly rose through the ranks of the FOP. He believed that Black officers belonged in this union because the union handled collective bargaining to determine the terms and conditions under which we worked. Black officers deserved to have a voice. He stood side by side with us in that fight.

He began by reaching out to two or three or four officers and encouraging them to vote to allow Blacks into the Fraternal Order of Police. Initially, there might be 20 or 30 blackballs against Black officers being admitted to the union. Then there might be four or six "whiteballs", which meant there were white officers planted within the FOP who wanted to admit Black officers. It came about because Martin was the second or third vice president of the FOP.

He said, "we ought to let them in." Martin was a radical to some of the officers. I was also a radical to some of them. But it was a much different thing when you looked at my color and looked at his color. He got harassed for being a "nigger-lover."

Chapter 51:
BLACKBALLED

During my time as a Negro policeman in Jacksonville, I spent more time and energy fighting to get into the police union than I did trying to arrest criminals. For us Black officers, the thin blue line of union membership seemed unbreachable, and just like the Jim Crow segregation that ruled our lives, unbreachable.

In 1957, I became president of the Jacksonville Police Benevolent Association (PBA), an all-Negro officer association. Ours was a charitable organization. We collected dues from our fellow officers to support worthy causes. We promoted youth athletics. Despite our good works and great intentions, we were without any of the authority represented by the Fraternal Order of Police. We were not allowed FOP membership.

The FOP was founded in Pittsburgh, Pennsylvania, in 1915 as a lodge rather than a union, because of the anti-union sentiments in America at the time. Three years after it was founded, the FOP went national. Its constitution pledged that "race, creed nor color shall be no bar." But clearly, that didn't apply to chapters in places like Jacksonville and other cities across the Jim Crow South. There was no place for us Negro officers among the union ranks. We were kept out of the FOP. In the North, white police officers long remained hostile to Black membership, which prompted Black officers in New York City to form the Guardians.

· · · · · · · · · · · · · · · ·

One of the things white officers always brought up when we mentioned FOP membership, was socialization. We didn't share the same space with white officers. We were separate in our roles and our authority. They policed white Jacksonville; we policed Black Jacksonville. But their fear was also rooted in one of the bogeymen theories white Southerners never seem to be able to escape. Like so much of Southern racism, their opposition to Negro police officers joining the FOP was rooted in miscegenation. They feared us coming into close social contact with white women.

The FOP had their major fundraising ball every year. It was the annual highlight of the social season. White officers were afraid we wanted to dance with their wives and girlfriends at the annual ball.

"Do you want a Negro to dance with your wife?" They asked each other. That was their motivation behind keeping us out. Their motivation, like so much of what was behind whites' attitudes toward Blacks across the South, was protecting white women. That became their rallying cry. That was the motivation for keeping us out. All I was looking for was the opportunity to be a member of the union that determined my salary and my other benefits as a policeman. I wasn't necessarily interested in being a union member to socialize with white folks.

But while their opposition was ostensibly social, I was motivated by economics. I wanted to join the FOP because the FOP was the collective bargaining agent for police officers both white and Black. The union set the rules that governed my salary, benefits, and retirement, my economic well-being. I wanted to join the FOP so I would have a say in my future. They argued that whatever they got, we would get. That wasn't the point. I wanted to have a voice in the conversation. They didn't know what I wanted. They didn't know what was best for me. They didn't know what I thought I deserved.

· · · · · · · · · · · · · · ·

I kept pushing my fellow Black officers to apply for FOP membership. I didn't want to make it a public issue, so I called the FOP president, a patrolman, who was riding on a beat adjacent to mine. We met at a barbecue stand and I asked him for his help. I asked for his support of Black officers. I didn't want to make it a public issue. If I could get his support as president, it would have made things far less difficult. He looked at me and smiled and got in his car and drove off. I stood there and watched him drive away; I marveled at his arrogance, at his disdain for my basic claims of brotherhood and humanity.

Meanwhile, through the grapevine, I received word from an assistant chief. Said they knew, because of the FOP's nondiscriminatory policy, they couldn't keep out Black officers forever. "But woe to the man who forces us to let them in."

Undaunted by the threats, in 1957, I made arrangements to fly up to meet the national president of the FOP in Pittsburgh, Pennsylvania. My fellow Black officers collected money to help pay my plane fare. All but one of the Black officers contributed $5 to my air fare and other expenses.

That officer supported my quest, but he was too cheap to come up with five bucks. The day I boarded the plane, I mailed a letter to the local FOP president, outlining to him what I planned to say to the national president. I planned to tell him we were being blackballed because of our race despite the FOP's policy of being open to all races. I called ahead and made an appointment, but by the time I arrived, I learned that an officer had died, and the president had to attend the funeral.

The National President received me well at his office and acknowledged that the national policy on membership was non-discriminatory, but he didn't have long to talk with me. He gave me the excuse that he had to attend a funeral and didn't have time to talk to me. He was noncommittal. I never heard any more from him or the national organization.

After I returned from Pittsburgh, my name became mud, but having ventured that far, made an impression on my fellow officers. They were inspired by my determination. They realized I was unwilling to take no for an answer. But my stance earned me the disdain of white officers because of my insistence on being a member of their union.

"Stay in your own organization. Why are you trying to join ours?" they asked. Contrary to what I expected, their look was not hatred. It's hard to explain the expression on their faces. They were very sincere, almost religious, in their fervor to keep us out of their union. I could not understand that kind of separateness and how badly they wanted to keep us from belonging to an organization that played such a determining role in our employment and benefits.

• • • • • • • • • • • • • • • •

As the years passed and Martin Garris joined the department, he became a staunch ally of Blacks trying to join the FOP. He kept trying. The objections to our membership became fewer and fewer, but we continued to be blackballed by the FOP. I can conservatively say that I applied for membership in the FOP at least 20 times and was blackballed each time. The way the system works is that the FOP had a set of black balls and a set of white balls. Members would select a white ball for yes, acceptance, but a black ball for no, rejection. Each time the name of Charles Scriven came up for a vote, the result was the same. They no longer have the system of white balls and black balls, but it was effective against me for 40 years.

• • • • • • • • • • • • • • • •

I made enemies because of my agitation to join the police union. I became a target. My detractors tried to set me up by offering me bribes two or three different times. They used Black folks to do it. One day, I pulled over a motorist who was drunk. As I walked up to his vehicle, another man appeared. He had a specific request.

"The man in the car has a pistol," the man said to me. "He's drunk. All I want is the pistol. I'll give you some cash for it."

The Black man was trying to get me to take the money. I called the station to take the man to jail and impound his car. Meanwhile, an unmarked Florida Department of Law Enforcement car was parked nearby. It wasn't easy. They tried to set me up, but I wasn't one to grab the money. If I had reached out and given the pistol to the guy, he would have given me some money. If I had taken the bait on any of the things they set me up with, I would be in prison today.

And that FOP annual ball — once they began admitting Black officers to the union, the annual ball was discontinued.

Chapter 52:
A BULLET ABOVE MY HEAD

I can still hear that bullet. It hummed on the night air, coming in my direction. The hairs on my arms and head stood at attention. My adrenalin surged. I sensed the danger, that moment when my life hung in the balance. There was no time to duck or dive. My service in the military was of no use at that moment. Like a sniper, my assailant could see me, but I couldn't see him.

Even as the echo of the shot rang in my ears, I felt a slight heat near my forehead as the bullet grazed my thick black eyebrows and lodged in a brick wall above my head.

Someone was trying to kill me, I thought to myself. I had made enemies. I could never prove who it was. I was one of 27 Jacksonville Negro police officers. They excluded us from the police union. We wore the uniform and carried the badge, but had no voice about our working conditions or our wages. We lacked the power to chart our own future.

I had heard through the grapevine that there were folks who were unhappy with me. They were upset with me for going to Philadelphia to see the national leadership about being kept out of the union. I sent the local president a letter telling him I was on my way to Philadelphia to complain about the discriminatory practices in the local union. It was not my intention to create a controversy. I had appealed directly to the local president personally about allowing Negroes into the Fraternal Order of Police. I wasn't looking for a fight, but I wasn't about to back down. I had no way of knowing if any of this was connected to those shots in the night.

• • • • • • • • • • • • • • • •

It was a weekday evening. I was working a security shift for a basketball game at old Stanton High School in Jacksonville. Stanton and I had lots of history. It was my high school. I had returned time and time again since I graduated in 1951. Its hallways and stairways were pathways on my long journey to becoming a Negro policeman in Jacksonville. I knew the teachers. Head football Coach J. P. Small had coached me during my three years of playing football. Providing security for basketball games allowed me to mingle with the people who had shaped me, and in turn allowed me to provide an example for other young people who needed to see that their future had more options than the street corner or the chain gang or the janitor's closet. Putting in for a freelance assignment earned me some extra dollars to provide for my wife Jeannetta and our two young children.

• • • • • • • • • • • • • • • •

Moments earlier, I was inside the gym with an eye on the crowd in the stands and another on the game, when I heard the familiar report of gunfire. In my seven years on the Jacksonville Police Department, I hadn't heard much gunfire. But I served as a military policeman in the U.S. Army, and had spent enough time around the shooting range and live fire exercises to recognize the sound of gunfire when I heard it. I heard one shot, then another. I immediately drew my pistol and ran outside.

That's when I heard the third shot. The first two shots drew me outside. That was by design. Somebody wanted to get me outdoors, in the open where I was vulnerable. The third shot was aimed at finishing me off. Someone wanted me dead. I froze, waiting to see a flash, a shadow, any sign of movement from the shooter. But nothing. Dead silence. I waited for a few minutes before I could breathe normally again. The pounding of my heart in my chest slowed. I could feel the tension of the blood pressure in my head drop. I returned my pistol to its holster and took out my pocketknife.

I looked up at where the bullet had lodged in the wall above my head. I pried the metallic fragment from the brick and placed it in my pocket. I then went back inside to watch the end of the game. I wanted to have it in my pocket just to remind me, like a favorite coin. I wanted to keep it, but I eventually lost it.

• • • • • • • • • • • • • • • •

As I drove home in my Volkswagen Bug that night, I replayed the evening's events in my head. There was no doubt in my mind: the shooter was a Black man. It had to be a Black man. That was the most likely scenario. You could pay a Black man a few dollars to kill another Black man. As a Negro policeman, my life would fetch a higher price, a premium even, and I was sure it was a Black man who shot at me, not a white man. A white man in that neighborhood would have stood out; he would been too obvious. But who hated me enough to harm me? I couldn't think of anyone.

It was almost 10 years after the Supreme Court ruled against separate but equal public schools. Stanton High on Broad and Ashley streets sat in the heart of the Black neighborhood. Jacksonville, like all cities in the South, remained segregated. Sharp lines separated Blacks from whites. We lived in two different worlds. Rarely did our lives intersect. And when they did, it was often with negative consequences. If a white face showed up in my Black neighborhood, and he was not a store merchant or an insurance salesman, everyone looked at him with suspicion. White folks didn't casually walk among us. Whenever white police officers appeared, they did so unsmilingly, in the black and white patrol cars, like two-man military transports in an occupied zone. If my shooter was white, he would have drawn attention to himself, raising suspicions for just being there.

A Black man had tried to kill me. Of course, if in the unlikely event the suspect got arrested, the case would have been investigated by the white police department. All the detectives were white. There were no Black detectives conducting investigations. Black officers were patrolmen. Years earlier, when Sgt. Charlie Sea, one of the first Jacksonville Negro officers, was killed, there was very little effort initially to find his killer. But we did, by luck, find him. And even when he was caught, the suspect served less time than normal for a cop killer.

I didn't make any report about that shooting. What do you say? There was nothing to be made of it. It wouldn't have done me any good.

But who wanted me dead? What enemies had I earned in the seven years since I joined the ranks of Precinct 3, the City of Jacksonville Police Department's Negro division? That evening when I arrived home, I gave Jeannetta an extra tight hug and recalled what happened.

There was no doubt in my mind that the shooting was connected to my efforts to join the Fraternal Order of Police. I was a troublemaker. I was agitating to get membership in the FOP.

I didn't think the FOP tried to hurt me. But I understood the hostility of white officers toward the Black officers wanting to join their union. Someone wanted to send me a message. It didn't have to be sanctioned. I got the message, but it didn't stop me.

BOOK VIII:
THE 60s

Chapter 53:
AX HANDLE SATURDAY

As the new decade of the 1960s dawned, Blacks in Jacksonville were restive. It had been six decades since we enjoyed police power and economic standing commensurate with our size and ability. Despite *Brown v. Board of Education* and other measures, Jim Crow segregation remained in force. The old white power structure remained unapologetic in its stance. In 1959, the school board named a new high school in honor of Confederate General and Ku Klux Klan Grand Wizard, Nathan Bedford Forrest. That insult sparked sit-ins and other protests. Like Black folks in Alabama, South Carolina, Mississippi and across the South, Jacksonville's Black population was tired of the heavy hand of racial oppression. Sit-ins and protests became a way of life in downtown Jacksonville.

As Negro police officers, we were not assigned to patrol white downtown. Our beat and assignment were restricted to Jacksonville's Black residential areas and business community.

In 1960, I was promoted to sergeant and placed in charge of the school safety patrol for Black schools. My normal routine took me away from street patrol and reporting to Precinct 3, so as a result, I didn't come in contact with the young Black folks who were protesting.

One of the darkest days was what became known as Ax Handle Saturday. On August 27, 1960, a group of white men wielding ax handles attacked Black demonstrators who were protesting segregation of a downtown white public park.

We had Black and white parks. If you were Black, you were not allowed to sit on the benches in the white park. The young Black demonstrators decided they were going to sit in protest.

We heard about the violence the following Monday. My role was working with young Black officers who were assigned to work in the Black community. The white supervisors might have known about what was going to happen, but none of that was communicated to the Black officers. We would not have gone out of our Black community without direct orders from our white supervisors.

There was a question about communication even with white officers assigned to downtown. Why wouldn't white officers control the disorder? Sheriff Carson was conveniently out of town that weekend. Some believed Mayor Haydon Burns was still catering to his white supporters.

While the demonstrations were going on, I was working in the schools. I was not standing on the front lines of the conflict. Negro officers were not put into positions where they would've been in opposition to Black demonstrators.

The demonstrations were led by Rutledge Pearson, a young history teacher. We lived about four or five blocks apart in the same neighborhood. He was a few years older than me, and was in my older sister and brother's age group. I had a great deal of admiration for him and supported everything he did. He led the NAACP and made it vibrant. I had a NAACP membership even then, when Southern white folks considered the NAACP to be a Communist, subversive organization. Pearson's story ended tragically as it seemed to happen with transformative special Black leaders. After he left Jacksonville, he went to work as a labor organizer. On his way to organize Memphis, Tennessee laundry workers in May of 1967, Pearson was killed in a traffic accident. Just like another Jacksonville native, James Weldon Johnson.

Chapter 54:
THE GAS STATION

I learned entrepreneurship from my father, J. L. Scriven. Even as I rose through the police department and expanded my pastoral ministry, I built a service station in the black community because, then as now, motorists in the Black community always had to drive a long way to buy gas. My station, the Magnolia Phillip 66 Service Center, was located at Edgewood and Avenue B in the heart of the Black community called Magnolia Gardens. Three of us went into business. Teachers Joseph Johnson, Elizabeth Jasmin and I formed the Magnolia Service Center Corporation. I served as the president, Joseph served as the vice president and Elizabeth served as the financial secretary and treasurer of the corporation. Each of us held a third interest in the business until I later bought them out. Johnson and I took turns working on the weekends while Elizabeth took care of the bookkeeping.

The three of us came up with the financial investment to acquire the lease for the property, that already had the building and underground tanks installed. Our business marked economic development for that area. Across the street from the station was a business area, a high-end Black home development, Magnolia Gardens. Streets were all named after flowers, like Rose, Carnation, Myrtle.

I had moved to Kinnard after the expressway arrived and the state acquired my property at Eighty and Venus. Kinnard was first developed in 1958 by Anthony Kinnon, an Adel, Georgia native who had moved south to Jacksonville in the 1920s. He had made a living as a pullman porter at the Jacksonville Terminal railroad station in LaVilla, a Black neighborhood.

With legions of Black veterans returning to civilian life and Black economic prospects improving after World War II, Kinnon became a building contractor. Kinnard was constructed as a Black middle-class rebuke to the ghetto-like neighborhoods that were being erased within the Jacksonville city limits to make way for Interstate 95. Kinnon employed Black architects and Black construction workers to create his oasis. In addition to the brick-style ranches, Kinnard boasted a physician's office, a laundromat, and a drugstore. Exxon later came and put up a station. We later moved to the Kinnon subdivision.

At first, our station just sold gas. Then we expanded and offered kerosene and heating oil. Customers called us and we delivered their oil or kerosene. That was our boast in our newspaper ad: "It's printed on the ticket. Immediate delivery Radio Dispatch."

Later on, we did repairs. I had a professional mechanic who would pay Magnolia Service Center for use of our garage. But my service station was a family operation. My son Lanse worked at the station pumping gas after school when he was in junior high. My dad, J. L. Scriven was an employee. He changed tires, pumped gas, and washed cars. But the main contributor was my sister, Mary. She managed the gas station. I was at the police station. I hired my brother George whenever he got sober. He had lost his job at the Post Office because of his drinking. When I paid him on Saturday, he would get drunk and disappear. Later my mother would call me and say, "George is sober." That was her signal for me to give George a job. She never gave up on him.

Gulf was the first company to build a station in the Black community. It was sold to Frank Hampton. Phillip 66 opened a station right across from the Gulf station.

When you operate a gas station, the secret to financial success is securing a contract for city, county, state, or federal employees to fill up their vehicles at your station.

The Duval County government gave the contract to the nearest service station. Frank Hampton owned Hampton Service Center at 16th and Myrtle. He was strong politically. He had the contract for the post office. His station and my station were a mile or two miles apart. He eventually got a second station. The second station was a mile away from my station. The vehicles that were being serviced by his station were less than a mile, which meant that under the rules, I should have had the contract, as by law, mine was the nearest station. I couldn't fight that opposition. I didn't fret. I called the director of the Postal Service and asked them why their vehicles were driving by my gas station to go to Frank Hampton's.

I owned the station for about 13 years. I sold it before I left Jacksonville and moved to Tallahassee. The property was leased from Phillip 66. After I left, someone else took it over. An investor needed a million dollars to open a Phillip 66 station. I didn't know too many people who had that kind of money. Today, the location is a still a gas station. Other commercial buildings have cropped up in the neighborhood. My old location appears to be chugging along.

Chapter 55:
FRANK HAMPTON

In our time, Frank Hampton was perhaps one of the most politically connected Black operatives to walk the streets of Jacksonville. Mayor Burns gave Hampton a job with the police department. He was in my group of officers who attended the police academy in 1955. He stayed for about five years. He walked the beat. He rode the car. He did his job. Bates, who was in charge of our Precinct, knew of Hampton's connections with Mayor Burns, who ran everything. He didn't give Hampton any special privileges. Hampton was just another policeman. Hampton took the sergeants' test but didn't make the cut. When Hampton resigned, I am sure Bates breathed a sigh of relief.

Hampton was, in every sense, a self-made man. He wasn't college-educated, but was schooled on the streets of Black Jacksonville. He married into a good family and was an astute businessman. At that time, the only gas stations in the Black community boasted one or two pumps but were off-brand. No big-name oil company allowed Blacks to own their station. No Blacks in Jacksonville owned and operated a large franchise gas station until Frank Hampton sealed a deal for a Gulf station. Across the street from Hampton's Gulf station was a white-owned Phillip 66 gas station.

On the national level, Hampton was a political force. He received invitations to presidential inaugurations and got federal grants to build subsidized housing. His politics were so strong on the federal level because of his connection with legendary Congressman Charles E. Bennett. Known as "Mr. Clean," Bennett championed ethical reform and sponsored legislation that placed the words "In God We Trust" on dollar bills. He represented North Florida from 1948 until his retirement in 1992. His redrawn district set the stage that year for Corrine Brown to become the first African American in Florida to be elected to Congress since Reconstruction.

Before he became a police officer, Hampton was a Black political boss in Jacksonville. If you wanted to be elected in Jacksonville and get straight with the Black community, you went to Frank Hampton. He hired people, but he also worked. He wouldn't just give people handbills and send them out. He was right behind them. The reason he was so powerful was because he delivered. He had the name and the reputation. If there were two people running for superintendent, the one who hired Frank Hampton won. They didn't just put handbills on doors. They knocked on doors and talked with members in the community. It was a machine.

When it came for political season in Jacksonville, Frank Hampton was the ring master. About 5' 10" and slightly overweight, Hampton was loud, outspoken, and bold, and you didn't want to engage him in an argument. He could talk loudly and laugh loudly, and was very persuasive. You couldn't bring facts and figures to him. He eventually did learn how to talk softly. A self-made millionaire, Hampton won a seat on the Jacksonville City Council in 1974, but lost his bid for re-election.

Politicians respected him. If they wanted to be elected, they would send him a $5,000 check. He would create a sample ballot and put their names on it. His workers would distribute the sample ballots in the Black community, and when Black voters headed to the polls, they took the ballot with them into the voting booth and voted the way Hampton told them to. He was a force to be reckoned with. He was a street fighter. He didn't get on the radio or go to churches to win over voters. He drove around the Black community with loudspeakers playing church music and encouraging Blacks to vote for Haydon Burns. The church didn't have that kind of influence within the Black community. Ministers carried a lot of dignity, but they didn't carry any weight when it came to voting, not like Hampton. Politicians visited churches and left $50 in the collection plate. Frank Hampton had political saavy. He organized fish fries and chicken dinners. Hampton could go into the Negro community and successfully get people to vote for Burns. He had seed money available to give his Black workers who knocked on doors and told voters who to vote for. Black ministers didn't have that kind of clout.

Hampton's experience being a Black man in a white political world was as good as gold. He wasn't very educated, but he was street smart. He was key to Mayor Burns' success with the Black community. After Hampton and Burns fell out however, he was as much a pain in Burns' side as he was welcomed when he was a supporter. He was just as much in opposition to

Burns as he had been for him, and used his influence against him as much as he could. He was formidable if he was for you, and if he was against you, you felt it. He could go either way.

In 1960 Hampton and a group of Black residents filed a lawsuit demanding the City of Jacksonville desegregate the municipal golf courses. As a compromise, the city offered to allow Blacks to use the golf courses certain days of the week. The suit was later amended to include the municipally-owned public facilities such as the Gator Bowl, the Civic Auditorium, Wolfson Park, the Jacksonville Zoo, and swimming pools and other parks and playgrounds. The initial response by the City of Jacksonville, like the City of Tallahassee and so many other cities in the South who faced such lawsuits, was to close or sell these facilities to private parties. Another suit was filed requiring desegregation of the Duval County Courthouse, Duval Hospital, the beaches, and the county jail and prison farm. To avoid the lawsuit, the County Commissioners eventually agreed to the desegregation of those facilities.

Chapter 56:
CLOSING THE NEGRO PRECINCT

The Negro Precinct remained open until 1966, but the signs of the end appeared years before it was finally shuttered. In 1963, the Jacksonville City Council contracted with the International Association of Chiefs of Police (I.A.C.P.) to make an in-depth study of the Jacksonville Police Department. The department needed modernization, and the recommendations made led to the Reorganization Act of 1965 and set the stage for the integration of the police department and the closure of our Negro Precinct.

The reorganization gave Chief Reynolds more authority, but also required his mandatory retirement at age 68 in 1966. As Chief Reynolds was heading out the door, the Negro police officers were moving into police headquarters.

· · · · · · · · · · · · · · · ·

When it first opened in 1950, Precinct Three was housed in the Wilder Park Civic Club Building. In 1953, Precinct Three was moved to 4th and Jefferson Streets below the public pool. When I joined, the precinct was still below the pool, but our growing number made the space inadequate. The Negro Precinct, which started with six officers, had grown to 14 by 1953, and had almost doubled in size by my cohort of 13 members in 1955. To accommodate our larger squad, the precinct was then moved to the Blodgett Homes Housing Project, located at 1205 N. Davis Street. By then, we had two patrol cars, which allowed us to drive into the Black residential community. By the early 1960s, I was a sergeant and focusing not on law enforcement, but on school safety. Jacksonville's Black community was clamoring for more opportunity.

In 1964 when Mayor Burns was running for Florida governor, he authorized an exam for the Negro precinct and actually appointed two Negro police officers as lieutenants because of the Negro lieutenants he had seen in the Miami Police Department, which hired its first five Black police officers in 1944.

He wanted to make sure he was not accused of discriminatory practices in Jacksonville. The officers took the exam, and they were promoted. But as soon as Burns won the governor's mansion in the 1964 election, he sent word that he did not need two Negro lieutenants. Those officers were demoted immediately.

To cover his tracks, however, Burns had the exams produced as proof that their appointments to lieutenant had been premature, as they had both failed the exam with the same failing grade — what a coincidence.

In 1964, the year when President Lyndon B. Johnson sat at the top of the Democratic ticket, Burns ran for governor and was elected to a two-year term. He served two years instead of four years because the cycle of gubernatorial elections was changed so as not to coincide with presidential election years. As governor, Burns is credited with supporting constitutional reform, recreation bills, and tax reforms.

In 1965, Lou Ritter, president of the Jacksonville City Council, became mayor when Burns finally won election as Florida's 35th governor. Louis Hampton Ritter graduated from Andrew Jackson High School in 1943 and went on to earn a bachelor's in public administration from the University of Florida in Gainesville. He was elected to the Jacksonville City Council in 1951 and served as President of the Council during 1953-1954. In 1955, he was elected as Commissioner of Highways, Sewers and Airports. After Burns was elected governor, Ritter served as mayor from 1964-1967.

Negro officers were Mayor Burns' political payback to the Black community. Burns had moved on to the Governor's Mansion. Separate and unequal police precincts had become an awkward legacy of the Burns years that city officials were eager to erase.

Our country was changing. The civil rights protests across the South were having an impact. The Civil Rights Act was passed in 1964. Jacksonville was feeling the effects of this wind of change. But old attitudes died hard. The proponents of Jim Crow didn't relent. In 1965, the state set up a commission to provide a report to help residents decide the issue.

The Negro precinct, Substation Three, was closed without fanfare and with the insistence of the local NAACP and the recommendation of the National Association of Chiefs of Police, without any ceremony. The Negro officers reported to main headquarters for their assignment without any disruption.

The 26 Negro police officers were assigned to the downtown police headquarters in 1966. We were assigned lockers. We reported to headquarters before we headed over to patrol the downtown Negro business district and Black residential areas. Personally, as the sergeant assigned to the safety patrol, I didn't report downtown. I reported to the office elsewhere before I headed to the Black schools for which I was responsible.

All law enforcement personnel were told to report to the main headquarters at 711 Liberty Street, the same building where they are now. The local Ku Klux Klan saw and understood the implications of closing Precinct 3 and the reassignment of Negro officers to main headquarters. Not surprisingly, they refused to go away without a protest. The KKK mounted a small demonstration over the merging of the Black and white officers. For us Black officers, it meant not being assigned to the subjugated Black precinct and restricted by practice to the Negro community.

The last physical symbol of discrimination had been removed. Weeks went by. With Negro Precinct Three gone, and all of us moved downtown, the Ku Klux Klan got involved. As long as the Negro officers stayed in their section of town, they were not seen, but now we were riding around in the white community, and that was not acceptable to the Klan. There were protests and finally, the question was asked of Mayor Lou Ritter, "Could Negro officers now arrest white offenders?" In answer to that question from the Klan's Grand Dragon, the Mayor simply said, "They all wear the same badge on their uniforms, and they all have the same authority."

In saying that, Ritter mentioned other cities that had Black officers with arrest authority, like Gainesville and Miami, which were far ahead of other cities in Florida.

There was never an order that said that blacks could not arrest whites. The only thing stronger were the community expectations and the limitations on us as to where we were physically. Once that was removed and Mayor Lou Ritter said our badge was the same as any other police officer, he removed that mythical barrier because all that was needed was for the Chief or the Police Commissioner to say that. That's how the barrier was removed.

The KKK was unhappy, but they couldn't stop integration once we moved downtown. Then we were assigned to calls across the city. When the dispatchers received a call, it was often impossible to decide whether the call was Black or white, or in a white working-class neighborhood or a Black middle-class neighborhood.

We were integrated but we still patrolled separately. White officers in one vehicle. Black officers in other vehicles. The question was, who would break the impasse? Who would have the courage to buck the wall of resistance? Who would be the first to defy a system of segregation that had defined Black and white lives for generations?

While they were all assigned to the main station, the problem of getting Black and white officers to ride together still existed. The challenge was finding a white officer who would run the risk of being called a "Nigger-Lover" and dare to be the first white police officer to ride in an integrated patrol car. It didn't take long.

It fell to Martin Garris. Martin had established a reputation for support of Negro officers to join the union. Martin had crossed the racial divide. We ate lunch together. We were friends on equal footing, something rarely heard of in Jacksonville at the time. Martin stepped forward and offered to share his patrol car with a Negro officer. He volunteered to ride with Negro patrolman Wilbert Wiggins. A 1954 graduate of Stanton High, Wiggins had a reputation among the guys because of his background for being comfortable around white folks. Among the Black officers, Wiggins was the most likely choice to partner with Martin and navigate the complexities of the situation. That solved the problem. Once Martin and Wiggins rode together, there were others who volunteered to ride with Black officers.

Wiggins became the first Black officer to ride a motorcycle. He remained on the force for forty-one years until he suffered a fatal heart attack while trying to hook up a trailer to a police truck. Wiggins, who played football for the Edward Waters College Tigers, was a big man. He was well-loved in the department. On the day he died, he and several officers were getting ready to conduct a traffic operation on a local interstate. He collapsed as he was pulling a trailer toward the police truck. His fellow officers found him on the ground. He died in hospital the next day, Friday November 8, 2002. Wiggins was only 66.

The year of police integration, a young man named Nat Glover Jr. joined the police department. As fate would have it, Martin and Glover's paths would converge almost three decades later. Martin, who was then the chief of the University of North Florida Police Department, provided a key early endorsement in 1995 for Glover as the Edward Waters College graduate launched his historic bid to become the first African American to be elected sheriff in Florida since Reconstruction. Martin's support, a white man backing a Black underdog against two better-funded white candidates, made Glover's election possible. But that's a story for later.

Chapter 57:
CONSOLIDATION

My hometown was a microcosm of so much of what was wrong in America. Despite Mayor Haydon Burns' efforts, the city's tax base was shrinking. Whites were fleeing the city to the Beaches communities. But many of those people lacked adequate municipal services offered by Jacksonville. During the early 1960s, the drumbeat of consolidation between Jacksonville and Duval County began beating more loudly.

Jacksonville tried to annex surrounding areas, but those who lived outside the city rejected annexation in six votes between 1958 and 1965. Whites resisted being part of an increasingly Black city.

But real-life circumstances intervened. Jacksonville City Council was hit by a corruption scandal. Many in the good old boy network got indicted. A restive Black inner-city population yearned for political power. Many of my neighbors wanted to have more say at City Hall. They erroneously believed that consolidation of the City of Jacksonville and Duval County governments would empower a Black population largely shut out from power since 1907, when the last Black elected official left office.

I heard the arguments, but I was unconvinced. As a child of Jim Crow, I remained suspicious. Whites fled the city for a reason. Why would they want to become part of Jacksonville again unless the terms were to their advantage? Whites would only support consolidation if it meant control of the levers of power and wealth.

Burns didn't support consolidation, but he was no longer part of the city structure. There was another political faction in Jacksonville who saw that they were losing Jacksonville because everybody was moving out. It was too important to be run by the Black community.

The trifecta of falling population, slowing economic growth, and rising property taxes made consolidation look like a life-raft to many

Jacksonville residents. On Tuesday, August 7, 1967, City of Jacksonville and Duval County residents voted overwhelmingly to consolidate both governments.

· · · · · · · · · · · · · · · ·

The merger took more than a year to become a reality. On Oct. 1, 1968, the City of Jacksonville and Duval County became one. For me, a law enforcement officer and member of the Jacksonville Police Department, that meant the end of the old JPD as we knew it. JPD and the Duval County Road Patrol, the arm of the Sheriff, combined the Office of the Sheriff and the Jacksonville Police. The Duval County Sheriff became the top law enforcement officer. Sheriff Dale Carson had been appointed by Governor LeRoy Collins following a corruption investigation and botched response from the incumbent. Carson selected D. K. Brown, who was JPD chief in the six months leading up to consolidation, as his second in command. D. K. Brown and Carson got along well because Brown had been Carson's supervisor with the FBI.

A second appointee, former FBI Agent John Riley Smith, was named the director of Police Services. I later learned that Smith had been Governor Collins' first choice as Duval County Sheriff, but he was older and nearing retirement and recommended Carson, who was next in line for promotion, to be rotated out of Jacksonville. Carson wanted to stay in Jacksonville because his wife, Doris, had a very successful medical practice.

The City of Jacksonville Police Department was now called the Jacksonville Office of the Sheriff and had three strong men at its helm. Consolidation meant further integration. JPD employed 26 Negro officers at the time of consolidation. Until that point, the Duval County Road Patrol was entirely white. The Duval County Sheriff's Department did not have any Black deputies in uniform, which was an established tradition for the county law enforcement; however, they did have several plainclothes Negro officers who had been hand-picked by long-time sheriff, Rex Sweat, in an attempt to patronize his Negro supporters. These half dozen officers did not wear uniforms. They were restricted to serving civil citations to members of the Negro community only.

Some prominent Blacks supported consolidation. Most Blacks like Frank Hampton opposed it. In June 1967, Mary Singleton and Sallye Mathis were the first African Americans elected to office in Duval County since the dark veil of Jim Crow descended on the American South. Although Blacks made up 40 percent of the city's population, the two Black women comprised our representation on the nine-member city council. Singleton opposed consolidation. Mathis voted for it.

Like the other Blacks who supported consolidation, Mathis must have believed the new system would give them the political clout they had so long been denied. There was also widespread fear that an increasingly Black city would not attract new industry and would become a mushrooming slum. Once we got consolidation, the promises didn't bear out. That's because the numbers were no longer in our favor.

Consolidation included all of Duval County except for three small municipalities along the Atlantic. The city swelled to 840 square miles and a population of more than 500,000 in 1970. In the old city boundaries before consolidation, Blacks made up 47 percent of the population. But after consolidation in 1968, the enlarged city's population grew to 455, 411 residents. Jacksonville's 121,170 Black residents only comprised 26.6 percent of the population. That was a drastic diminution and dilution of our voting power.

The enlarged City Council diluted our tenuous voting power even more. The first year in consolidation was 1968, and the Black community was promised they would have a certain number of representatives on the City Council, but the promises that were made by those who voted in consolidation were not kept. The Negro community was suckered into voting for consolidation and now they had to pay the price.

We had three Black council members, but they were overshadowed and outvoted by 20 council members. The Jacksonville Negro was not sophisticated in politics. We could have learned a few lessons from Black folks in Atlanta. You had Black people in Atlanta who had more sense about political power. I remember going up to Atlanta, and hearing a friend, who was an administrative aide to Mayor Maynard Jackson, say that Mayor Jackson told him how important it was to keep Blacks in power.

"Don't leave until you have another Black person who can take your place," Jackson advised him.

My fears about consolidation proved to be right. The well-connected Blacks benefited from consolidation as a reward for their support. The rest of the community didn't. As for me, becoming a member of an integrated Jacksonville Sheriff's Office opened doors for me to make history.

Chapter 58:
AFTER CONSOLIDATION

The City of Jacksonville Police Department was now called the Office of the Sheriff and had three former FBI agents at its helm.

The once-subjugated Negro police officer was now a police officer in the Office of the Sheriff with all the rights, privileges and responsibilities of other officers. I had no idea where I would be assigned in the new administration. Still a sergeant, I was chosen by Sheriff Carson to be a member of the newly founded Police Youth Affairs division.

The designated director of Police Youth Affairs was John E. Goode. A prematurely balding, blonde-headed man, Goode was intelligent and quick-thinking. I found him to be of unquestionable integrity, ability and competence. He had been in charge of the Officer Friendly Program in which I had been involved for some time. I was gratified to be working with him.

I am not sure why Sheriff Carson picked me for the Youth Affairs Division. But I no doubt came to his attention when on April 17, 1970, the Florida Times Union newspaper, highlighting my work as a pastor and law enforcement officer, wrote: "Officer, Pastor, Pacifier Has No Time for Insomnia."

The article referred to my heavy schedule as a full-time lawman in the police public affairs section and my full-time work as a pastor of a church in St. Marys, Georgia, a substitute teacher, service station owner and part-time graduate student. By then I was attending Stetson University in Deland, Florida, pursuing a master's degree.

I was part of the Officer Friendly program. Unlike safety patrol, this job was hard to define. It wasn't breaking down doors and frisking kids on the street. We visited Black Front meetings as representatives of the Sheriff's Office one night. The next day I would address an assembly of elementary students.

Sometimes I was a social worker directing people toward social service agencies to take care of children's needs. At other times I was a peacemaker and an ambassador addressing residents with racial and police brutality complaints against the Sheriff's Office.

I often talked to high school students to help them understand our role as law enforcement officers, and make sure they understood that a policeman does not just wait behind a sign to arrest someone. I loved the times when teens rode with a patrolman on a Friday or Saturday night. They got to see the rough side of the city.

Around that time, my office was trying to figure out how to deal with a near riot on the west side after a young black man had been shot by a patrolman. The officer claimed the youth had a knife, but no weapon was found at the scene when the first backup arrived. Later a knife appeared on the ground near where the dead youth lay. A white sergeant said he saw the knife, but I didn't. I was convinced the knife was placed there afterward. A knife drop was a common weapon in the patrolman's arsenal. After a questionable shooting of a civilian, especially a Black youth, knives and other weapons often miraculously appeared to support the officer's claim that the dead suspect was armed and hence a threat.

This incident was part of the ugly history of law enforcement in Jacksonville. Sheriff Carson had to be unaware. Officially, he looked into the complaint and set up dialogue sessions with various groups to ease the tension and allow residents to let off steam.

I found great satisfaction in my work. Every day brought new problems and new challenges. While working the day shift allowed me the opportunity to attend Lanse's basketball games and conduct Bible study at my church on weeknights, it meant substitute teaching of biology, mathematics, and other subjects was out of the question.

It helped that I liked my supervisor, John Goode, immediately. We were now working closely together leading a $150,000 federal grant that had been given to the City of Jacksonville. The project was called the Juvenile Delinquency Public Education Demonstration Project. Goode was the director. I was his assistant.

But he never acted like he was a director. We simply put our heads together and did what was necessary without any reference to where ideas came from, and focused only on the merit that it would bring. This unity brought us closer to accomplishing our goals. In my association with Goode, I often found myself in direct contact with Sheriff Carson, Undersheriff

Brown and their command staff, and got to know them personally.

Sheriff Carson was a man with a strong sense of humor and did not seem to be moved easily when strong criticism was leveled against him by the Florida Times Union newspaper or television stations. On the other hand, Undersheriff D. K. Brown, a Bishop in the Mormon Church, was very sensitive to the slightest criticism about his job or the Sheriff's office. John Riley Smith, the oldest of the three-man staff, had a very calming and pleasant demeanor. He never seemed rattled by internal problems within the department.

Unfortunately, my partnership with Goode ended when the Chief of Jails took his own life, and Sheriff Carson assigned Goode to fill the role.

Since Goode and I had worked so closely together and I more or less ran the program, I assumed Carson would appoint me as director of the new project. I was wrong. Instead, he chose a recently promoted lieutenant to head the Division of Youth Services. I could not hide my disappointment. I deserved the job. Although I was still a sergeant, I was qualified to lead the project and the Youth Services Division. After discussing my frustrations with Jeannetta, I walked into Sheriff Carson's office to find out why I was not given this assignment since I had been a part of it initially. Carson's reply was that he wanted to have a lieutenant in charge. When I heard his response, I could hardly control my anger. But I did.

"But Goode was a sergeant," I reminded Carson respectfully. "Sgt. Goode had headed the unit and the requirement didn't call for a lieutenant in charge."

The double standard was so obvious I didn't need to mention it. A white sergeant was qualified to lead the Youth Services Division, but a Black sergeant was not. Carson sat across from me, stone-faced.

I immediately understood what was being done. Carson did not want to have me, a Black man, in charge of this signature program.

· · · · · · · · · · · · · · · ·

My new supervisor didn't hang around long. Shortly after Lieutenant Al Kline became director of the Youth Services Division, he was selected by a South Florida police department to be interviewed as a finalist for a vacancy as police chief. He got the interview but not the job. While he was away, it became obvious that I had been overlooked. I did most of the work. I knew how to run the grant project. The project involved a different approach to police work which was a part of the new police community that was facing challenges during the late sixties and seventies.

It took Sheriff Carson seven months to correct his error. In December 1970, I was named director of Police Youth Affairs. As the director, the $150,000 grant put me more in the public eye than ever before. Becoming director of the $150,000 Juvenile Delinquency and Public Education Demonstration Project in 1970 was unique. It brought us more in contact with the entire City of Jacksonville and with Jacksonville University. Basically, though, the police department was not ready or sophisticated enough to face the community and the demonstrations that were happening on college campuses.

When Sheriff Carson appointed me director of Police Youth Affairs, I immediately named Martin Garris as my assistant. Martin selected the patrolmen to work with me in the program. The program involved Sheriff's Department officers, members of the school system, the Juvenile Court and young college students from Jacksonville University who were majoring in psychology and counseling. We put one of them into each of the four centers in Jacksonville. Everyone was paid by their respective agency, except for the college students, who were paid through the grant.

The four centers were within schools in the City of Jacksonville; one in the north side, one in the south side, one in the east side and one in the west side. We called them Police Youth Specialist Centers, and whenever we got troubled teens who were truant, rather than take them to a shelter or to the police department, the police officer would take them to the center where we had a member of the court, the school, and a counselor to work with them.

The police officers loved the program because if they picked up a delinquent student, generally more time was involved. But in this instance, they were taken directly to a center and turned over to the youth specialists. The counselors at the center would work with them anytime between the hours of 8 a.m. and 4:30 p.m. This was attractive to the police officers because of the short hours and the non-threatening environment. Most of the police officers wanted to work there.

Martin was the person dedicated to hiring white officers to work in the centers. I gave him authority to select officers because he knew them. It was an attractive job which did not involve riding around on a rotating shift at night or possibly being in danger.

The centers were a unique approach to delinquency and crime and received a great deal of good press for the work that was being done. The Sheriff got accolades and was pleased.

Each of our four centers was a one-stop center, with a police specialist, college counselor, a member of the court and a representative from the Duval County School System. Sheriff Carson received letters of commendation. There was follow-up at home, and it was working. The program really gave Sheriff Carson some political clout. Through me, he got positive notice from the voting community, but there were still plenty of challenges.

It was only my Christian faith that kept me on track through all the promotions and challenges. Martin Garris made a big difference in my life and in my career in the police department. I never had a man love me and help me and respect me as much as he did. We worked together on the centers and on diversity training, and I knew I could trust Martin to choose the right police officers for the Centers. He always had my back.

Since the police officers were being paid at the centers, I asked Martin to select a person who would work with the Police Athletic League. I would let that police officer work a half day at the center and a half day with the youth at what we called, during the first year, The Sheriff's Athletic League. I wrote my own personal check to have it incorporated and later, the officer I let work at the center a half day and spend the other part of the day organizing kids all over the city to play competitive sports, tried to say it was his idea. Norm Demers said he started a PAL. All he did was he got some balls and bats, and found some kids. I later challenged him. He was at a banquet where Martin introduced me and said that he had picked Demers for a special position under me.

The record will show that back in 1957 I was president of the Police Benevolent Association, and we started a PAL program. Then there was no association with the white community, nor could we apply for a national charter as a Black police precinct with a city police department. I got the kids uniforms, but they did not play in integrated leagues. We were a Black substation in a Black neighborhood and couldn't participate in other parks.

PAL proved to be the best public relations project in the city, and an excellent tool for curbing juvenile delinquency. Having attempted to form the youth organization back in 1957, I was once again instrumental in getting PAL going. And this time, we made it stick. My $5 personal check to the Secretary of State to charter PAL is evidence of my involvement. I also have a photo of Martin, several other officers, and me with a PAL group of youngsters.

It was during this period that a lieutenants' exam was scheduled. With no racial qualifications or previous conditions of servitude, I knew it was time for a long-awaited promotion. I had spent 10 years as a sergeant — six years in the Negro precinct, two years in the integrated Jacksonville Police Department and two years in the Office of the Sheriff under Carson. I was determined not to miss this opportunity. I had taken the lieutenant's exam before but had failed. This time I was going to be prepared.

Chapter 59:
LIEUTENANT SCRIVEN

The first time I took the lieutenant's exam, I failed. My preparation was lacking. When Sheriff Carson announced the test was coming up in 1971, I decided not to be caught unprepared again. Jeannetta and I and the children had planned a vacation that conflicted with the exam schedule. I was determined not to be denied. I decided to use my vacation time to study, instead of having fun with Jeannetta and children. It was a sacrifice I felt compelled to make. I took drastic measures. I didn't leave anything to chance. I was going to study in isolation with no one to interrupt me.

So, without consulting my wife, I packed everyone up, drove them to Atlanta and booked them in a hotel for a week. I flew back to Jacksonville and holed up in my house for a week. Jeannetta was not a happy camper. I didn't ask her permission. I can take a vacation anytime. If I am going to get promoted, I have to put in the time. Once I studied and got promoted, it was OK. Everybody said, "Look at your husband." She felt good about that.

I was never the kind of husband who let other people decide where I needed to go. I came back and studied for the exam. If I passed, there would be good recognition.

Jeannetta wasn't pleased at first about my not joining her and the family on vacation, but she later came to understand that sometimes sacrifice is required to get ahead. As a man and as a husband, there were decisions I had to make. She didn't have a say in the matter. I felt it was the right decision. Jeannetta and the children would benefit if my plan succeeded.

When I passed the exam, Sheriff Carson seemed to have taken some delight in being able to name the first Black lieutenant in the history of the Sheriff's department. On January 1, 1972, the Jacksonville Chronicle ran a short blurb with my photo under the headline "Man on a Hot Seat?" The one paragraph story reported that the writer had it on "good authority that

Sgt. Charles Scriven, who heads the Youth Affairs Division of the Sheriff's Department, will be promoted to lieutenant on Friday."

In addition to that, I became recognized as an administrator and program director — crossing over the different disciplines of schools and courts, and that brought additional compliments to the Sheriff's Office. I was more in the presence of the Sheriff, and if something came up, I became his go-to guy.

・・・・・・・・・・・・・・・・

I was the first Black officer to rise to the rank of lieutenant in the Sheriff's Office Jacksonville Police. At the time, the Office of the Sheriff employed 40 other Black officers including six sergeants and more than 30 patrolmen. At integration, we had about 26 Black officers, including more than 20 patrolmen and three sergeants, including me. We had a tough time of recruiting Black officers in an open and competitive market. At the director of Sheriff Carson, I was responsible for increasing the number of African Americans in the agency to reflect the size of the Black population in Duval County. A large corps of Black officers could help improve the rapport between the Sheriff's Office and the Black community.

Since consolidation, Sheriff Carson did nothing specific about expanding opportunities for the Negro police officer. It's a debate whether that was the wisest way of handling things. Whenever the Sheriff's Office had an exam, we simply posted the police vacancy and the requirements for a police officer. That was the way the police department dealt with consolidation. But several years in, Carson personally put me in charge of recruiting Negro officers. I wasn't limited by budget. I could go from Jacksonville to Atlanta or anywhere to recruit Negro officers because we were still undermanned with Black officers in terms of Jacksonville's Black population.

In the open market, there was a problem because when you looked at a white recruit, he might have had a white police officer living in his neighborhood. Even little things like that figured into the competition when you started recruiting. Because of the historical animosity between the police officers and the Black community, young Black men were not attracted to careers in law enforcement. That became evident with my recruiting efforts. But that was only one hurdle.

The other issue was the entrance test. Black recruits struggled to pass the police officers' exam. To remedy that, what I did later, with the help and permission of Sheriff Carson, was to use a grant to help prepare officers or cadets and put them in a special training program so that they could take the test to become a police officer. The cadet program was run in collaboration with the Jacksonville Urban League, which was led by Clanzel T. Brown for seventeen years. Brown had the reputation for getting things done and for fighting on behalf of the downtrodden.

Despite our best efforts, we struggled to get Black recruits through the test because one of the downsides of the educational system was the inequity prevalent in our Negro community schools. You cannot take a student from a major white high school and compare him with one from our Black high school. All of the books we had were handed down from white schools. We didn't have any new books. This was not only in police work but other critical areas without any racial restrictions. Test-taking is a skill many would-be Black recruits didn't learn. The Urban League Cadet Program was designed to help our young Black men overcome that hurdle.

∙ ∙ ∙ ∙ ∙ ∙ ∙ ∙ ∙ ∙ ∙ ∙ ∙ ∙ ∙

A Negro lieutenant supervising white policemen was something that had never happened in the Jacksonville Sheriff's Office, so when I eventually began doing that, it raised a lot of problems from just the practice and policy in a Southern police department. It wasn't easy for me to do certain things. White men who were working under me resented the fact that they were working under a Black supervisor. Normally, if I had a patrolman that I wanted to meet with, I'd just call them on the radio and tell them I wanted to meet them at Third and Main. Sometimes they would do all sorts of tricks. They would pretend they didn't receive my communication to meet me somewhere. As long as I held that microphone down, I was transmitting, but if I want to break that transmission, I could double-click the mic and stop the transmission. When I called them and they responded to me, they could double-click the mic and break that transmission. It would be as if they hadn't heard. But then, I could call Central headquarters and ask them to transmit the message. All I had to do then was ask Central to call them, and if they did not respond to Central, they could be written up and subject to disciplinary action. Once I saw what was going on, I would simply ask Central headquarters to call them. They knew what was coming after that, and they didn't have an option.

Another problem which came about was in the selection of personnel. For example, any sergeant or lieutenant, when they get ready to select the men working in their squad, knew them because they'd been around them. But when I went to Central headquarters, they knew each other, but I didn't know them. The supervisor had a choice as to whom he selected, but if I didn't know them, the person who had the choice of selecting would get the men with a more favorable record. So, I got the ones who no one wanted, those everyone knew performed poorly and had poor records. When my squad went out, I had the poorest rated officers because I didn't know them. That made a difference in terms of my supervision.

They did little things, and had I known of their poor performance, I would not have selected them, and I would not have been left with poorly performing officers. Unfortunately, Martin wasn't assigned to me then.

Of course, I always had to watch my back because I didn't know how they were going to respond to me. They were afraid sometimes. Every police officer likes to know that who he's working with has his back. I had officers who had problems with me as a Black man. I had to be careful.

In my first few years as director, I had sergeants under me who I supervised administratively. That was not the case in my first assignment. I had to be on the street and supervise police officers as everyone else did. I'm thankful that I was able to go through that period, and did not have that street experience where I had to depend on others behind me. You get to know who you can trust after working with people for a while. When you're in a dangerous position, you want to make sure you are with officers you can trust. We had some Black officers who were afraid of their shadows. Everybody knew who they were. That's where my friend, Martin Garris, was an invaluable asset.

For instance, ninety percent of the city police cases went to City Court because of our jurisdiction. The usual police work — domestic problems, fights, traffic tickets, DWI, misdemeanors, and bar fights landed in the municipal court. The courts were all very harsh on Black offenders and there was literally no defense available. For instance, if white women were arrested, they would stay in back in a separate area until they were called before the judge. But when Black women were arrested, they were intermingled in the holding section with Black men until their case was called. There was no defense. If the police officer said you did it, the judge charged you. Half the time the judge was drunk. He knew nothing except "90 days."

With consolidation, we had a new police department and a powerful and professional sheriff. Some of the rackets, like the petty corruption, taking kickbacks and bribes from street hustlers and numbers runners, came to an end, or so it appeared on the surface since the action probably went further underground. Sheriff Carson was a man of integrity. He had to run a lot of people away and he cleaned up the police department, but unfortunately, that did not extend to the courts.

What the Black community needed was protection from a corrupt police department that took advantage of the Black community. With consolidation and a professional sheriff in charge, a lot of that professionalism had a good effect on the old corrupt system, but the city judges were elected. Black men and women were sentenced unfairly compared to white offenders. They were finally able to get the FBI to investigate a particular judge for corruption, so the next time the election came around, he was gone. That was Municipal Judge Charles Miller. Miller was in the news back in 1955 when his primary opponent in the election charged voting irregularities. A city council canvass found no erroneous and fraudulent returns in the 14 voting districts.

The city county and state law enforcement officials met to devise a plan to clean up the dumps, dives and juke joints as part of Mayor Haydon Burns' plan to eliminate blight of taverns on Bay, Main and Ocean streets, the Times Union reported on May 7, 1955.

Chapter 60:
CHIEF SCRIVEN

A year and a half after I became the first Black lieutenant in the history of the Jacksonville Sheriff's Office, I made history again. On Friday, July 20, 1973, the Jacksonville Journal evening newspaper reported Sheriff Carson's announcement of the formation of a new, one-man division within his department and my appointment as Jacksonville's first Black police chief to head it. The Journal reported that I would serve alone in the new division for an unspecified time period. He told the reporters that he could not determine how many men would be needed in the new division or when the first would be assigned to work for me. There were no uniformed Black women in the JSO department until Retha Smith was hired in 1973.

In my new role, I would act at staff level to "create and maintain closer lines of communication between the Black community and the Sheriff's Office," Carson said. He did concede there might be some overlap between my division and the public affairs unit, but he didn't think there were going to be any problems that couldn't be handled. My efforts would be "directed mainly at the Black community."

"Things are fairly quiet at the moment. This move is not being made under any pressure," Carson said at the press conference as Jeannetta and I sat smiling next to him. I wore my nicely-pressed uniform with the JSO badge proudly pinned on my left breast. Looking back at my wry smile that Friday morning, as Jeannetta leaned toward me beaming, I can imagine what was going through my mind. I was very political in my comments. I told the newspaper and television reporters that I planned to begin my duties by visiting other cities which had community relations projects and report my findings. Carson said my initial task was a "travel survey of the community and minority relations programs in other cities."

After I returned, Carson expected me to work with community leaders to develop programs that could bridge an existing gap between the Black community and the Sheriff's Office.

"We don't know how large a division this will require. There is no way to tell, really," Carson told the Times Union reporter. "Chief Scriven has worked the streets. He has worked men. He is a minister. We have chosen him because he can do the job to keep peace and racial harmony in the community. Some cities have a community relations unit which is no more than window dressing. We want something that will work on an operational level."

The Times Union that day described me as a soft-soften officer who has "long been cultivated by my superiors as an ambassador from the police force, first for the former Jackson Police Department and then the Sheriff's Office, to the Black community." They also acknowledged my role as the primary recruiter of Black officers. I had also served as a liaison officer between the Sheriff's Office, the City Council, and the Black community.

Carson did most of the talking that day.

While I was proud of my promotion, at the time I had greater ambitions than the Sheriff's Office. I didn't keep them a secret. I said I had planned to retire in two and a half years, in 1975, and pursue a law degree at the University of Florida law school after I finished my master's at Stetson University. Perhaps I wanted to allay any of Carson's fears that I was a potential challenger waiting in the wings.

Jim Davis, the Journal reporter, alluded to the politics of my appointment in the last paragraph of the three-column Journal article. Carson had created a new division for me and named me chief even though it was well known that Chief of Investigation R. L. Starratt was scheduled to retire in August, the following month. By naming me chief of a division without a staff, Carson wouldn't have to be worried about how it would look if I was overlooked for the job of Chief of Investigation.

That Carson was giving me a title without real power was obvious to the media gathered for the event. The Florida Times Union described me as "a chief without Indians." Also, by giving me an office without staff, Carson avoided having to deal with the hurt feelings of white officers who I would have to supervise.

At that news conference, Carson acknowledged that my appointment must be included in the mayor's general budget and required approval from the city council before I could get my four stars and be sworn in as a Chief. My appointment required confirmation before the end of August from the

Jacksonville City Council, which Carson was rightly confident he could secure without much opposition.

· · · · · · · · · · · · · · · ·

Carson promoted me to Chief to get around having to promote me into a position where I would directly supervise white officers. At that time, I had not only passed the captain's exam, but I was No. 1 on the captain's promotion list. The next captain's vacancy would result in my promotion. Given the civil service rules, Carson would have had no choice but to promote me to a position supervising white officers. That would have been a bold move, and Carson didn't have a track record of making bold racial moves. By appointing me Chief, he side-stepped disrupting the social structure within the department. He was doing himself a favor and eliminating me from a promotional position that automatically put me in charge of white patrolmen. Eventually, white officers came to work for me because they saw the advantages. Coming into my division was a position that took them away from a rotating shift, so they were home at night. It was less threatening. Some racist officers saw it was to their advantage to work in a job that didn't involve a rotating shift or chasing criminals. Officers had their own assigned car to take home each day. We worked in the schools, working with a social worker, the court, the juvenile prevention liaison, and college students. We were not dealing with violent offenders. The racist white officers might not have liked having a Black man as their supervisor, but they found the perks of the job irresistible.

Many times, people create a small position, and once you get into it, it remains small. I saw in the position more than Carson did. I had an audience that I wouldn't have had under normal circumstances. I wasn't just another captain working a watch. I could play it the way he thought it would have been played. I was a Black representative to the Black community. I saw something in that position that gave me an audience that he didn't realize. When you attach the Chief title to me, they were not seeing "Negro chief." They saw the title "Chief." The title made 100 percent difference when I applied to the Parole and Probation Commission. I wasn't the chief Negro representative to the Black the community, I was the first Black Chief in the history of Jacksonville.

I've always believed that you can give a small man a small job, and he could let it stay small. I saw within the job larger opportunities than the sheriff saw. He was looking at it from a political standpoint. He wanted to keep the good ole boy system in place, but he wanted to appease a restive Black community frustrated by the pace of change in Duval County. My being Chief meant I was the Sheriff's Office representative to the Black community. I had some input within the management level of the Sheriff's Office. The sheriff didn't see it that way. He was satisfying a political section of a community.

Carson did what he thought was the best thing to do at the time. He was meeting a local community demand in having a Black chief. He was smart enough to know when I made such an impact that position never changed. Nobody white could ever get into that position. Martin wanted it. He deserved it, but he didn't get it. With that position that I had been given, he saw where he made the biggest achievement in putting a Black man in it. When I moved to Tallahassee, he couldn't bring a white man into that position. When other chief positions became available, they were filled by white officers. He told Martin Garris that it was a Black position. He wouldn't put him in it.

I developed relationships with the business community — Maxwell House Coffee, Rock Company, Southern Bell. Your political community was your business community. They wrote checks for political contributions. Carson didn't realize the real value of my position. Some of the officers said to me, "You have a chief and no Indians." That was true. I had no real staff. Martin volunteered. I didn't have a structure until we got that federal grant. The grant allowed us to bring officers into that division. When officers saw the advantage of working for me and the conditions under which they worked, they took advantage of it. They were home every night and had the use of a private police car. What more could they ask for?

• • • • • • • • • • • • • • •

Although my staff was small or non-existent, my mandate was huge — be a peacemaker between the Sheriff's Office and Jacksonville's restive Black community. The relationship between the Jacksonville Sheriff's Office and the Black community was never good, and had not improved in the years after consolidation. In the ensuing year, I came to understand the magnitude of the obstacles I faced and the sacrificial, token nature of my position. Improving relations between the Sheriff's Office and the Black community was not a priority for Sheriff Carson. I was his one-man band-aid to a problem that the entire country struggled to solve.

Chapter 61:
CIVIL RIGHTS COMMISSION

The issue of police/community relations in Jacksonville had received national attention. The Florida Advisory Committee to the U.S. Commission on Civil Rights described the relationship in terms reflective of the times — the Cold War between the U.S. and the Soviet Union.

The Committee's report, "Toward Police/Community Détente in Jacksonville," was submitted to the Civil Rights Commission in June 1975. Created in 1957 following the passage of the Civil Rights Act of 1957, the Civil Rights Commission is an independent, non-partisan agency of the federal executive branch charged with addressing issues related to the denial of equal protection of the laws based on race, color, sex, religion, national origin, voting rights violations, and other similar issues.

The Florida Advisory Committee was chaired by Ted Nichols, an administrator at the University of Miami. The State Advisory Committees, made up of men and women volunteers reflecting various racial, political and age groups within each state, were often referred to as "the Federal Presence" within each state.

"These committees became the eyes, ears and arms of the Civil Rights Commission through the Nation at the grassroots level in matters of civil rights, whether the issues affected American Indians who until then were a wholly forgotten group, Mexican Americans in the Midwest, Blacks in the South or other groups," Nichols later testified in spring 1978 during a House Judiciary Committee hearing on legislation, to extend the life of the U.S. Civil Rights Commission. Nichols and other state chairmen fought to block regionalization of the state committees.

The Florida Advisory Committee didn't mince words about the Sunshine State or Jacksonville. "Florida was not immune to the urban turbulence that followed the killings of the Kennedys and Dr. King. With large compressions of poor and minorities in the cores of its glittering resorts and seaport cities, Florida was ripe for the mass expressions of frustration and rage at bright promises left dangling — and for the repercussive Law and Order," read its 1975 report. As part of its work, the Committee had also visited Tampa and Miami. Its Tampa study was released in December 1972.

During its investigation, which included an opening meeting in Jacksonville on March 8th and 9th 1974, the Advisory Committee, led by Chairman Nichols, examined allegations of police ill treatment of Black citizens and studied the Office of the Sheriff, focusing on hiring and promotion policies, human relations and public contact, complaint procedures, and Law Enforcement Assistant Administration (LEAA) funding.

The office of the sheriff currently has jurisdiction over all aspects of law enforcement, including the operation of the city jail and county prison work camp. The range of crimes the Sheriff's Department deals with has expanded along with the city. Unlawful activities that regularly reach the police docket range from moonshine and cattle rustling to such urban sophistications as syndicated vice and drug-dealing.

The Committee conceded a sad fact I had admitted to myself in the five years since consolidation: Black/White relations in both rural and urban areas, each with its own ugly history of discrimination, had become even more complicated.

"Blacks remember the rural counties' reluctance about granting them so basic a right as the ability to vote. In the inner-city, deteriorating ghettos and idle youths are evidence of the economic repression that is a byproduct in any region where commercial gains outstrip education and services to the entire citizenry. Jacksonville's long record of confrontation with its black citizens, town and county are not laudable," the FAC report said. That statement was an acknowledgment that Jacksonville's prosperity with the relocation of major corporations to the city has brought wealth for whites, but had left many of the city's Black residents behind.

Black officers had been hired ostensibly to reduce white police brutality against Black residents, but clearly based on the committee's report, that experiment had failed miserably. I had done well as a Black police officer. I felt I had made a difference in the lives of the people with whom I came into contact. But the vast majority of my fellow Black residents did not share my views, and the committee's report reflected that.

Jacksonville's history was not encouraging. The Committee recalled the racial tensions that erupted in 1960 at the Woolworth's lunch counter that devolved into what white Jacksonville residents called the "Hemming Park" riots when Black students who had been conducting a peaceful sit-in were beaten by whites armed with ax handles.

The night of April 14, 1968, hours after Dr. King had been assassinated, Jacksonville erupted along with numerous other cities throughout the country, and the police made ample use of tear gas to control the unrest, the report reminded us.

Several days of widespread disturbances follow the Halloween 1969 shooting of a Black youngster by a white salesman who thought the lad was stealing from his truck. Many members of the Black community who witnessed the outbreaks claimed that the members of the Sheriff's Office made the situation worse rather than quell the disturbances. Unfortunately, the Black community had come to expect nothing better from Jacksonville police.

The Advisory Committee strongly criticized the overwhelming superiority of whites in numbers and rank in the Sheriff's Office. They saw that issue as exacerbating the tension between Black residents and white police officers. They recalled the period of Negro police officers and the all-Black substation when it was understood that Black officers could not arrest whites for whatever reason. Prior to consolidation, there were no uniform Black deputies under the County Sheriff. No Blacks were allowed membership of the Fraternal Order of Police, bargaining agent for police officers, until 1969, the committee found. I was all too familiar with all these sore points.

In preparation of its report, Committee members interviewed Jacksonville residents who had experienced harassment or had witnessed it personally. They complained that the Sheriff's Office made it hard to log complaints and that officers often tried to punish those who tried to file complaints by charging them with resisting arrest with violence, a felony that could result in a five-year sentence. The Office of the Sheriff conducted its own investigation of brutality charges but did not feel obliged to report back any disciplinary action, and the case files were virtually inaccessible to the public despite Florida's generous open records statutes.

The committee held its open meeting on March 8th and 9th 1974 at Edward Waters College. A few days before the meeting, 18 blacks, alleging they had been victims of police brutality, joined with the head of the local chapter of the NAACP in announcing the intent to file suit against Jacksonville city officials. The purpose of the class action lawsuit was to guarantee constitutional rights to members of the Black community.

As a result of the impending lawsuit, four of the scheduled witnesses declined to testify at the open meeting on advice of counsel. Both Sheriff Carson and Mayor Tanzler, who had earlier accepted invitations to speak and to give open statements, didn't show up.

In all, 30 invitees spoke at the meetings. People from city agencies and civic organizations and residents of the minority community gave their personal viewpoints, sometimes conflicting on the causes and cures for the poor police/community relations. Even though the NAACP litigants did not attend, several alleged victims gave accounts on how police had abused the authority and had applied force unduly and unfairly.

Some also claimed that charges such as resisting arrest with violence were used by officers as devices to discourage them from filing complaints. Sheriff Carson had agreed to present his overview of police minority relations and to respond to any substantive issues raised during the meeting. Instead, Carson sent me to fill his time slot before the committee. As the highest-ranking Black person in the Sheriff's Office and one of three Blacks in the entire agency above the rank of sergeant, I did not purport to speak for Sheriff Carson or the agency.

I only presented my own views.

Carson never told me about why he didn't show up for either of the two days of sessions. However, his quoted statement in the Florida Times Union several days later, told me exactly what he thought of the proceedings. It reflected his aloofness and insensitivity to the problems and concerns of the community's Black residents.

"The fact that we haven't had any disturbances for several years is a far better indicator of race relations than a suit filed by an organization which needs conflict to survive," said Carson in an obvious dig at the NAACP and an indication of his dismissal and disregard for the Committee's work.

The Committee wanted to hit Jacksonville where it hurt. The report noted Jacksonville's success in securing grants for law enforcement under the Omnibus Crime Control and Safe Streets Acts. Since 1971, Jacksonville had obtained $3 million in federal funds for police services and the judicial system that included the $150,000 that was secured for the juvenile program that I headed. Some of the past programs have included installation of a communications network, halfway houses for prisoners, alcoholics and drug addicts, training, minority recruitment and jail renovations. The Committee believed that in order to get Sheriff Carson's attention, federal funding should be cut.

The Committee took issue with the overwhelmingly white, male make-up of the Sheriff's Office. The study found that the Office of the Sheriff had disproportionately small percentages of Blacks and women on the sworn force, and these groups were underrepresented in the higher echelon officer ranks. As of July 1974, exactly a year after I was promoted to chief, the representation of Black women on the force was zero percent, Black men 5 percent, white women 2 percent, and white men 93 percent. For officers above the rank of lieutenant, there were no Black women or white women. Five percent were Black men and 95 percent were white men, the study found.

The charge of ill treatment was not leveled at the entire police force, but a significant number of complaints have been made against a small cadre of officers. Some complaints have resulted in lawsuits.

On March 12, 1974, a class action suit was filed by the local chapter of the National Association for the Advancement of Colored People (NAACP) naming Sheriff Dale Carson, Mayor Hans Tanzler, Community Relations Chairperson Nathan H. Wilson, and 22 policemen, 17 of who were identified by name, and five John Does, as defendants. Charges against the defendants ranged from misconduct and abusive authority to use of excessive force and brutality. Subsequent to the open meeting of August 16th, 1974, members of the Advisory Committee and staff from the Committees' Commission's Southern Regional Office met with representatives of the Black community and with Sheriff Carson and Undersheriff D. K. Brown.

During the informal hearing, a public information officer for the Sheriff's Office submitted a statement to the Advisory Committee in response to an allegation of police brutality made by an attorney on behalf of a client. The statement began with the classic "no admission of wrongdoing by members of our department" caveat but announced that the officers had been either dismissed from the department or have tendered resignation to the department in relation to other areas of misconduct.

"The Jacksonville Sheriff's Office is fully aware of problems with some (a very small number) of our officers in connection with improper relations with members of the community. However, we must work within the framework of law and prove beyond a reasonable doubt, the guilt or innocence of an officer before terminating him for cause."

Because it was so difficult to fire officers for excessive force, the statement said the Carson administration was taking alternative measures.

"Within the past week, four officers who have been continuing problems in the area of improper conduct with respect to Black citizens, have been separated on charges of theft of firearms, and a fifth officer has been recommended for firing on charges of sleeping on duty, damage to a city vehicle and falsifying his work log," the Sheriff's Public Information statement read.

While it's gratifying to me, a lawman, to know that the bad apples were being weeded out of the Sheriff's Office, those allegedly harmed by those officers got no comfort that their tormentors and abusers were fired for other reasons. They got neither justice nor satisfaction.

The result was the initiation of dialogue between the Black coalition and the Office of the Sheriff, the first meaningful communication between the two groups. The Advisory Committee also urged Carson to step up the recruitment and hiring of Blacks and women. Like Community Relations with the black community, that was part of my portfolio.

Chapter 62:
APPROACHING THE END

Unlike the Negro community, the Black officer profited by consolidation. I would never have been a division chief had consolidation not occurred. I think Sheriff Carson and Undersheriff Brown knew the temperament of the white police officers, and I knew it well too. They would hurt me when I was promoted to Chief if I was in the position of supervising them.

When I was promoted to Division Chief, Sheriff Carson did not put in white officers under me. They had their biases too, and knew the kind of racial disharmony that would have happened in the city if they had put white officers under me. My life would probably have been in danger. I worked in the position where I knew how to handle the mentality of white police officers.

The other thing that made a difference was that after consolidation, there was a kind of different system. You didn't have that same group that could influence and do things — you had the system with Dale Carson and D. K. Brown, the undersheriff. You had a professional management running the police agency. The old boy system had been largely dismantled. Prior to that, if you were the cousin of the chief and you passed the exam, you might have been tenth on the list, but you could be up for the next promotion.

We had professional police officers in charge. Carson and his command sent officers to Quantico for FBI management training. Initially, they just sent white officers to the six or eight-week course, but eventually, Black officers got the same opportunity. A training certificate from the FBI was often a prelude to a management promotion. Nat Glover attended the 130th Session of the FBI National Training Academy.

D. K. Brown was responsible for me going to the FBI Academy in Quantico, Virginia for diversity training. At that time, the FBI Academy was top of the line when they started acknowledging there needed to be training for police officers in sensitive areas. Some police departments included that in their curriculum, from one to two to four hours. Now you must have a minimum of ten or twenty hours in diversity training, and they will bring in people from New York or people who specialize in this area, to learn the temperament of the community and how to train. When I went, there was a question of police legitimacy all over the nation. The FBI led the training to make police departments more professional. One of the crowning glories was to be designated to go to the FBI Academy on six to eight weeks paid leave to be trained. It meant I was among the elite.

• • • • • • • • • • • • • • • •

Being the first African American to be named Division Chief in the Jacksonville Sheriff's Office brought its share of notoriety. Most of the time, the media coverage was positive. But it wasn't always. When you are prominent in the community, your relatives are often unwittingly thrust into the limelight. That's what happened with our daughter Reenee. On September 6, 1974, the following headline appeared in the Florida Times Union: "Chief's Daughter Arrested on Stolen Check Charge." The five or six paragraph story stabbed my heart like a dagger. "The daughter of Jacksonville Police Chief Charles Scriven has been arrested at her home and charged with passing more than $700 worth of stolen checks."

By then Reenee had moved out of our home where she had lived since she was in elementary school. In excruciating detail, the newspaper reported the following about Reenee who was 19 at the time: "Miss Scriven reportedly went on August 30th to the Lake Forest Atlantic Bank where she formerly was employed and went to the ground floor drive-through where she cashed two checks for $393.73. She then allegedly drove to the top level and cashed three more checks valued at $345.53. Police said the checks were returned to the bank and listed as stolen by the Jesco Corp. Scriven heads the Community Relations Division of the Sheriff's Office."

The article's final sentence was like a slap in my face. I had nothing to do with the crime. But the media found it convenient to include my name. I guess that's how they sold newspapers. That incident was very painful. By then, Reenee had moved out of our home and was living on her own. The officers arrested her at her home. They took her to the bank. When I heard she had been taken into custody, I went and asked to drive her to the station. I didn't trust the officer who were taking her in.

Later on, as chief of the Community Relations Division, I started sitting on the police Oral Review Board. These officers had passed the written test, and the psychological test was the final hurdle before they were either rejected or accepted into the police department.

I often took a position that if a man didn't have some experience with other races, he would not make a good police officer. We began with one hour on race relations and when we started having problems nationwide, we increased it to two hours of diversity training. Then later on, police command said the problems were culturally related, and we found that when we hired police officers, they had no idea about race relations. We almost had to teach them about race relations in order for them to effectively perform their duties.

We found that many white officers actually were afraid of Black people, and they would overreact. There were officers we sent to predominantly Black communities who did not have the temperament to deal with a different culture. One bad incident happened when a police officer shot a kid. We knew the problem was he had never been in a Black Baptist Church when they start getting happy, doing dances, shouting and looking all crazy.

The judge asked the policeman if he had his pistol with him when he saw them shouting. I've been to sanctified churches, and they get wild. As boys, we used to look through the windows and laugh and make fun, but it was a different culture. It was not dangerous. When you put somebody with a lack of understanding in a Negro neighborhood, he can be rattled anytime.

I was sitting on the Police Oral Review Board. I did background investigations. This board was the one with the final decision as to whether you would get the job within the department.

It got out that I was asking real questions centered about relationship between Blacks and whites and having a relationship with the Black community. I remember asking, during an interview with a white police officer, "Have you ever been out with a Black person?"

I suspect they put a hidden microphone on one of the applicants. I was trying to ascertain if the person had any interracial interactions when I asked "Have you been out with a Black person?", It caused some fury. They painted me as being a liberal. This was 1970, when Richard Nixon was in the White House and Republican conservatives were on the march. America, ever a reactionary country, had turned its back against what it viewed as the liberal excesses of the 1960s. To be a liberal in law enforcement was not an asset.

Sheriff Carson called me into his office and showed me a stack of about 400 or 500 petitions calling for my firing. He ignored them all.

My enemies sent an applicant into the interview with a wire and recorded the interview. When the conversation was leaked to the Florida Times Union, they blasted me for it. I had broached a taboo subject. They reacted as if I was asking the applicant if he dated Black women.

One of my colleagues asked an applicant how he would feel if he discovered that one of his ancestors was Black. That didn't make the news.

I had no such intention. Given the racial history of the Jacksonville/Duval County Sheriff's Office and the demographics of the people the agency served, I wanted to know if the applicant had any history of relating to people of color in his daily interactions. I had no interest in his romantic life. I wanted to know if he had any understanding of the culture of the people he would be hired to serve and protect. But the union and others jumped all over me. They called the mayor and city council members saying Scriven asked an applicant if he had ever dated a Black women. They demanded that Sheriff Carson fire me. He showed at least 500 petitions, including some from members of the department who wanted me fired. They were part of the anti-Scriven lobby. They sought, through that episode, to get rid of me finally. But it wasn't that easy. Sheriff Carson stood firm. He said they wanted me fired because of my racial views. He couldn't fire me. He had invested in my career. I was his spokesman to the Black community. He understood the opposition was coming from the old white, narrow-minded Jacksonville. My question was not about dating and social mixing. I wanted to know if these officers were prepared to police my community.

Unfortunately, that was my last appearance on the oral review board. I was the only Black person on the board, and I was removed after that. Carson didn't announce my removal from the Oral Review Board. I just didn't get any more meeting notices.

I wasn't asking if he had ever been on a date with a Black woman. I was simply trying to find out his experience with another race. This would make a difference in his ability to police in a minority or Black community. We were able to get diversity training into the Sheriff's Office. We received a $150,000 grant, and we had to have police officers sit in these classes. Some of them would not come unless they wore their uniforms with the pistol. The Sheriff had to order them to participate in the sensitivity training without their pistols. When you're sitting with a man with a pistol, how many issues are you going to raise?

We continued to advocate diversity training for police officers. We were late in training them to handle verbal abuse. When college students started protesting, we found that we had a police department that was not trained for combat other than using a stick. They needed some real diversity training. It was not enough to have a degree in accounting and know how to speak to people on the telephone. The police were caught flat-footed in cities like New York, Los Angeles, Chicago, and they didn't know how to deal with verbal abuse. The Sheriff did not quite know what to do with this problem.

• • • • • • • • • • • • • • • •

I was serving as Chief of the Community Relations Division, for less than a year when the Civil Rights Commission hearings were held. That episode laid bare the impossibility of the challenge I faced in my role as the Sheriff's Office ambassador to the Black community. No matter what I needed, there were too many circumstances beyond my control. As the summer of 1974 turned into fall, I saw an announcement that caught my attention and gave me new focus. A year earlier I had begun to look to my future outside the Sheriff's Office. In March 1975, I would have put in my 20 years, making me eligible for full retirement. I was on schedule to complete my master's at Stetson, and planned to apply to the University of Florida law school. God, however, had other plans for me.

BOOK IX:
PAROLE AND PROBATION COMMISSION

Chapter 63:
GOING TO TALLAHASSEE

After he was elected the 37th Governor of Florida in 1971, Democrat Reubin Askew was committed to tax reform, civil rights, integrity, and the financial transparency of public servants. Although he was a white man born in Muskogee, Oklahoma, Askew was committed to breaking down the white male bastion of law and justice and admitting Blacks and women, especially white women.

Askew was committed to doing all he could to create a fairer legal system. In 1975, the former state legislator appointed civil rights lawyer Joseph Woodrow Hatchett as the 65th Florida Supreme Court Justice and the first African American Florida Supreme Court Justice.

At the time, Askew's hands were tied with the appointment of judges, so he sought to use his executive power through appointments on the Parole and Probation Commission. In 1974, after the Legislature expanded the number of seats from five to seven, Governor Askew announced his intention to appoint a minority and a woman on the Commission. Since its founding in 1941, the Commission had been a bastion of white male power, privilege, and racial oppression. The expansion gave a non-voting seat to Division of Corrections Director Louie Wainwright, a white man.

• • • • • • • • • • • • • • • •

At the time of the announcement, I was in the Jacksonville force for 19 years. The following spring, March 1975, would give me 20 years of service, and I would be eligible for my full pension. I enjoyed being a member of the Sheriff's Office. In 1973, I had been made Chief, the first African American to rise to that rank in Duval County Law Enforcement. Sheriff Carson had appointed me Chief of Community Relations. But I understood the limits of my ambition as long as Carson was sheriff. Although I had earned my master's degree at Stetson University, and although my work in the community was lauded and I had earned Carson substantial support in the Black community, I knew I would never be the boss. It was time for me to venture elsewhere.

So, as soon as I read about Askew's plan, I immediately claimed the job. I had an overwhelming desire to take my conviction to criminal justice reform to the Parole Commission. It was like my call to the ministry. I felt called to bring new ideas about reform and rehabilitation to those who were lost in the prison system without hope. Like me, many of them were Black. Setting prisoners free was another way I could live out the Gospel message. That became my mission and my ministry. During most of my law enforcement career I was not locking people up behind bars. Most of my efforts were spent trying to steer juveniles back to the straight and narrow. Seeing so many of our young men, and women behind bars, inspired me to do more. Being on the Parole and Probation Commission would give me another opportunity to help those I couldn't help in my previous role. After 20 years of seeing young black men and women thrown behind bars, often for minor misdeeds, I wanted a chance to reverse the pipeline going into Florida's growing prisons.

Immediately, after I saw Askew's announcement, I claimed the position. Some call it magical thinking. I called it faith. I posted signs around our house in Jacksonville, "Going to Tallahassee." In recent decades we had become accustomed to the "name it and claim it preachers" like Reverend Ike. If you want something from God, you just have to speak as if you received it. My thinking might not have been articulated in those words at that time, but I was convinced that the historic appointment was mine even though I had not yet applied for the job, and the vetting process was still months away.

Jeannetta and the children must have wondered if I was losing my mind. But my mind was made up. I told them, "We would be moving to Tallahassee. I am going to be appointed to the Parole Commission."

I filled out my application and sent it in. My resume was impressive enough. I had served in the U.S. Army as a military policeman. Following my honorable discharge, I had come home to Jacksonville, started a family, and joined the Jacksonville Police Department. Since then, I had never stopped learning and educating myself. My bachelor's from Edward Waters College and my master's from Stetson University were my academic proof. I had strong character references. I had dedicated my life to helping young men and women find alternatives to a life of crime. Throughout Jacksonville, the productive lives of legions of young Black men attested to my efforts. My life was scandal-free. There were no extramarital affairs or bastard children. Given my position as a police officer and my increasing influence and visibility in my community, the temptations never stopped. As a man of God, I was determined not to get entangled the way many good Black men had become tainted and ensnared by scandal.

• • • • • • • • • • • • • • •

The Commissioner's job was full-time. It paid well — $27,600 a year. It was prestigious. It was coveted. The jockeying for the two positions started immediately.

Established in 1941, the Parole and Probation Commission was also controversial. It was powerful. Its members decided which inmates got early release from prison, who got parole and who remained behind bars. The Commission also had its many law enforcement critics who felt it was too lenient on criminals. Many justice reform advocates argued that since most Florida prison inmates were Black, the all-white male Commission couldn't adequately address the needs of the prison population. Law Enforcement advocates and sheriffs from across the state threw their support behind me. I was a veteran lawman and part-time minister. The Associated Press reported that my "appointment may soothe disgruntled sheriffs and policemen who say the commission has been too lenient on offenders."

Hundreds of people applied. The state announced it received 272 complete, valid applications. Mine was among them.

The Cabinet appointed a special screening committee chaired by Leon County Circuit Judge James Joanos. The committee's mandate was to select six finalists and present them to the Cabinet. The committee personally interviewed 110 candidates. I drove to Tallahassee for my interview.

Jake Gaither, the retired legendary former FAMU football coach was the only Black member on the interview committee. The interview took place at the Capitol in what might have been Judge Joanos's office. The session lasted about a hour. I was apprehensive about the questions.

What would I do under certain conditions? My position was that I would look at the time the inmate spent in prison and the offense he committed, and I would make a judgment about what danger he posed to society if he was released from prison. They seemed to like my answer. Coach Gaither asked me a question. I don't remember what he asked me, but I am sure he didn't try to trip me up. Gaither had unquestioned integrity. He was a leader. When Askew appointed the largely apolitical Gaither to this committee to select a minority commissioner, he picked someone with an abundance of credibility and goodwill with the state's Black and white residents.

Although he had retired from coaching in 1969, Gaither was still, without question, the most influential Black man in Florida. His fame was nationwide. For my part, I had made a name in law enforcement and had avoided political controversy during the tumultuous 1960s. He didn't oppose me getting the job.

· · · · · · · · · · · · · · · ·

Early on, I had picked up some major endorsements. The Florida Sheriff's Association saw me, chief of a division in the Jacksonville Sheriff's Office, as representative of their thinking on the expanded Parole Commission. They saw my badge and my uniform and counted me as an ally. They were wholly unaware of my belief that the Florida prison system needed to balance punishment with compassion. They didn't see me as a threat to the punishment regime. I was not a "lock 'em up and throw away the key" law enforcement officer.

The Sheriff's Association's support was viewed as a robust, tough-on-crime endorsement. The Florida Chiefs of Police Association also threw their weight behind my appointment. Mayor Tanzler backed me. State Attorney Ed Austin also endorsed me.

Although considered as tokenism by some detractors, my title as the first Black Division Chief gave me a leg up. To other law enforcement officials, my title meant I had input within the management level of the Jacksonville Sheriff's Office. My being Chief meant something to them. Perhaps Sheriff Carson didn't always see it that way. He satisfied a political section of a community.

But when I applied to become a Parole and Probation Commission member, my title stood out. It said I was qualified for the new role. After 20 years of being on one side of the law enforcement coin, I would address the other side of crime and punishment. My supporters didn't know that I was not the tough-on-crime hawk they imagined me to be. I believed people should be held accountable for their actions. At the same time, I always believed in addressing the roots of crime rather than the fruits of crime. I was prepared to take that philosophy to the Parole and Probation Commission.

· · · · · · · · · · · · · · · ·

On Thursday, January 16, 1975, my hometown newspaper, the Florida Times-Union, reported "Chief Scriven One of Six Eyed for Parole Post." I made it out of committee. I was elated. I just needed a majority of Cabinet members to support me. They didn't know it yet as the final selection had not yet been made, but I knew I was going to Tallahassee. It was a done deal,

I told Jeannetta. We need to pack up and get ready to move.

Among the other five finalists was Mrs. Annabel Mitchell, former Superintendent of the State Prison for Women in Lowell. She was the only woman named on the list. The other Black man was Maurice Crockett, Superintendent of the state facility in Trenton for unruly youth offenders. The other finalists were Charles H. Lawson, Administrator of the Interstate Compact for the Parole and Probation Commission, a white man, Robert Bolkcom, District Supervisor and regional coordinator for the State Parole and Probation Commission, and Gerald L. Mills of Plymouth, Wisconsin. Other than Mills and me, all the other finalists lived in Tallahassee or were employed by the state in some correctional or parole/probation capacity. The deck seemed stacked in favor of insiders.

Although Askew was the governor, the choice was the Cabinet's. That included Askew, Attorney General Robert L. Shevin, Commissioner of Agriculture Doyle E. Conner, Commissioner of Education Ralph D. Turlington, Secretary of State Bruce A. Smathers, and State Treasurer Philip F. Ashler. Askew held only one vote. He did not have veto power over the selection. I just needed to get a majority to send my appointment to the Florida Senate for confirmation in April.

I soon received word that Gov. Askew already had a pick in mind. He had thrown his support behind Maurice Crockett, then a 44-year-old long-time state Division of Corrections employee. At the time, he was Superintendent of the Lancaster Home for Boys. Crockett was a fine man. He was my stiffest competition. He had the inside track. But I had law enforcement credentials. I had spent the last two decades trying to keep young men and women on the straight and narrow. I was the "new face," a dark horse candidate out of Jacksonville. Given Askew's reputation for integrity, he was unlikely to go back on his word. If he promised Crockett his support, Askew would give it, even in a losing vote.

Shevin had also announced his picks which were Crockett, Mills, Mitchell, and me. His aide was careful to say they listed the names in alphabetical order. But reading the newspaper account, I couldn't help but infer Shevin's preferences from the list. I was listed dead last among his four preferences.

Gathered in the Cabinet Room on Monday, February 17, 1975, the six white men — Askew, Shevin, Conner, Turlington, Smathers, and Ashler, considered six finalists from the 272 applicants.

Even as the Cabinet debated, I carried on with business as usual. I stayed close to the phone to hear the news. I was confident the seat was mine. If not, I would look silly in front of my wife and children. I had assured them we were moving to Tallahassee.

Then I received the call. The Cabinet had decided. I don't remember who called, but I think it was Roy Russell, then the longest-serving member on the Commission. I thanked him. I felt my prayers and desires had been answered. I was looking forward to making the move to Tallahassee.

Annabel Mitchell and I would make history. As the only woman on the list, Mitchell's selection was inevitable, given Askew's announcement a year earlier. She received all six Cabinet votes. But the Cabinet was divided when selecting the first Black commissioner. Askew and Shevin backed Crockett. Turlington, Conner, Smathers, and Ashler voted for me. Governor Askew had committed to supporting Crockett, and was true to his word. The next time there was a vacancy, Crockett got the seat. Lawson also was appointed to fill a later vacancy.

· · · · · · · · · · · · · · · ·

On the night of Monday, March 24, 1975, I stood next to Jeannetta at the front of Bethel Baptist Institutional Church and took the oath of office administered by Judge Everett Richardson. Jeannetta wore white gloves for the special occasion. I wore my favorite suit and tie that night. I watched all those in attendance to celebrate the swearing-in of Florida's first Black Parole and Probation Commissioner. Councilwoman Sallye Mathis was there that night. Sheriff Dale Carson gave me an award that night, as did the Edward Waters College Alumni Association. The Reverend Richard L. Wilson gave me a plaque from the Ministerial Alliance.

But amidst all the festivities and the applause, I couldn't help but think of my lowly beginning and just how far I'd come. But I also was heartened that all those years of striving, of showing integrity, and of standing apart had finally paid off. I was going to Tallahassee. My children saw that faith paid off. Their father was not just a dreamer, but a visionary, a prophet, even. I understood my date with destiny. Like the biblical Joseph, like the biblical Esther, I was being positioned for a time like this.

Chapter 64:
THE LAST LUNCHEON

The night Judge Edwin Richardson swore me in at Bethel Baptist Church in Jacksonville, the Sheriff and Mayor and many members of the City Commission all came to talk about me and congratulate me. I received plaques and commendations and that should have been enough, but my departure from the Sheriff's Office was not complete.

There was a longstanding tradition in the Sheriff's Office. When a command officer departed, the officer would be honored at a luncheon where his badge would be presented to him on a plaque, and good things would be said about him, about what a good job he'd done and how much he'd be missed, etc. This luncheon was considered to be my official exit. The event was catered at the Sheriff's Office's main conference room. Usually, colleagues told anecdotes and jokes about the person who was leaving at such an event. But at my luncheon, no one said a word. Most of those fellas I had known, with a few exceptions, from the time I went to the force. It was only after consolidation my movement started. I ended up in the same room with them with comparable rank. Early on, my division didn't allow promotion. After consolidation, my rapid rise from a sergeant to a lieutenant to Division Chief was under Sheriff Carson. Their respect for me was not a professional one. They looked at me as a Black chief who was promoted for Carson's political benefit. I didn't have the experience of being close with them in rank and relationship. I was a sergeant, and after consolidation, I was a lieutenant, then a chief. Meanwhile, they moved to sergeant, lieutenant, captain, then division director. There was no camaraderie with me as they moved up.

I met them at the end of the political trail with my rank. My ascendancy was more political and community-related than theirs. We didn't have a period when we built a working relationship. This luncheon was the first time any senior command staff was in my company socially. They had a problem sitting and eating with me. It was the first time Sheriff Carson and I had lunch. However, it was not his first time in a social relationship with Black folks. He could chew a little better than others who had never been with a Black person in a social situation. This was 1975. This was their first time being with me in a quasi-social setting. No one came and shook my hand or congratulated me. They had trouble eating and swallowing and making small talk. An awkwardness hung over the room. Their discomfort made me uncomfortable. I didn't eat much. It was a most unpleasant affair. The attendees drifted off to go about their business. Soon afterward, Martin and I left to have lunch.

Looking back, almost fifty years later, the details of that day are vivid in my memory. They still irritate me. The farewell luncheon was an established tradition of the Sheriff's Office. This was my goodbye. The event usually involved anecdotes and jokes and a recollection of good memories shared. This was not an easy thing for them. At the same time, they couldn't avoid it. Here I was, selected by the Governor, Cabinet, and Legislature to one of the highest positions in the state. I brought them accolades. My name, title, and new salary were all announced in the newspapers. What do you do when a Black man who you socially and professionally ignored for years is selected by the state for such a prestigious position?

The significance was too evident for them to ignore: "We have chosen one of your Black officers to go to one of the highest positions in the state." In doing that, you have the governor, the state representatives and the senators calling and saying, "Look what you have."

The local newspapers, the morning Florida Times-Union and the evening Jacksonville Journal, published articles about me. City Commissioners, the mayor, and the state attorney were all in the papers saying what a fine fellow I was. I didn't know I was that famous. TV reporters came to my house on Ribault Street. They talked to my wife and my neighbors.

The Sheriff's Office top brass didn't have a choice in this farewell, best wishes luncheon. If I had brought discredit on the department, then there would be no send-off. Instead, I had brought them honor and positive attention. Unfortunately, they didn't know what to make of it, because such an honor had been bestowed on me. My honor was Jacksonville's honor. Other cities had hoped to have the first Black man on the Commission. The only question was who. My outstanding achievement was being named the first Black chief. No other city had that recognition in Florida. That separated me from everyone else who had applied.

Chapter: 65
LEAVING ST. MARYS

In the spring of 1975, I had been pastor of First African Baptist Church of St. Marys for almost nine years. The congregation had blessed me with the honor of my first pastorate. My first day was June 12, 1966. The assignment fulfilled my desire to be bi-vocational, that is, a preacher and a policeman. For nine years of Wednesdays for Bible study and Sundays for worship service, I had driven thirty-six miles from my home in Jacksonville north on U.S. Highway 1 to St. Marys and east to the red brick building on Wheeler Street.

My time at First African Baptist in St. Marys had allowed me to develop my preaching style. I became a preacher and teacher. I was not a whooper and hollerer. I had to plant meaning in a man's mind. My desire was to plant a thought or idea in your mind that is more convicting than when it's over and your emotions wear off.

My preaching style, then as now, was to prepare my sermon during the week. I used many of the theological books I received from Dean Morse to hone my message. I was not a manuscript preacher. I didn't believe in reading from a prepared text for half an hour. I prepared the man. I prepared myself for the task ahead. I took notes and wrote down an outline of the highlights I wanted to hit. I never finished a sermon until I reached the pulpit. I needed to keep my mind and heart open to the spirit of God. There might have been something that happened when I walked into the pulpit that I might have included in the message, but I hadn't thought about while I was in the study. I wanted to prepare the man and to have such a command of the language so I wouldn't be dependent on the manuscript when I got in the pulpit. There might have been an illustration I saw on my way to church that I might include in the sermon. I was never a manuscript preacher. I used notes but I don't read from a script.

My average sermon was about twenty minutes to a half hour. Service started at 11 a.m. and we were usually out by 12:30 p.m. One of the members of the church, Rosa Parrish, was designated as the person who would prepare my diner. She was a widow and one of the best cooks in Georgia. She was appointed and paid by the church to provide a Sunday meal for me, my family and guests. After dinner I was provided a place to rest. I employed her daughter as part of the special police project in Jacksonville. She commuted daily from St. Marys to Jacksonville to the center five days a week.

There were members who invited me to dinner from time to time. As it was a small community, there were always more invitations than there were Sundays to fill. But Ms. Parrish had the primary responsibility of caring for us. There was a Sister Gracie Green, wife of Dean Bernard Green, who also prepared our meals. She made a shrimp salad that was unforgettable. Her son, Bernard Greene Jr., and Lanse became close friends after college and reconnected years later in Tampa.

St. Marys is a seaport town. One member of the church owned a shrimp boat, so fish and shrimp were plentiful. I was blessed to enjoy the delicious bounty every week

Most Sundays after service, Sister Parrish prepared a sumptuous meal for me and the family to eat and a guest room to rest. If I had evening service, I would return to the church. If not, we would drive home to Jacksonville. At first, Jeannetta was a little hesitant about me enjoying somebody else's Sunday dinner. But eventually she came to enjoy being catered to. The food and the cooks were excellent — country food, and southern Christian hospitality. Every month, I was getting invitations, not just from First African Baptist members, but from other congregations. That was just part of St. Marys community life. I had deep roots in that area. My father's family is from Camden County. My grandmother was a Polite, a common surname in the area. Another grandparent was a Sullivan. My grandfather and great-grandfather are buried in Camden County. I am deeply rooted there. It almost seemed inevitable that I was called to preach in St. Marys.

The first year I went to St. Marys, Sister Carrie Alderman, one of the deaconesses, baked me a fruitcake for Christmas. When I came to preach the Sunday before Christmas, she hand delivered a fruitcake neatly wrapped. Every year after that without failure, my family enjoyed Sister Alderman's fruitcake for the holiday season. Decades later, even after I left for Tallahassee, the tradition continued, and my fruitcake arrived at my house in Lafayette Oaks. After Sister Alderman died, her daughter Jackie Alderman-Moses, whose wedding I officiated, continues the tradition even today. Every year without exception, our fruitcake arrives. We share it with Lanse and our granddaughter, Danielle, Rosemary's daughter.

My predecessor, Rev. Patterson, had built an elegant new edifice in 1965, the year before I arrived. Seven years later, I led the congregation's one hundred and twenty members as we burned the mortgage. That Sunday, I was delighted to share the moment with a former pastor, the Rev. Gilbert Mizell, who had led First African Baptist from 1909 to 1935. Imagine the struggle of those dark years for the Negro race. But Rev. Mizell remembered them as a period of God's blessing and spiritual growth. He served the church in the years before Social Security was introduced. Despite his long tenure, at First African Baptist, he was not receiving a pension from the congregation. Discovering that, I convinced the church board to provide him with a pension until he died. At age one-hundred-and-two, Rev. Mizell was still visiting the sick and comforting the dying. He occasionally was invited to preach at area churches.

That Sunday, we celebrated burning the mortgage, my sermon topic was "Who built First African Baptist Church?" The answer is "the Lord built it."

Unfortunately, a year after I left, fire destroyed the building.

· · · · · · · · · · · · · · · ·

During my time as pastor of First Baptist, moments of joy and euphoria alike were interspersed with occasions of pain and tragedy. I cannot forget preaching the Sunday after Dr. King was assassinated in 1968. I recall the enormity of the task of helping my rural small-town congregation navigate the troubled time when cities all across the country burned with Black anger. The pain of the tragedy of Dr. King's death had begun to recede in our collective memories, when on February 3, 1971, my congregation was rocked by another unspeakable loss.

St. Marys and much of Camden County was an economic landscape scarce of well-paying jobs. Some men made a living on the water, others in agriculture. The Thiokol chemical factory in Woodbine was a major source of employment for many of the Black women in Camden County. Woodbine was the Camden County seat about seventeen and a half miles from St. Marys as the crow flies.

Opened in 1960, the plant prospered during the next decade, building rockets for the space program. When budget cuts kicked in after the 1969 moon landing, the factory focused on munitions manufacturing in support of the Vietnam war. Employees began the production of the CS-2 gas, 81mm, and 40mm for our military. In 1969, Thiokol was awarded a

U. S. Army contract for the production of 758,000 trip flares. Their workforce grew to 600 employees. The plant operated three shifts and was a twenty-four-hour operation. On the morning of February 3, 1971, a fire broke out and was followed by an explosion heard as far away as Jacksonville. Twenty-five workers died as a result of the initial blast and four others later succumbed to their injuries. Fifty others were injured in addition to the twenty-nine who lost their lives. My cousin Cheryl Sullivan was among the dead. Among my congregation, the explosion claimed the life of Mae Hazel Davis. The mother of two was planning to close on a house the day she died. She took the down payment for her mortgage with her that day. The conflagration took her life and her family's dreams of homeownership that day. I was not among the Jacksonville police and EMS personnel who responded to the tragedy that chilly Wednesday morning. I was working far from the front lines. But in the ensuing days, weeks and months, my skills as a pastor and counselor came to bear as I comforted the grieving families in St. Marys and surrounding communities. A year after the tragedy I, along with high school principal Peter Baker and the pastor of the First Baptist Church in Woodbine, organized a memorial service to remember the dead and to honor those who survived. A faded newspaper clipping from that day reminds me of my role during that difficult time.

·················

In 1974, when I became aware of the imminent vacancy on the Parole and Probation Commission, I told Jeannetta about my plan to apply and my conviction that the position was mine. I had told no one else. My children were aware since the "Going to Tallahassee" notes were all over our house. I had not shared my vision for moving to Tallahassee with anyone at First African Baptist, not the deacon, not the board, no one. I was honored to be their pastor and shepherd, but I felt God had led me in another direction. My selection as the first Black man on the Parole and Probation Commission was confirmation that my faith was not misplaced. I knew my ministry there was coming to an end.

·················

We had a church business meeting after the morning service. I told them I had accepted a position on the Parole and Probation Commission and that I was moving to Tallahassee. They were disappointed when I told them I was leaving. They wanted me to stay. I could not. I would not try to pastor a church in southeast Georgia and live in Tallahassee. It was one thing to commute 36 miles from Jacksonville, but another thing to commute for

200 miles from Tallahassee to St. Marys. They were willing for me to have an associate and assistant pastor, but that was impractical. But there were no hard feelings. They respected my decision. On the night I was sworn in at Bethel Baptist Institutional Church in Jacksonville, the chairman of the First African Baptist Church of St. Marys' Deacon Board spoke on the program. The congregation gave me and my family a silver plate tea set, one we never used. From time to time, Jeannetta pulled out the cloth and the cleaner to remove the black soot coating the pieces, and polished the silver set to its shiny best. Decades later, we gifted it to our daughter-in-law, Lanse's wife, Federal Judge Mary Scriven, the first African American woman appointed to the federal bench in Florida. It had sentimental value. After I was sworn in, I preached a few times before I left for Tallahassee.

Although moving to the Parole and Probation Commission was the right decision, it was difficult leaving behind my small community church. I was held in high esteem. Jeannetta didn't cook on Sundays. Members competed with each other for the chance to host me and my family after Sunday service. They treasured my leadership and wanted to shower love and generosity on Jeannetta, the children and me. During most of my tenure, it was six of us — Jeannetta and I and the children, Rosemary, Reenee, Lansing, and young Leonard. After lunch, there was always a place for me to rest. I was attached to that community. The children and adults regarded me as their spiritual leader. They treated me with dignity and respect. My leaving was a very emotional experience I had not experienced before. At that time, that was my first and only pastorate. I had developed a deep relationships with people all over the Camden County community. I was getting ready to say farewell to a ministerial and pastoral relationship that had existed for nine years. How do you say goodbye after that kind of experience?

This was the congregation that gave me a chance to fulfill my calling. You can be a preacher, but being a pastor gives you a certain professional identity within the ministry that you would not otherwise have. You have people that God have asked you to shepherd. That's an honor.

For nine years, I christened their children, married them, buried their parents. I baptized them in the indoor pool when they found Jesus. I saw their children grow up in Sunday school and then go off to college. I officiated at weddings. I buried too many members to count. I comforted them in times of grief and sickness.

I had preached the Sunday after Dr. King was killed in 1968 and the members of St. Marys were looking to me to find answers at that moment when others were erupting with violence and frustration over the death of the Black prophet.

• • • • • • • • • • • • • • •

I left St. Marys on March 24, 1975. I moved to Tallahassee leaving behind Jeannetta and the children. At the time, her father was battling cancer. He died on my one-year anniversary at the Parole and Probation Commission. And Rev. Mizell? In the ensuing years, I returned to St. Marys time and again for special occasions when members personally asked me to come. But I didn't return as official Pastor. I returned to St. Marys to participate in Rev. Mizell's funeral in March 1976. He was 106 years old.

Chapter 66:
ALONE IN TALLAHASSEE

In the spring of 1975, when I was appointed to the Parole and Probation Commission, my older son Lanse was attending Episcopal School of Jacksonville. He was a lanky six foot, two inches. He played center and was the leading scorer on the Eagles basketball team. He was a good player for a white private school. He was a star and fostered basketball dreams of perhaps playing the game in college. But I was realistic. My son was good enough for Episcopal. He was captain of the team. I wouldn't ask him to leave his quality private high school to come to Tallahassee to attend Lincoln or Leon High. He needed to focus on academics instead of athletics. Still, he thrived at Episcopal, so I didn't want to uproot him. Jeannetta was still teaching in Duval County Schools, but she would have been happy to quit and come with me. Rosemary, my older daughter, was off at the University of Florida. Reenee, the daughter we had adopted, had moved out and was living on her own. Leonard, our youngest, was still in elementary school. It didn't matter where he went.

When I drove west on Interstate 10 and moved to Tallahassee, I left the rest of the family behind. An acquaintance, Josh Williams, who taught journalism at FAMU and wrote for the Florida Star, a Black newspaper based in Jacksonville, found an older, single woman who had a room with a private entrance. I rented a room and I stayed with her.

When I came to Tallahassee, I was at a disadvantage. I was wholly unprepared for domestic life without my wife. I grew up with three sisters. They did the cooking and the cleaning inside while my older brother and I were responsible for keeping the yard clean. During my twenty years of marriage, Jeannetta had always cooked. I didn't know how to boil water. I couldn't boil an egg. The Probation and Parole Commission Office stood on Thomasville Road next to Whataburger, the Texas-based chain that sold the best hamburgers around. There was also a Morrison's Restaurant nearby. My basic meal every day was whatever Whataburger was serving. Thankfully, when I went home on the weekend, Jeannetta would pack up food for a few days.

After a few months, I found and bought a dilapidated duplex on Pasco and Saxon streets, just south of the Florida A&M University campus. The structure was raining on one side and pouring down on the next. I had it fixed up, moved into one unit, and I rented the next. I didn't tell my wife because I knew she'd object. But that summer, when she and the kids were out of school, they came to Tallahassee to stay with me.

I struggled socially in those early days. Here I was in Tallahassee, one of the highest-ranking African Americans in state government. With FAMU, the city had a sizable Black middle-class population. But I was an outsider from Jacksonville who was accustomed to sitting and eating with my wife and children, but here I was, eating alone. It was by choice. I didn't want to eat lunch with other commissioners. We had spent enough time together already. I wanted to have lunch with someone other than the people with whom I worked. But at the same time, I had to be circumspect. I was a forty-one-year-old, healthy, powerful, married Black man living alone more than two hours away from his wife and children. It would have been easy for me to accept the company of a young woman who wanted to share my lunch table. But I was mindful of scandal. I had just received a history-making appointment. I had to be careful. I must say it's only by God's grace that I survived with my integrity intact and my reputation untarnished.

One of the young women in the office asked to borrow $40. I haven't gotten that money back. I didn't take that bait. Occasionally, women asked me if I wanted them to join me for lunch. I always said no, even though I hated eating alone. I wanted a meal with somebody who was not part of the staff. If I invited someone out for lunch, I was not looking for a date.

One big test was choosing an executive secretary. There were no Black executive secretaries except those employed at FAMU. I was not tempted to hire a young white woman with blue eyes, blond hair, and a miniskirt. I saw myself being in a situation driving alone at night with a young white woman in my car. Even in 1975, that raised eyebrows in certain parts of the state. So instead, I selected a homely, older woman to be my executive secretary. She was competent and efficient, but she was no looker. I don't mean to be sexist or offensive, but it was important for me to find a secretary that would raise no eyebrows. If anyone said I was going out with her, I would have been doing her a favor. For my executive assistant, I also opted for caution.

I hired a young man who had graduated from FAMU Law School but had never passed the Bar exam. He had a learning disability. I couldn't teach him the elementary things of doing the parole hearings. He struggled to keep up and to handle hearings. I got a lot of criticism for not hiring an assistant who could help me. But I stood by my decision. I was looking at my white colleagues. They would have a problem with me driving around with a young white woman. I didn't doubt my ability to avoid an extramarital relationship. I just didn't want to take the chance of traveling around with a young white woman in my car and causing suspicion. If I had this young man, it wouldn't be a problem, I figured. All the other commissioners hired a secretary who knew the system. They would have been working closely with me daily.

As a minister, I made it a rule to protect myself from sexual entrapment. I didn't associate socially with people with whom I had a professional relationship. Jeannetta stayed in Jacksonville for six years when I went to the Parole Commission. Many women knew that. They tried all kinds of things to trap me. I didn't know women could be so devious. Living alone in Tallahassee taught me more about the opposite sex than twenty years of marriage. I stayed away from young white women and Black women. The Black women I associated with were older, mature people who were not attracted to me nor me to them. That helped me. During the summer, Jeannetta came to Tallahassee, and my conduct was always above board. I couldn't have lasted without the Lord watching over me and friends who knew I didn't want dinner and something else when I said, "let's go to dinner." Even though I was in my forties, I was still naive. I didn't know women played that game. Maybe, I just wasn't that smart.

Being the first Black person appointed to the Parole Commission, I could not afford to be identified with any problems or scandal. I had to be careful. My ministerial responsibility and Christian commitment served as a buffer. Other than the summer times, I lived in Tallahassee and drove home to Jacksonville every week. I commuted home every week for the first six years.

One lifeline during those early years was a Sunrise Fellowship prayer breakfast I had with other Black men and women who worked in supervisory or managerial positions with the State of Florida. Among the group was state Supreme Court Justice Hatchett. We were both members of Bethel Institutional Baptist Church in Jacksonville and were friends. Many Sundays we sat in the same pews to hear pastor Rev. Rudolph W. McKissick Sr.

We were part of the Black leadership within state government as Governor Askew tried to bring more Black folks into positions of authority in the traditionally lily-white state bureaucracy. Others were James Matthews, attorney Harold Knowles, and Herbert Alexander. A professor of education and business ethics, Alexander was FAMU's first vice president for Student Affairs and followed in the footsteps of his mentor, the Rev. C. K. Steele, as pastor of Bethel Missionary Baptist Church in Tallahassee. Alexander died of cancer in 1994. Among the group was Sharon Wynne, who worked for a state agency.

The group met at 6 a.m. on the first Monday of each month. We studied a Bible lesson, and a member of the group would make a presentation. We met once a month for the fellowship breakfast and reading the scripture, and once a year we sponsored a family seminar to encourage men and women to be better spouses. We were not competing with churches. There were some people who might come to a fellowship breakfast who were not part of a congregation. Our purpose was to try to get men, especially, to be more involved in their spiritual development. We met at the Howard Johnson on Apalachee Parkway for breakfast. Afterward we went to work.

The staff reserved space in the dining area for about twenty or thirty. We would invite members of the fellowship to speak. Occasionally, we would go outside of the fellowship and bring someone in to speak to our group. When circumstances changed, we found another place that served breakfast where we could meet.

That prayer breakfast fellowship was a defensive weapon that helped us survive and thrive in an environment that was not accustomed to dealing with Black men and women in positions of authority. Our friendships deepened even as some of us got other positions and left Tallahassee. As the first Black State Supreme Court Judge, Judge Hatchett had to be very careful with whom he had lunch. We were favorite lunch partners. He was very instrumental in the development the spiritual prayer group.

Judge Hatchett and I were born the same year. The Clearwater native graduated from Florida A&M University in 1954 before entering Howard University law school. In 1959, when he took the Florida bar exam, Hatchett couldn't stay in the segregated hotel where the test was administered. He and Leander Shaw, another legal giant, were not allowed to sit with the white test-takers, but were assigned to sit in another area.

Like me, Hatchett was appointed by Gov. Reubin Askew in 1975, the first African American to sit on Florida's highest court in its history. Hatchett was a civil rights legend in our state. He championed Black voting and equal rights in state and federal courts before becoming an assistant U.S. Attorney. He had served as a federal magistrate in the Middle District of Florida before Gov. Askew elevated him to the Supreme Court. A man of integrity and generosity, Judge Hatchett mentored Lanse and his future wife Mary, who both graduated from Florida State University law school.

During his first year of law school, Lanse had a problem with one concept in his Civil Procedure class. Lanse and his fiancée, Mary Stinson, were both first year law students at FSU when I arranged a visit for them to meet Judge Hatchett. I don't know how the subject came up, but I told Judge Hatchett Lanse was struggling with the concept of specific personal jurisdiction in his Civil Procedure course.

When a plaintiff wants to file a claim, the court must have personal jurisdiction over the party being sued. If someone sues a Texas resident in Florida, it is very difficult unless that Texas resident meets certain criteria, such as owning property in Florida or breaching a contract for services due in Florida. If not, it's a due process issue. Florida courts don't have jurisdiction over non-residents except in certain circumstances.

Once Judge Hatchett explained it to him, Lansing said the lightbulb immediately went off.

Lansing and Mary met at Duke and entered law school together. They were married in 1988, the year after they both graduated law school. Lansing later served as clerk to Judge Hatchett, before entering private practice.

Mary Scriven also went into private practice, but her destiny was public service. She was appointed a federal magistrate in 1997, a decade after completing law school. Like Judge Hatchett, Mary Scriven is a pioneer. She was the first female African American appointed to the federal bench in Florida. Eleven years later, after three tries, Mary was appointed to be a federal judge in 2008. She has said in interviews, that seeing Judge Hatchett gave her "the audacity to dream and believe that she could ascend to a similar position." She strives to provide the same inspiration to others.

I am happy to say that my friendship with Judge Hatchett enabled Lansing and Mary to get to know that great man. They really benefited from his mentorship.

Chapter 67:
THE OUTSIDER

When I was appointed to the Parole and Probation Commission, I joined a group of white men who had been rewarded for their decades of service to the agency with a governor's appointment.

Chairman Ray E. Howard had been a Commission employee since 1956, longer than Commissioner Armond R. Cross. Like me, Howard was a native of Jacksonville, a husband, and a father of four. But unlike me, Howard was the ultimate insider. A University of Florida graduate, he had worked for the Parole and Probation Commission in various roles since the year after I joined the Jacksonville Police Department. He rose through the ranks to become a regional coordinator for the Commission in 1968. He was appointed to the Commission on October 20, 1971. Commissioners J. Hopps Barker, Cale R. Keller, and Roy W. Russell had been Commission employees since 1942, 1945, and 1941, respectively. Russell had the distinction of being the Commission's first professional employee.

Newly appointed Commissioner Anabel Mitchell, a Division of Corrections employee since 1958, had risen through the ranks to become a deputy director for inmate treatment. An eighth Commissioner, Louis L. Wainwright, served as an ex officio member of the commission. He could vote on policy matters but not on parole or probation decisions. A former Gainesville cop, Wainwright had served as head of the Division of Corrections since 1962. When it was renamed the Department of Offender Rehabilitation on July 1, 1975, he was named secretary.

As the other new appointee, I was not just the only non-white commissioner, but I was also a distinct outsider career-wise. I was the rookie, a virtual newcomer to Florida's vast punishment apparatus.

• • • • • • • • • • • • • • • •

The Parole and Probation Commission was charged with reviewing the parole status of inmates. Commissioners weighed the fate of inmates by sifting through hundreds of case files prepared each week by hearing examiners. These white employees visited the inmates behind bars and questioned them to judge whether they were fit to be released back into society.

The nature of my job and the difficult task that faced me when I joined the Commission in spring 1975 were vividly captured in the 34th Annual Report sent to Governor Askew and the Cabinet that fall. Our mission was summed up in the 85-page document: "The total function of the Florida Parole and Probation Commission is maximum protection of society, coupled with dedicated efforts to rehabilitate every offender who is willing to do his or her part to return to the outside world."

The Commission's "compassionate" philosophy sounded progressive enough — "Every human being deserved a second chance" to be guided back into the mainstream of society. Commission Chair Ray E. Howard believed commissioners had always given men and women that chance after intensive study of the probability that the offender could be rehabilitated.

When I came aboard, it was a time of change and tensions over budget cuts and legislation aimed at splitting the Commission's staff. That spring, the Legislature passed the Correctional Organization Act of 1975 that split off the field staff from the Parole and Probation Commission and triggered a legal fight over whether the legislation was constitutional. While the question remained unanswered, the Commission's corridors and offices were rife with uncertainty, anxiety, and apprehension.

Howard's letter to Governor Askew and the Cabinet reflected the issues his commission faced. "Activities this year have been hampered by travel limitations, freezing of positions, and curtailment of programs such as the Multiphasic Diagnostic and Treatment Centers, which are alternative programs for the courts to imprisonment," Howard wrote.

The Chairman complained that the austerity budget had affected all areas of the Commission operation. The average parole and probation officer caseload remained almost double the National Professional Standards, which seriously hampered the Commission's "rehabilitative effectiveness." The result, Howard found, was a "leveling off of the statewide caseload" that resulted in fewer cases placed on probation by the courts and a drop in the number of parole releases.

At the same time, our state's prison population continued to soar. Howard warned that overcrowded conditions posed an ever-increasing threat to the welfare and security of the correction system. Because of budgetary cuts, the demise of the Commission's misdemeanant program was projected to decrease the total parole and probation caseload in the next fiscal year, generate further overcrowding in the county jails and cause court backlogs. Howard's predictions were right on the money.

Chapter 68:
THE KNOWLEDGE OF SOCRATES, THE WISDOM OF SOLOMON

Under Florida law, inmates were eligible for parole the day they began their sentence. That was unless they had been sentenced to life without parole. The fact was that 98 percent of all inmates would be released back into society. The Commission's job was to decide who deserved to be released early on parole.

Our parole process began with the field staff preparing an exhaustive pre-sentence investigation or evaluation of the offender's background and history. The report provided the Commission and prison officials with a composite of the inmate's prior criminal record, circumstances of the offense, employment history, reputation, social background, family history, medical and psychiatric evaluations, education, and a host of other information that helped to classify the type of custody, to establish rehabilitative programming and to provide information for parole consideration.

Regularly scheduled interviews of the inmates provided safeguards that "there were no forgotten men or women in prison." This safeguard ensured that each inmate and their case were studied and reviewed for possible parole release. The information was regularly updated. Commission Parole Examiners conducted interviews that provided for face-to-face contact with inmates within six months if they had received a sentence of five years or less. Those sentenced for more than five years were guaranteed an interview within a year of being sentenced. After the initial parole interview, inmates were interviewed at least once a year.

The Commission's field staff was the lifeblood of the parole and probation system. My fellow commissioners and I relied heavily on the staff for numerous reports, verified field investigations, and proper supervision of parolees and probationers. That was a vital and integral part of the parole decision-making process. Success or failure depended on the reliability of these factors. We had to trust the information we were given before making life or death decisions about inmates.

We also had to be confident the staff could carry out the conditions of parole supervision according to the Commission's intent. Since the Parole and Probation Commission was created in 1941, it had decided that parole matters were totally removed from political influences — a very different environment from what preceded it.

In the Commissioner's Tallahassee office, we read the files of inmates who would be up for parole. I was handed a batch of 100 or 200 files to review each week. Each file represented a husband or brother, son, mother, sister, or daughter with anxious relatives awaiting their fate.

I had to read those files on Monday and Tuesday. I have to vote for paroles on Wednesday. The inmates we agreed on are processed immediately. The Commission established two panels with four commissioners to expedite the parole decision-making process. Three Commissioners served on each panel, and the Chairman served on each panel. Parole decisions required at least four votes. If the first panel failed to garner four votes, the case was then referred to the second panel, which assured that a minimum of four votes were cast either for or against parole. If there was disagreement, the chair cast the deciding vote.

・・・・・・・・・・・・・・・・

The Commission had its own rhythm. The field staff prepared our cases. We received the case files on Thursdays and began reviewing them with the help of our executive assistants. I spent many weekends reviewing files. We had a responsibility to review all the files to be ready to vote on Wednesday. If that meant working Saturday and Sunday nights, we had to have read those files so we could vote yea or nay on each case. Defendants had attorneys to represent them; law enforcement or victims who opposed an inmate's parole also appeared. We set time limits for the defense, then those on the opposing side spoke for equal time. It was a tribunal hearing. We listened to the pros and cons and could ask questions like judges on the Supreme Court. We had nearly as much power, just without the black robes.

Every Wednesday morning, we gathered to weigh whether one inmate should be released while another should remain behind bars. We met Wednesday mornings at eight and worked through until lunch. After lunch, we'd return and deliberate until six or seven in the evening. Since the

Commission meetings were public, they usually drew a crowd of reporters, especially if an inmate whose crime had gained notoriety was coming up for parole. The state's most prominent newspapers and the wire services loved to cover sensational cases.

We had parole sentencing guidelines that were later introduced by the legislators who were upset by the release of inmates who went on to commit more crimes.

The public was also invited. Parents, siblings, and spouses came to talk to us about their sons and daughters, fathers, and mothers. Attorneys were also there representing inmates. One woman called to say we shouldn't release her son. We did anyway, and he went home and killed her.

It was difficult when a state attorney opposed parole for someone they had prosecuted in court and had sent to prison. If the court has already determined a sentence of twenty years, it's up to the Parole Commission to determine how much of that twenty years the inmate should serve. The sentencing judge might send a letter opposing parole. You might also. Once a judge called me and said "I think the jurors got it wrong. I don't think this man should have been convicted. You men don't have to run for re-election, but I do."

The only way a commissioner could be removed was for malfeasance. Our six-year terms overlapped the four-year terms of the governor who appointed us. That was designed to protect commissioners from political interference. Crime and punishment were a potent political mix.

The recidivism rate went up sometimes, and sometimes it went down. The longer a man was in prison, the less likely were his chances of ever returning to being a productive citizen. Sometimes, depending on the case, someone famous showed up, and the cameras would be on you. We got a lot of interest from the newspapers.

If we released a woman inmate on parole and she didn't re-offend, we were credited with her success. However, if a man or woman was released early and victimized someone, that often resulted in a public outcry and "Willie Horton" moments. It exposed the Commission to political pressure and public displeasure. It undermined the whole system of probation and parole. If the inmate re-offended, he hadn't failed, but we did.

We had to weigh the evidence in front of us to decide. You cannot predict a man's behavior. It was a weekly Solomonic role. Be compassionate and release an inmate, or be harsh and protect society from a likely repeat offender. In Chairman Howard's opinion, ours was no easy job. He believed the decision to parole or not to parole was a sensitive, tedious, and time-consuming process. To be a good commissioner, Howard felt, required "the knowledge of Socrates, the insight of a clairvoyant, and the wisdom of Solomon."

I possessed none of the three. But as a Black man, a preacher, a father, and a former police officer, I brought a level of understanding of the nature of crime and punishment, particularly as it affected Black folks. None of the white men who had occupied the commission seats in the previous 34 years had. I am not saying they were unjust commissioners. They were not equipped to give my people justice. They were conservative. That meant Black inmates rarely received the benefit of the commissioners' doubts. It was well-documented that Black men served longer sentences than whites for similar or lesser offenses.

Chapter 69:
JUSTICE AND MERCY

The Parole Commission was an exciting place to be deciding who would be released from prison. The prison population was high. Each week we made decisions that allowed men and women to walk free. But the prison pipeline was never-ending. When one prison bed emptied, another inmate was ready and waiting to occupy it.

The Commission not only evaluated case files for inmates. Sometimes we would get a call from an institution, "You need to get an inmate out of here because we need to have two or three inmates guarding him to protect him from other inmates."

Prisons are brutal. Most of the people in prison are victims of the system of inequity. Certain things were evident in the profiles of people in prison. Most of the people behind bars lacked education. Most of them were poor. That always stood out. Suppose we could eliminate some of the socio-economic factors contributing to crime. In that case, we could reduce the number of imprisoned people. The person's age when he is first arrested, his first encounter with the prison system, his color are all factors. Blacks were arrested and incarcerated earlier in their experience than whites. When a white officer stops a white kid, and he identifies with him, he sees himself in that kid, someone, who needs and deserves a second chance. When that white officer arrests a Black kid, he rarely has any mercy. He sees someone very different. He feels he needs to protect society from that Black kid, so he arrests him. The charges and incarceration are the likely outcomes when an overwhelmingly white criminal justice system processes that Black kid.

• • • • • • • • • • • • • • •

The year 1975 was what we called the post-Watergate period. Republican Richard Nixon was long gone from the White House, disgraced by his paranoia and criminal proclivities. Gerald Ford was president in his stead. The war in Vietnam was winding down to its inevitable conclusion. The fall of Saigon on April 30, 1975, provided a sad backdrop to the chaos at home, especially of Black America. The riots were mainly behind us, but our neighborhoods remained unsafe. The FBI reported that the crime rate jumped more than 18 percent over the previous year. Tough on crime rhetoric won elections and filled prisons. There were more men and women in prison than at any time in the country's history, their report stated. Crime and punishment were expensive solutions. It costs taxpayers millions to house and feed inmates, construct new prisons, and provide rehabilitation so former inmates can become productive, law-abiding citizens. Building prisons was expensive. Building a new prison in 1975 cost at least $22,000 per bed.

It was cheaper to pay a young man's tuition to any one of Florida's public universities than to keep him locked up in prison. The Commission reported that it cost about $6,000 per year to house an inmate in an institution. It cost $15 a day to house a prisoner. Florida prisons were bursting at the seams because of overcrowding. The Department of Correction erected tents on prison grounds to provide temporary housing to handle the overflow. New prisons couldn't be built fast enough to accommodate the influx of new inmates.

Before I arrived in 1975, the general public regarded white men on Florida Parole and Probation Commission as conservative. They were seen as one of the tightest paroling agencies in the entire country. When you consider our Southern neighbors, that was quite an ignoble distinction. Commissioners were criticized for not doing enough to ease the state's prison population crisis.

Some facts did not support the Commission's conservative reputation. The statistics showed that the Commission was releasing more and more inmates on parole with each passing year before my arrival. In 1969-70, the number of released inmates who had served their entire sentences was similar to the number of those released on parole. By 1974-75, the balance had shifted to almost three times as many inmates were released on parole as those released after serving their complete sentences. The numbers couldn't hide that Black inmates were being denied parole at much higher rates than whites. That wasn't surprising since the examiners were white, and prison officials and guards were overwhelmingly white. Until I arrived at the office on Thomasville Road in Tallahassee, all the Parole and Probation Commissioners were Southern white men.

Chapter 70:
PRISON VISITS

Another of our responsibilities as commissioners was to hold hearings with released inmates who had violated the terms of their probation or parole. Any former inmate arrested for a violation was detained in jail. We would hold a probable cause hearing to determine if he had violated one or more conditions of his parole. That's a violation hearing. If the Orange County Sheriff's Office arrested him for robbery, that's prima facie. We still had to hold a hearing.

Suppose his probation officer issued an order revoking his parole. Perhaps he was supposed to be home by 8 p.m., and he wasn't there, or he was supposed to have a drug test, and he didn't show up, or showed up and tested positive. What if he didn't have a job so he couldn't afford to pay his restitution? These are technical violations. If the ex-inmate committed a technical violation, the parole officer could recommend he be found guilty of a violation but returned to supervision. He would remain free but would have to follow the rule of his release. If it was a technical violation, what was in the best interest of society?

What if he committed a criminal violation? What if he was arrested for robbing a service station? If the ex-felon committed another crime, there would be a probable cause hearing to determine if he committed a criminal violation and to decide whether the person's parole would be revoked. If the hearing determined he had committed a criminal violation, we would issue the order to revoke his probation, and that inmate would serve the remainder of his original sentence before he starts to serve the new sentence if he's convicted of the latest crime.

We have an investment in him. We released him from prison. What are we going to do with this investment? If we return him to prison, we have to take care of him and take care of his family. Do we want to take responsibility for his health and care? Which action would be in the best interest of the state? We have no choice. By re-offending, that inmate is saying he's not ready for his freedom.

Decision of prison or freedom became a political thing. Let's execute people, and that would stop crime. Let's lock them up. We had more people in prison, but the crime rate was still increasing. Are we still going to continue with the idea that long sentences deter crime?

What we have lost are men and women who have a vision of the problem and a solution and who are willing to stand by their convictions regardless of public criticism or the political cost, even if it means losing an election.

• • • • • • • • • • • • • • • •

The probation hearings were at the Processing Center at Lake Butler, about 45 miles from my home in Jacksonville. Commissioners rotated the assignment, but I volunteered whenever it became their turn. It was to my advantage. It was no inconvenience for me. They would have to spend two or three days at Lake Butler. It was a short trip home for me, and it gave me a few more nights at home in my own bed.

Commissioners drove to Lake Butler for hearings on Thursday and Friday. During the weeks when it was my turn, I went home to Jacksonville on Wednesday night. On Thursday morning, I would drive to the facility at Lake Butler to interview inmates and conduct hearings all day, then return to Jacksonville. That way, I could attend Lanse's basketball game and other activities. At least, the Scriven household on Ribault Road felt normal for a few days. Since it was convenient for me to drive home and go back and forth to Lake Butler, I volunteered to take other commissioners' turns. After all, since they didn't live nearby, they had to stay overnight in a hotel while they conducted hearings. My weekly routine would later become a source of controversy and generate unwanted headlines.

• • • • • • • • • • • • • • • •

The Lake Butler Reception and Medical Center was a state prison and hospital for men. Located in Union County, the facility was built in 1968 as an intake and processing point for all-male state prisoners and a secure medical facility.

Everyone taken into custody in the state prison system had to go to a reception center to be processed. Each inmate was classified to determine which prison they would be assigned to. Their classification determined where they served their sentence, and where they were locked up was dependent on the offense they committed, length of sentence, age, and rap sheet.

If an inmate received a 20-year sentence, that inmate would be sent to a maximum-security facility. If the inmate has a murder conviction, we could not send him to a low or medium-security facility. We didn't send younger inmates to institutions where older inmates could take advantage of them. A 17-year-old inmate would not be sent to a high-security institution to be preyed upon by older inmates housed there.

Chapter 71:
CHAIRMAN SCRIVEN

I had served on the Commission for just one year when the chairmanship became vacant. Howard's two-year term was over, and all the other longtime Commission members had already served as chairman. There was left the newbies, Anabel Mitchell and me. There was a sense that the white men didn't want Mitchell to get the gavel. Wainwright, the eighth commissioner, was ineligible to be elected chairman. The role carried real authority. The commission chairman possessed administrative duties. He could make hiring and recruitment decisions, in addition to casting the tie-breaking vote on parole and probation decisions.

Charles Scriven had made a good impression on the other commissioners from the public perception. I was Black, and I had a police background, so my law enforcement cred was in great shape. There was some suspicion that Mitchell's close ties with the director of the Department of Corrections made her vulnerable if she had become chair. He would have been able to run her. I was newer, and some commissioners believed they could manage me. I was confident I could handle the job. While I was new in the ballgame, my management and administrative skills were proven. The rules were different from being in a police department.

Governor Askew was in my corner because it made his administration look good. I could not have done it without the Governor who believed that the system needed a Black voice who could understand the plight of the thousands of black men and women sent to Florida's prisons. We didn't have any Black parole examining officers visiting inmates in state penitentiaries or executive secretaries working alongside those who made life-changing decisions. We were not getting Blacks paroled because we were not getting recommendations from the prison or the examining officers who were white. White parole hearing examiners didn't understand the issues of Black inmates who might be returning home to share a room or an uncertain job situation.

The Commission used 14 general factors parole examiners considered in making recommendations for parole. As commissioners, we considered those same factors in making our final decision. The factors included:
1. The prisoner's personality, including his maturity, stability, sense of responsibility, and any development in his personality which may promote or hinder his conformity to laws.
2. The prisoner's conduct in the institution, particularly whether he has taken advantage of the opportunities for self-improvement afforded by the institutional programs.
3. The prisoner's ability and readiness to assume obligations and undertake responsibilities.
4. The prisoner's family status and if he has relatives who display an interest in him, or whether he has other close and constructive associations in the community.
5. The prisoner's employment history, occupational skills, and stability of his past employment.
6. The prisoner's attitude toward law and authority.
7. The prisoner's conduct and attitude during any previous experience of probation or parole and recency of each experience.
8. The prisoner's attitude toward parole.
9. Observations of the court officials, law enforcement officials, and other interested community members.
10. The type of crime(s) and surrounding circumstances for which the prisoner was imprisoned.
11. The prisoner's prior criminal record, including the nature and circumstances, recency, and frequency of previous offenses.
12. The prisoner's past use of narcotics or past habitual or excessive use of alcohol.
13. The type of residence, neighborhood, or community in which the inmate plans to live.
14. The adequacy of the prisoner's parole plan as well as other factors.

My sitting on the Commission made a difference in how Black men and women were treated. Here we have a "colored man" or a "nigger" up for parole. Should we release him?

When I came in, all of that changed. The other commissioners had never seen anybody like me. I was in a position to make decisions. My philosophy was one of compassion, not just punishment. Many people sought revenge instead of rehabilitation. The fact that I had been in the ministry brought a complete change of attitude to people coming up for parole. The others' backgrounds were in Corrections. My ministerial background helped me to look at a man as more than a criminal, but as a man with a soul that needed redemption. That made a big difference. But there were some instances when my colleagues agreed to parole those I never would have paroled.

Chapter 72:
MURPH THE SURF

Some people got long sentences in prison. Most were Black. When they came up for Parole, the press was there, and depending on the case's notoriety, you had the television cameras as well.

The most famous case to come before me on the Commission involved Jack "Murph the Surf" Murphy. This con man killed two women accomplices in the theft of negotiable bonds in South Florida. In 1969, Murphy received two life sentences plus 20 years. He never expected to leave the notorious Starke Prison alive. His first parole date was in 2005. But after years of selling drugs and running all kinds of illegal schemes behind bars, Murphy found Jesus in 1974. The former con man began to participate in the prison chaplaincy program. He led Bible study and mentored other inmates. Soon his fame extended beyond the prison walls. A female television reporter out of Gainesville told his story, and Murphy became a cause celebre.

The people who supported him had connections in high places. The president of the Southern Baptist Convention called me and recommended he be released from prison. They were making phone calls to the Governor's Office. They were bombarding Cabinet officers with phone calls.

I never got a call from Governor Bob Graham saying he would not object. Although Murphy ran a prison ministry, I couldn't bring myself to grant parole. A white minister from Jacksonville called me and said, "This man has been redeemed." I said no to him. I couldn't parole Murphy.

Sometimes a letter of recommendation came from an organization with credibility, and someone from that organization would even show up at the Parole Commission. Even Secretary Wainwright spoke on Murphy's behalf when the convict was invited to appear before the Parole Commission.

Although Murphy found Jesus in prison, he had lured these women and killed them. I couldn't vote for him. I think I was the only one who voted against releasing him.

I believe in forgiveness. I believe in redemption. But I also believed the nature of his crime deserved more punishment. I am a Christian. I believe in the forgiveness of Christ. But I didn't think his finding Jesus exonerated him from his actions.

Murphy walked free in November 1986.

In retrospect, I can't get over how white folks so easily see redemption in other white folks. When Black men were in a similar situation, instead of redemption and sincerity, parole and prison officials often saw a con. They believed the Black man was pretending to be reformed or pretending to have found Jesus, just to get out of prison early. I was not impressed by Murph the Surf, but I was out-voted. History has proven that society would benefit from his release. Jack Murphy is still running a halfway house where inmates can live after their release.

Fourteen years after his release, seeing the impact of Murphy's prison ministry and other efforts, the Florida Parole Commission ended Murphy's lifetime parole in 2000.

Chapter 73:
CRIME AND PUNISHMENT

When I came to the Commission, the prison population was growing. The big question facing us was what could be done to reduce crime? Someone came up with harsher, longer sentences as the answer, with no chance to be paroled. The state legislature bought that. They did away with parole. They reduced the Parole Commission to three members from seven. There was no more parole. When an offender was sent into prison, he or she served ten years minus gained time. That was supposed to be the answer to crime.

I've always said: "You've got to deal with the roots of crimes, not with the fruits." When you look at the people in prison, there is a profile. When was the first initial arrest? What was his level of education? In the average person's profile in prisons, education is the key. If he dropped out of school, elementary or junior high school, that was one factor. Another factor was the character of the community in which he lived. There is documentation on the profile of a criminal. Regardless of where he was or who he was, it was expected whether he was Irish or Italian. Any population with a high crime rate all had the common factors of poverty and a lack of quality education. If you started a program that helped you overcome some socio-economic problems, there's an opportunity for real change.

The parole commission dealt with thousands of cases. The judge sentenced men and women. Once they have been convicted and sentenced, they fell under the Parole & Probation Commission's jurisdiction to determine how much of their sentence they would serve.

Later, sentencing guidelines were introduced after people saw disparities in the people being released. The Legislature wanted to ensure that everyone who committed the same crime would serve the same sentence.

Prisons should not be about retribution. The Parole Commission's main thing was to determine whether a man could be released back to society and live a law-abiding life. It's not touted much, but the best chances for rehabilitation were the people who committed murder. Many people are in prison for murder, but it was a crime of passion. If a man comes home, he and his wife argue, and he kills her, the object of his passion is gone. Once he has served his sentence, he can live a law-abiding life.

But what we want is retribution. The person you need to keep in prison is a burglar. He has a pattern. If you keep him in prison, you are doing society a favor. If a man kills, if you put him on parole or probation he will do well. The burglar is just looking for a chance to rob and steal.

We would put a young man in prison, and after six months, we would shock him with parole. The longer you keep a man in prison, the less likely he will adapt. He loses his support system, and he loses his ability to adapt to the technology. Imagine being in prison for 20 years.

All we were teaching him in prison was how to make license plates, which were illegal on the outside.

Someone proposed teaching prisoners to write. Some people objected to that. Teaching him life skills would help him survive when he got out. Some members of the Legislature and community didn't want to do that.

A work-release program was proposed. Some legislators complained it was competing with the free market. One of the worst things to happen was eliminating parole. Then there was no release system that would gradually let a man back out and there was no way to monitor him when he was out.

If you put a man in jail for ten years, he serves eight years. What's going to happen to him now? There is no monitoring. He must eat. Every man must eat, but suppose he can't get a job. Once he has a felony record and has been in prison, he might have difficulty finding employment. The system right now is guaranteed to fail.

· · · · · · · · · · · · · · · ·

The prison population has more than tripled since they eliminated parole. The way to be tough on crime is to nip it in the bud. Sentencing a twenty-seven-year-old to life doesn't deter him. Crime is expensive. When you incarcerate a man, you must pay somebody to keep him and watch him. You need a doctor and a dentist to treat him. You must take care of him in prison, and take care of his family and his children. If you let that man out, he could take care of himself. He could get a job. You don't have to pay for child support.

Are you going to keep building more prisons? A man in prison gets the poorest treatment.

Florida was periodically infected with the get-tough-on-crime fervor. In 1995, "Truth in Sentencing" emerged from one of those episodes in the wake of the $10 billion federal crime bill and much talk about super-predators and other offenders. The legislation pushed by then-Republican State Senator Charlie Crist required inmates to serve at least eighty-five percent of their sentence.

Someone thought it was an excellent idea to sentence men to fifty years even before even considering parole. It became a matter of prison control. If inmates have no incentive to improve their behavior, it causes another problem. The longer you keep that inmate in prison, the harder it is for him to adjust to life on the outside.

Thankfully, these changes happened much later, after I had left the Commission. Because we were appointed to six-year terms, we had the independence to make apolitical decisions that elected officials found politically risky. Sometimes we could surprise a man with parole. We were not subject to the kind of political scrutiny that exists now. If we built more prisons, the judges filled them until the federal government intervened and insisted on doing something about prison overcrowding. That sowed the seeds for the billion-dollar, politically powerful private prison industry that operates today.

Chapter 74:
THE HAZELTON CONTROVERSY

When I was appointed to the Parole and Probation Commission, I moved to Tallahassee. I had left Jeannetta in Tallahassee to allow my son Lanse to finish high school at Episcopal School. By then, Rosemary was 21 and attending the University of Florida. Because Jeannetta was a teacher, she and the boys, Lanse and Leonard, could stay with me in Tallahassee all summer long. Initially, I rented a small apartment but eventually bought a house. I didn't cook, so I ate out every day. I missed Jeannetta's home-cooked meals. I went home to Jacksonville as often as I could. I arranged my schedule so that while I was in Jacksonville on weekends, I visited the Lake Butler Reception Center to interview inmates for violation hearings.

My trips never caused a stir until they came at cross purposes with the ambitions of a politician, Representative Don Hazelton. Hazelton, who served the voters of District 78 in West Palm Beach, accused me of wrongly seeking reimbursement for trips to Jacksonville. Hazelton was a former religion teacher who was first elected to the Florida House of Representatives as a Republican in 1970. After being elected twice as a member of the GOP, Hazelton switched parties. At the time, Florida Democrats had long controlled the House and Senate and the Governor's Mansion. Democrat Gov. Reubin Askew occupied the governor's mansion, and Democrats made up the entire Cabinet. Hazelton's defection was largely against the tide. In the wake of the passage of the federal Civil Rights Act of 1964, many conservative Southern Democrats were becoming Republicans in protest of liberal Democratic policies.

Hazelton was handed the gavel to chair the House Parole and Probation Committee by the Florida State House of Representatives in exchange for his defection. That committee controlled our budget and could make life difficult for us. Hazelton was a sort of oddball. At age 47, while he was a member of the Legislature, Hazelton was one of a dozen and a half hopefuls who showed up in Tampa to try out to play as a placekicker for the Tampa Bay Buccaneers in May 1976. Imagine that. He told a newspaper reporter that he liked to kick footballs.

• • • • • • • • • • • • • • • •

A year after I was appointed to the Parole and Probation Commission, I was elected chairman by a unanimous vote. Again, it was history-making. I was the first Black man to head a state commission. My high profile naturally made me an easy target. Hazelton decided to use me as a political football in his quest to be elected the next state treasurer.

After being appointed to the Parole & Probation Commission, I commuted for six years. When a person was brought back to the institution for a Probable Cause Hearing because he violated his probation or parole, all the hearings were held at Lake Butler. Living in Tallahassee and going home to Jacksonville on weekends, I would volunteer to take their place. I could go to Jacksonville on Wednesday, spend Thursday and Friday interviewing inmates, and return to Tallahassee on Monday. My fellow commissioners didn't complain. If they took their turn, they would have to drive hundreds of miles from home and sleep in a hotel for one or two nights. Inmates were brought back regularly. I was doing them a favor and doing myself one. I had a chance to spend two or three days extra with my family. I could attend school activities in the evening. Then I would get up in the morning, drive to Lake Butler, hold hearings until 3 p.m., and drive the seventy miles back to Jacksonville.

• • • • • • • • • • • • • • • •

After all Hazelton's fuss and fury, the state auditor said I was entitled to financial reimbursement for trips to Jacksonville dating back to September 1976 if I had proper documentation, which I did. I had kept my receipts. Chief of the Comptroller's Bureau of Auditing, Joel Martinez, said he found nothing wrong with my travel vouchers. But that announcement didn't deter Hazelton. His committee persisted with its investigation. He even called on Governor Askew to suspend me. He questioned why I had recently sought reimbursement for 14 trips between Tallahassee and Jacksonville, some dating back to September 1976.

I paid for the 320-mile round trip out of my pocket for a long time. I didn't ask the state to pay. However, I asked state auditors if I was entitled to reimbursement since I did state work on that trip to Jacksonville. I was told unequivocally, yes. I could get reimbursement, and I did. So here comes

Hazelton. He was looking for notoriety; he was looking for a scalp, my history-making Black scalp, to jump-start his campaign for State Treasurer.

I was upfront. I didn't try to hide anything because I had done nothing wrong. As the first Black appointed to the Commission, I was always careful that my actions were above board. I received reimbursement for trips to Jacksonville dating back to 1976 after talking to officials from the comptroller's office and examiners working for Auditor General Ernest Ellingson. I kept a home in Jacksonville and conducted business while traveling back to Duval County on weekends. I sought no reimbursement for the trips until after I spoke to the auditors.

On May 21, 1978, the media reported that Hazelton, who apparently wasn't getting enough traction, had asked Governor Askew to suspend Commissioner Armond Cross and me. A native of Bristol, Florida, Cross was a U.S. Air Force veteran who then studied at Florida State University. He worked his way up the Parole & Probation Commission ladder before being appointed commissioner in 1971. Hazelton accused us of abusing our positions. Hazelton didn't make any specific charge. He claimed that his Committee found extensive improprieties during their investigation. They filed a report in early May 1978 criticizing us for travel and other management policies.

In the wake of the criticism of our travel expenses and policies, the executive director and one of his assistants resigned. The furor erupted soon after the Florida Senate confirmed Commissioner Cross by a unanimous vote to a four-year term. Cross was re-appointed by the governor and cabinet over Hazelton's objections.

· · · · · · · · · · · · · · · ·

The Parole Commission had a lot of critics because of our growing prison population. At that time, there were 15,000 inmates behind bars. In 1978, the prison population issue was like the gun issue in 2022. Once a man or woman had been sentenced, the Parole Commission determined how much time he or she would serve in prison. In some instances, if a man did less time than he was sentenced, granted parole, and then recommitted a crime, that created political backlash. Parole and Probation Commission hearings often got live television news coverage since Florida tended to have the most horrific crimes and most notorious murderers, like Ted Bundy.

Hazelton, as chair of the House Committee, used the position to criticize me so he could be in the spotlight and run for statewide office. As the first African American to sit on and chair the Parole and Probation Commission, I became an object of contention. Because I was the chairman, I became even more of a target. After I stepped down from being chairman, I was no longer the target. I was no longer an object to be used to run against. Ironically, we became friends.

The Hazelton controversy disrupted my own plans. I was thinking about running for a legislative seat out of Jacksonville. But this controversy dragged on, and it hurt me because of coverage in the media. It gave the false impression I had done something wrong. It was a classic smear campaign to throw around just enough mud to sully my name.

I never did run for office. The messiness of the controversy changed my attitude about politics. I saw that running for political office required me to do and say things I wanted no part of. I wanted no part of that blood sport. Also, when I saw the personal moral compromises required of politicians, I decided that was not my calling. I preferred to devote my time and energy to the ministry.

After leaving the Legislature, Hazelton had a second act as head of the Florida Athletic Commission. He was head of the Florida Boxing Commission from 1987 to 1996.

When Hazelton died in September 2012, he was hailed as a reformer in matters of prison and parole. Although we became friends, I remember him not as a reformer but as someone willing to come after me to score political points. I forgave him. Professionally, that's an entirely different matter. He was 83.

Chapter 75:
IN HINDSIGHT

Serving on the Parole and Probation Commission was one of the highlights of my working life. My reward was when I heard from a man who wrote me saying, "You paroled me back in 1987, look where I am today. Things are going well."

I felt good about that. I got letters occasionally from people I had paroled. Some had gone back into the system whom I could not help. I didn't have the wisdom of Solomon. I was just a man sitting in judgment of another man. Except for the grace of God, he could be there sitting in judgment of me. My greatest joy was whenever I went somewhere, and I encountered a man, and he'd say, "Do you remember me?"

I'd say no.

"You paroled me twenty or thirty years ago," the man replied. "I am doing well." I appreciate it. That has been one of the joys of my life, seeing people who were given a second chance and who took advantage of it and made something of their lives.

When some of my fellow commissioners didn't grant parole, a person might have stayed in prison for another eight or ten years. It's a serious and delicate thing to sit in judgment of another man. All we have on this earth is time. I am not taking another man's time lightly. When you can determine a man's fate for him to spend nine, ten, or twenty years in prison, that's a heavy thing. I spent time on my knees praying that I had made the right decision.

Other commissioners often disagreed with my position. Maybe they were trying to protect society from this person. It was a tough thing sitting in judgment of another man's conduct and behavior. The most challenging thing was predicting his future behavior. Predicting the behavior of a man who is a killer or man who raped or assaulted another person and violated his probation or parole caused a lot of grief in my heart and mind. But I had the opportunity to make a difference. I tried with some compassion and love to make that judgment based on the best information I had at the time. I decided with the mind, heart, and understanding of a Christian man.

Sometimes it was good. Other times, it was not so good. You can never measure your judgment about a situation and condition in your own time. That judgment's fruition is not made in our lifetime for some decisions. I made a judgment in 1987, and a man was released in 2000. That man's life and the contributions he will make might not be evident until many years later.

What did you do? You did the best you could with what was before you at that time. Wouldn't it be nice if we were all-seeing and all-knowing? We are limited in our foresight, but we are not limited in our hindsight. You could always see what you should have done. If I had known then what I know now, my judgment would have been different.

Chapter 76:
THE LAWSUIT, STILL FIGHTING

After two full terms, I retired from the Parole and Probation Commission in 1987 and went to work with the Department of Business and Professional Regulation, Division of Alcoholic Beverages & Tobacco. I worked as an ABT agent until 2003 when I retired as a captain. For my service, they bestowed on me the courtesy promotion to major.

Retirement from the state didn't mean I went home and sat on the back porch with Jeannetta. I worked on a doctorate at Florida State University. I pastored Corinth Christian Fellowship in Midway in Gadsden County, Florida's only Black majority county.

Being retired from full-time work allowed me to serve in areas that mattered. That was the Parole and Probation Commission. Retired commissioners on a voluntary and rotating basis can serve on what is now renamed the Florida Commission on Offender Review (FCOR). This provision was made for commissioners who retired. Some chose not to get on that rotation basis. The Commission sent me a form asking if I wanted to participate each year. They told me what the salary was going to be. I didn't have to participate. I didn't have to return the form. But once I sent back the form, I had the right to participate. Commissioners were called on a rotating basis.

Did I need the money? No, I did not, but I wanted to serve. Issues of justice and mercy get me out of bed every day. I went on the Parole Commission in 1975 as the first Black person in a system that was overwhelmingly white male for generations. There were disproportionate numbers of Blacks in prison. There still are. For generations, there was no one on the Commission who looked like them to speak on their behalf.

After my retirement, I was summoned to serve a few times. I would drive to the office and discuss cases with the staff and other commissioners. It reminded me of my 12 years as a full-time commissioner and how I was able to affect the lives of young black men and women especially those who had made bad choices and desperately needed a second chance.

Then as the years progressed, the invitations to serve dried up. At first, I quietly tried to find out what was going on. But in frustration, I had to go public. In 2008, I published a column in the Tallahassee Democrat saying that I had served once in five years while some of my other retired colleagues had served as many as 20 times. Those were the days when Jeb Bush was governor and Republicans and conservatives had taken over the reins of the executive branch. My views on crime and punishment were no longer in line with Jeb and his ilk. Jeb learned his political lessons from his father, George W. H. Bush. In his 1988 campaign for president to succeed Ronald Reagan, George Bush effectively used the Willie Horton television ad against Massachusetts Governor Michael Dukakis. Demonizing Black criminals and parolees made for good politics.

I always believed in examining the roots of crime rather than the fruits of crime. My ideology had become out of fashion. Getting tough on crime was the way Republicans wanted to get elected. The rational and reasonable days of Governor Askew were long gone.

································

In 2012, FCOR Chair Tena Pate included me among the six retired commissioners who would substitute for absent commissioners. Pate was a veteran of the Bob Martinez, Lawton Chiles, Buddy MacKay, and Bush administrations. She was first appointed to the commission by Jeb to fill a vacancy in 2003. She received six-year appointments from Governors Charlie Crist and Rick Scott. FCOR staff interviewed me and three others on the list. But when Commission Chair Pate submitted the list to Governor Scott and the Cabinet in 2013, my name was nowhere to be found. When I asked Pate why my name was omitted despite my credentials, she said the Governor's Office decided to keep me off the list. I was not a supporter of Rick Scott, the millionaire former hospital executive elected governor as an outsider in 2010.

When I learned my name was kept off the list, I even went to Attorney General Pam Bondi and told her I was being discriminated against. Bondi shook her head. She said that's right. One gets used to politicians shaking their heads, and saying they would get back to you later. She never did. The Governor's Office knew it too. Theirs was a position they couldn't defend. I tried not to make the issue too public for years but got no results. Finally, when they refused to do anything about it, I decided to take legal action.

I went to see Marie Maddox, an attorney in Tallahassee. Maddox has an impressive record of suing the state over discrimination and other employment-related claims. We pulled up the record showing I was getting called every tenth time. In late 2014, she filed a suit in federal court saying my name was taken off a list of prospective temporary commissioners submitted to Gov. Rick Scott and the Cabinet for approval in 2013.

They found my name was coming up every six weeks, but Commissioner James' name was coming up every two weeks. I asked "Why? Why were you not calling me? What's your explanation?" My credentials were the same as his.

As we prepared to go to court, the inconvenient question remained unanswered. Why was I not being called? The lawyers didn't have an acceptable answer. Rick Scott's Office didn't have one either.

Was there any reason some were being called twice a month, and Charles Scriven was being called every other month?

When that came up, their attorney said, "What do you want?"

They couldn't defend their position. The Parole Commission agreed to settle out of court in October 2015 for damages, lost wages, attorney fees, and other costs.

Marie said we should settle for $50,000. She got a quarter of that.

It's one thing if you could conceal something. But there was a record. My name was there, but the next person in line was called. "Why didn't you call me?" There's no explanation. There's a right and wrong principle. The Tallahassee Democrat even picked up the story under the headline "First Black parole commissioner settles lawsuit."

It was established that they discriminated against me based on my race. I proved my point. I wasn't looking to make a public statement. We got what we wanted.

I wasn't in it for the money. I was in my 80s. My needs were being met. I didn't have to serve. Like Caleb, there's always another mountain to climb as long as I am alive. It's a principle I live by.

It wasn't easy. Some people I respected and trusted told me to let it go. They said it wasn't worth the trouble. I disagreed. I've been discriminated against all my life. I have been treated differently because of the color of my skin for the better part of the twentieth century, and no matter how old I am, discrimination still feels the same. It dehumanizes me. It hurts. The pain is never diminished. But more importantly, I needed a good fight every now and then to keep me in shape.

There's nothing else but the principle. If you are taking advantage of me, I can't ignore that. That was a principle I was fighting in the police department to get into the union. I had a right to determine who would represent me. The fact that I would get what other officers are getting didn't impress me. I had no say in the matter. I was not part of the discussion of bargaining. Somebody else spoke on my behalf. They said, 'Scriven, whatever we get, you are going to get."

It's not alright with me. I want to be part of whatever is being done.

I kept fighting while others accepted that. It was my choice if I wanted to participate, but you can't tell me I cannot participate. I was a member of a department with a union, but I couldn't be a member of that union.

· · · · · · · · · · · · · · · ·

Florida has changed to a Clemency board. They're not releasing inmates the way they used to. At best, the board members are like clerks. The board no longer has executive power. If a person was sentenced under the Parole system, he stayed under that system until his release. If you were sentenced under the parole system, they couldn't go back and treat you retroactively as if you were sentenced under the new system. Under the reformed system, twenty-five years was the mandatory minimum. You served twenty-five years in prison before you were eligible for parole. The sentencing in Florida has become even tougher with successive Republican legislators and governors. Now it's fifty years. Tougher sentences don't deal with the roots of crime.

The real power to grant pardons now rests with the Governor and the Cabinet made up of the Governor, Attorney General, Chief Financial Officer, and Agriculture Commissioner. They are all elected by the voters. Justice and mercy lose whenever you have politicians in charge of punishment; politics always wins.

Chapter 76:
AN OVERDUE APOLOGY

When does a man stop fighting? When does the struggle for vindication end? When should a man ignore past wrongs and embrace all the benefits life has made rightfully his?

These are questions I have long struggled with. My long working life has been productive. I have enjoyed successful careers as a Negro Jacksonville police officer, Florida's first Black parole and probation commissioner, a pastor, and Department of Business Regulation/Division of Alcohol Beverages and Tobacco agent. For a while after retiring from the Parole and Probation Commission I flirted with the idea of returning to Jacksonville and running for political office. I was still a well-known commodity in my hometown. My years of service in the JPD and the Sheriff's Office stood up well in law enforcement and religious circles. But the more I dealt with politicians and those who moved within the political class in Tallahassee, the more dismayed I became. Throughout my life, I have lived by the maxim that my word is my bond. I learned that in politics a handshake and a promise are as worthless as a three-dollar bill. I quickly dropped the idea of running for office.

I soon joined the Department of Business Regulation's Division of Alcohol Beverages and Tobacco as a law enforcement agent, where I remained for almost 15 years. After I retired, I taught criminal justice part-time at Florida A&M University.

Meanwhile, I never stopped preaching. For nine years, after I moved to Tallahassee, I was the shepherd of Beulah Baptist Church in Gretna, a small town in western Gadsden County. That was followed by a two-year stint as interim pastor of First Elizabeth Baptist Church in Quincy. After that I was pastor of Corinth Christian Fellowship in Midway.

Although I stopped working for the state, I never considered myself retired. I even worked on my doctorate at Florida State University. I finished my coursework but never got around to completing my dissertation. I was content that I had climbed enough mountains. I was 86. I had outlived all of my older siblings. God had blessed me with long life, provision, and good health. However, one remaining issue still galled me — my lack of membership in the Fraternal Order of Police. After decades in law enforcement, I remained an outsider. As far as I knew, after applying at least 20 times, I was still not a member of the FOP brotherhood.

•••••••••••••••

There was a reawakening. I don't know what prompted it. Maybe it was something I saw in the newspaper or a conversation. Perhaps it was an issue, that I disagreed with the FOP's position. Even if I disagreed, I had no say in the matter. Maybe it was my restlessness. Even though Jeannetta said let it go, I couldn't. It was that nagging feeling, gnawing at my bones, that this was unfinished business. I had been rejected on the basis of my color. That wrong needed to be corrected.

In September 2018, I decided to address my concerns about my lack of membership in the FOP to Steve Zona, the current president of the Jacksonville FOP. Built like a middle linebacker, the goateed Zona began his law enforcement career with the Jacksonville Beach Police Department in 1988. He was a patrol officer for two years before switching to the Jacksonville Sheriff's Office. In his twenty-six years with the Jacksonville Sheriff's Office, Zona rose from patrol officer to sergeant over the K-9 Unit, Sex Crimes, Robbery, and Homicide.

Zona joined the FOP Jacksonville Consolidated Lodge 530 in 1990 once the Jacksonville's Sheriff's Office hired him. He was elected Lodge secretary in 2013 and was first elected Lodge president in 2015. He retired from the Sheriff's Office in 2016, but was still the FOP Lodge president. Zona serves on the Florida State Lodge Legislative Committee, the National FOP Urban Policing Committee, and is the Florida State Lodge District 2 director. Zona has gained a reputation for being reasonable and getting things done to help law enforcement officers. As Lodge president, he had been credited with helping pass the Corrections Law Enforcement Officers Safety Act (CLEOSA). That legislation allowed sworn corrections officers to be considered qualified law enforcement officers and to carry concealed firearms anywhere in the country, just like other sworn law enforcement officers. He helped successfully push for Officer Rights in the Florida Legislature, created a Jacksonville Public Safety Health Insurance Trust Fund, and negotiated funding in the amount of $180,000 per year from the City of Jacksonville to go to the Fallen Officers Fund. But Zona could also be like so many other police union presidents. During the height of the equal justice protests in June 2020, after a massive peaceful demonstration in Jacksonville calling for police accountability, Zona took to his Facebook page to target a Jacksonville school teacher who organized the protests.

But at the time, all I had was a name and my long-held grievance. So, I did what I did best. I didn't call. I didn't email. I sat at the desk in my study and wrote a letter. On Sept. 10, 2018, I wrote Zona a letter.

Mr. Steve Zona, president
Jacksonville Consolidated No. 530
5530 Beach Blvd.
Jacksonville, FL 32204-5161

Mr. Zona:

I was the first black police officer to apply for membership to the Jacksonville Fraternal Order of Police (FOP) in June 1957. I wanted to be a member of the organization that was the recognized bargaining agent for police officers in the City of Jacksonville. I was unequivocally rejected (blackballed) as were several other black officers in July or August of 1957. The local Lodge Officers refused through manner and demeanor to discuss the possibility of membership for black officers in the local FOP Lodge. Being subjugated in a segregated black precinct did not negate that desire.

I took a flight to Philadelphia, Pennsylvania, and spoke with the then President of National FOP, John Harrington. He acknowledged that the national FOP prohibited discrimination in Membership; however, he did not suggest or recommend any steps I should take, nor any that the national office would take, to correct this discriminatory violation by the local lodge. I never heard anything from the national FOP officials.

We continued occasionally submitting requests for membership for the next twelve years. Membership was finally granted to all black officers who qualified but me in 1969, once city and county government were consolidated and the black precinct was abolished. I was surreptitiously granted associate membership in 1993. I believe that the local lodge owes me a public apology for having denied me (blackballed) membership in the FOP for over 35 years.

Your immediate response would be appreciated.

Charles J. Scriven

To Zona's credit, he took my letter seriously. Maybe it was two weeks or a month, but he responded soon afterward. He called me back. I told him my complaints. He said he would come up to Tallahassee. He suggested we talk. I didn't ask him. He set the date. It was within a month of when we first talked.

The response to that letter was more than I had ever received and more than I ever expected. Soon afterward, Zona and Vontez Wright, the only Black member of his FOP Board of Trustees, drove to my home in Tallahassee. We sat in the living room and talked for about four hours.

Between my letter and our meeting, Zona researched and discovered that I had been accepted into the organization in 1996, twenty-two years earlier. Somehow, no one had ever informed me. I was not hard to find. I was a law enforcement agent for the state. Everyone in Jacksonville knew I was in Tallahassee.

Zona apologized on behalf of the FOP and invited my entire family and me to a dinner in my honor. My only caveat was that the dinner and apology had to be made public. I wanted the world to know what they did to me. I wanted the world to hear the apology.

Zona agreed to my demands. The dinner was scheduled for Tuesday, June 18, 2019. The event would be held at FOP headquarters. He apologized to me personally. When I said I wanted a public apology, he said that was fine. He called the TV station from my house. He apologized for their behavior. He wanted it corrected. He offered to send a police officer for Jeannetta and me. The FOP would provide lodging in Jacksonville for anyone I wanted to invite to the event. There were eight or ten of us, including Lanse and his wife, who is a federal judge in Tampa; my younger son, Leonard; Rosemary's granddaughter, the Deslets, our neighbors for more than 20 years; our granddaughter Danielle and her husband, and other friends of the family.

The day before, Zona sent a car to pick up Jeannetta and me for the dinner. They put us up in a Jacksonville hotel. When we arrived, the hall was filling up. Nate Glover, the former Jacksonville Sheriff, and Edward Waters College president were there. The Sheriff who preceded Glover and the incumbent Sheriff weren't there, but hundreds of people showed up. There was a good representation of African Americans from the Sheriff's Office.

Former chiefs and elected officials filled the room. I sat on the rostrum as Zona stood at the podium and uttered the words I wanted to hear. I got my apology.

"On behalf of myself and the Fraternal Order of Police, we are truly sorry for what happened to you back in 1957," Zona said. As he spoke, he was flanked by a phalanx of mostly white union members and officers from the Jacksonville Sheriff's Office. Most wore polo shirts with the insignia badge of the Sheriff's Office.

Hearing Zona's words more than sixty years late brought some measure of satisfaction. A public apology was necessary for the public record. Most people would rather forget and pretend that none of this happened, as if racial discrimination was a figment of our imagination. That apology was essential to show that even organizations that were supposed to support brotherhood across racial lines failed again and again when faced with the chance to do the right thing. Tears filled my eyes as I listened to his words. So many images of the past flashed through my mind — the first day I saw the ad in the newspaper advertising for Negro police officers; the day I took the test; weeks later, coming home from the Maxwell House Coffee factory to find the letter announcing I had passed the test; the days of showing up for work in Precinct 3 below the public swimming pool for negroes; the day someone shot at me; and each promotion, from patrolman to sergeant to lieutenant to chief.

• • • • • • • • • • • • • • • •

The dinner was excellent. The officers received me well. I felt welcomed. I felt vindicated. But as I listened to Zona's words and looked around the audience, one white face was conspicuously missing. Martin P. Garris IV was not there smiling behind his glasses. Martin had fought this battle alongside me, but he was absent for the victory ceremony.

Months after I left the Sheriff's Office for the Parole & Probation Commission, Martin left to become the Director of Public Safety and Chief of Police at the University of North Florida. During his twenty-year tenure, Martin, who was divorced, met his second wife Betty, who also worked at the Jacksonville campus.

In January 2006, I had attended a ceremony for the naming of the university's police building in honor of Martin's "dedication to ethics and integrity," which set the foundation for professionalism in the UNF Police Department. Unfortunately, Martin missed that ceremony too. In 1995, he left UNF to return to the Jacksonville Sheriff's Office to serve as chief of community affairs under Sheriff Nate Glover, who had won a historic election thanks in part to Martin's early endorsement. Martin stayed for four years, but he quit in disillusionment. Several years later, with Glover term-limited, Martin decided to run for sheriff to clean things up. Had he won, and I believed he would, I promised to be his undersheriff. But Martin's life was cut painfully short. On the morning of Sept. 5, 2002, Betty went to check on him to find that Martin had gone to his eternal rest. Martin was only sixty-six years old. I officiated many funerals in my career as a pastor. I buried my daughter Rosemary in 2012. But no funeral was as painful and emotional as Martin's that Monday morning at Kernan Boulevard Baptist Church. His burial at H. Warren Smith Cemetery with full police honors brought tears to my eyes. Martin and I shared so many great memories in uniform. For more than forty years, Martin and I spoke almost every day, even in retirement. He was my true friend and brother. Twenty years later, I still miss my friend.

• • • • • • • • • • • • • • • •

After Zona spoke, I rose to respond. That evening, I spoke my mind. I held nothing back.

"All I wanted was to have a chance to be a part of an organization that played a major role in my livelihood," I told the gathering. All eyes were turned toward me. I could hear a pin drop as I spoke. I spoke from the heart. I told them exactly what I had been saying for the last six decades. I wasn't trying to join a club. I wasn't interested in dancing with their wives at the annual ball. I wasn't trying to go on their fishing and hunting trips. I wanted a say in the organization that negotiated my salary, pension, and other benefits, that played a vital role in my professional life. Without membership, I didn't have a voice. The lack of membership didn't stop my progress, but being a member, I would have been able to advocate for other Black officers who couldn't speak up for themselves.

It was a special dinner. I was the guest of honor.

There was news coverage of the event on local television stations. Jenese Harris, a reporter from News 4 Jax, WJXT, followed Jeannetta and me around all day long and featured my story in a newscast later that evening. We walked the old neighborhoods of my childhood, where we bought our first house in 1957, the same year I first tried to join the FOP. Lanse accompanied us. He spoke about his happy childhood and called me his role model. Each time he said that, my heart was overcome with emotion. Lanse is a credit to my commitment to family, to Black manhood at home and in the workplace.

Mine was an improbable journey from the wood house on the dirt road in Durkeeville to the top echelons of the Jacksonville Sheriff's Office. I had always stood up for what I believed. I never compromised my honor as a Black man to make white folks comfortable. I was not a rabble-rouser, but I understood early on how to quietly and courageously stand my ground. My stance earned me a few enemies along the way, but none of them could say I compromised my faith, my family, or my race in the service of ambition.

After the banquet, an officer drove Jeannetta and me to a hotel for the night. The following day, the Sheriff's Office sent one of their vehicles to drive us home to Tallahassee.

Our driver was a Black female officer, Assistant Division Chief Deloris Patterson O'Neal. She had joined the Sheriff's Office in 1997 and made a name for herself in community policing.

As she drove, O'Neal and I talked. She said she was honored to meet me. She had even asked for the assignment to bring us back to Tallahassee. It was a gutsy call. It was a stormy day, and the weather was frightful. Rain fell in sheets. It was white outside the car. We couldn't see this much in front of us. Jeannetta sat in the back seat with her eyes closed, and her lips moved in silent prayer. If I were at the wheel, I would have pulled over at the side of the road until the storm blew over, but O'Neal drove and carried on our conversation as if it was a sunny day on Interstate 10. She sped us along, her foot heavy on the gas pedal. We couldn't see a foot in front of us, but she was calm like the professional she was.

O'Neal said she had heard about me. We talked about my career rising from the Negro Precinct to becoming a lieutenant, then division chief. She told me about the influence my name had on the department. I had made a difference in the Sheriff's Office. My decision to demand respect set the standard for the better treatment of Black officers. Sometimes you don't know what influence you might have on a situation. I still meet officers today who say, "You are a legend." I didn't know. Whatever I was able to do, I tried to do it. It wasn't a cakewalk. They tried to break me, but they couldn't. I wouldn't let them.

As we drove home on that stormy summer day, the battles of the past felt as if they had been worth it. I was uncowed and unbowed. I had fought for my apology and gotten it — publicly, and without reservation. I felt as if my spirit, the mantle of a pioneer, had been passed on to Assistant Chief O'Neal during that two-and-a-half-hour ride back to Tallahassee. We formed a special bond. I was the first Black man to be promoted chief in the Jacksonville Sheriff's Office. Two months later, on August 18, 2019, O'Neal would make parallel history. She was promoted to full chief. The first African American woman to reach that rank in the Jacksonville Sheriff's Office history came 130 years after Black officers were removed from the Jacksonville Police Department under Jim Crow.

But the march to full racial equality in America is far from over.

www.ingramcontent.com/pod-product-compliance
Lightning Source LLC
Chambersburg PA
CBHW061245230426
43662CB00021B/2437